Divorce Law and Practice
in Scotland

Divorce Law and Practice in Scotland

John C McInnes
Queen's Counsel, Sheriff of Tayside, Central and Fife
at Cupar and Perth

Edinburgh
Butterworths
1990

United Kingdom	Butterworth & Co (Publishers) Ltd, 88 Kingsway, LONDON WC2B 6AB and 4 Hill Street, EDINBURGH EH2 3JZ
Australia	Butterworths Pty Ltd, SYDNEY, MELBOURNE, BRISBANE, ADELAIDE, PERTH, CANBERRA and HOBART
Canada	Butterworths Canada Ltd, TORONTO and VANCOUVER
Ireland	Butterworth (Ireland) Ltd, DUBLIN
Malaysia	Malayan Law Journal Sdn Bhd, KUALA LUMPUR
New Zealand	Butterworths of New Zealand Ltd, WELLINGTON and AUCKLAND
Puerto Rico	Equity de Puerto Rico, Inc, HATO REY
Singapore	Butterworth & Co (Asia) Pte Ltd, SINGAPORE
USA	Butterworth Legal Publishers, ST PAUL, Minnesota; and SEATTLE, Washington, BOSTON, Massachusetts, AUSTIN, Texas and D & S Publishers, CLEARWATER, Florida

All rights reserved. No part of this publication may be reproduced in any material form (including photocopying or storing it in any medium by electronic means and whether or not transiently or incidentally to some other use of this publication) without the written permission of the copyright owner except in accordance with the provisions of the Copyright, Designs and Patents Act 1988 or under the terms of a licence issued by the Copyright Licensing Agency Ltd, 90 Tottenham Court Road, London W1P 9HE. Applications for the copyright owner's written permission to reproduce any part of this publication should be addressed to the publisher.

Warning: The doing of an unauthorised act in relation to a copyright work may result in both a civil claim for damages and criminal prosecution.

© Butterworth & Co (Publishers) Ltd 1990

A CIP Catalogue record for this book is available from the British Library.

ISBN 0 406 13210 0

Typeset by Kerrypress, Luton
Printed by Mackays of Chatham PLC, Chatham, Kent

PREFACE

The law with which this book attempts to deal is in need of codification. Some problems involve a considerable chase around the legislation. The book is not intended as a treatise on family law. I hope that it will be of use to lawyers and to students of law as a practical handbook. Much of our law is based on practice. The practice of our courts is not universally the same nor is practice rigid and unadaptable. I can only reflect practice as I find it to be at the time of writing.

I have not referred to all those cases which are nowadays briefly reported but which do not seem to raise matters of principle. Nor have I attempted to deal substantially with the earlier authorities many of which have been superseded as a result of the extensive and recent legislation in this field. One practical problem was how to tackle the subject. I have settled on a chronological order by topics as if there was an imaginary divorce action in progress. I have assumed that the user will not read the book from cover to cover and would prefer not to be referred constantly to other parts of the book. This has led to a certain amount of repetition for which I apologise. In the text I have assumed that those seeking divorce are almost invariably female. Otherwise I have written in the masculine, for brevity and for no more chauvinistic reason.

I would not dare to dedicate a book on divorce to my wife. I hope that my children will never have the need of it. I am very grateful to my wife for the use of her word processor and for putting up with the consequences of my gross underestimate of the time which it takes to write even a short book.

I am also grateful to Mr M G Bonar, Deputy Principal Clerk of Session, Mr Brian Sullivan, Sheriff Clerk at Cupar, and his then Depute Mr Ian Foote for many helpful comments. I would be obliged if the many errors which I have no doubt missed could be pointed out to me, lest there be another edition. I have attempted to state the law as at 25 October 1990.

J.C. McI.
Cupar
October 1990

CONTENTS

Preface v
Table of Statutes xi
Table of Orders, Rules and Regulations xix
Table of Cases xxiii

1 A Client Comes In . . . 1

2 The Situation Before Divorce 6
Presumptions 7
Obligations to adhere 7
Legal capacity 8
Aliment 8
Rights by succession 10
Wedding presents 10
Gifts between spouses 11
Matrimonial home 11
Immigrant spouse 11
Polygamous marriage 11
Parental rights 11

3 Taking Instructions 13
Simplified procedure 13
Choice of court 13
Other considerations 14
Cases where simplified procedure not appropriate 14

4 Ancillary Orders — Orders for Financial Provision 22
Ancillary Orders — General 22
Aliment 24
Orders for Financial Provision 28
Orders for Periodical Allowance 42
Termination, Variation and Recall of Orders for Periodical Allowance 45
Relevance of the Conduct of a Party 45
Taxation of Maintenance Payments 46

5 Other Ancillary Orders 49
Parental Rights 49
Custody 50
Access 53

Jurisdiction in Relation to Custody Orders 54
Disclosure of the Child's Whereabouts 56
Restricting the Removal of a Child from the Jurisdiction of the Court 56
Obtaining the Authority of Court to Remove a Child 57
Orders for Delivery of a Child 57
Orders Under Matrimonial Homes (Family Protection) (S) Act 1981 ... 58
Interdict 64

6 The Writ 68
Choice of court 68
Jurisdiction in Scotland 68
Simplified procedure 71
Styles of initial writs and summonses 72

7 Raising the Action 94
Mental capacity of the parties 94
Simplified procedure 95
Recovery of documents before an action is raised 98
Applications for an order under the Administration of Justice (Scotland) Act 1972, s 1 ... 98
Commencing an ordinary action 99
Transfer, remit and sist of actions 107

8 Interim Orders 118
Obtaining interim orders prior to service of the writ 118
Interdicts 121
Orders for the interim possession of property 121
Matrimonial Homes Act orders 121
Hearing of motion for interim orders 122
Interim custody 123
Interim access 124
Interim aliment 124
Reports 125
Obtaining evidence of welfare of children 126
Other orders which may be granted ad interim 126

9 Defended Action 128
Entering appearance 128
Arrestment on the dependence 128
Inhibition 128
Early hearing on interim orders 128
Where agreement can be reached 129
Where agreement cannot be reached 129
Where only aliment, periodical allowance, capital payment or transfer of property are disputed 129
Third party entering the process 130
Defences 130
Counterclaim or cross action 131
Sisting of third parties 132
Particular lines of defence 132

Procedure in a defended divorce 135
Recovery of documents 137

10 The Evidence Required 139
Burden of proof 139
Standard of proof 139
Sufficiency of evidence 140
Aspects of the evidence required 141
Practice notes relating to divorce affidavits 142
Proof of marriage 143
Proof of birth of children 143
Admissions 144
Divorce based on earlier decree of separation or in other matrimonial proceedings 144
Proof of extract convictions 145
Proof of adultery 145
Proof of unreasonable behaviour 146
Proof of the defender's consent to decree under section 1(2)(d) ... 147
Medical reports 147
Reports on custody and access 147
Evidence of welfare of children whose whereabouts are unknown 148
Evidence of the welfare of a child in the care of a local authority 148
Interviewing children 148
Affidavits 149
Evidence of the financial matters 152

11 Orders Made After Divorce, Variation and Recall of Orders 153
Orders made after divorce 153
Orders for financial provision following an overseas divorce or annulment 154
Restricting the removal of a child from the jurisdiction of the court 155
Orders for delivery of a child 156
Variation and recall of orders after divorce 156
Variation of pre-1985 Act orders for financial provision 163
Recall or variation of Court of Session decrees by the sheriff court 165

12 Enforcement 167
Breach of interdict 167
Civil imprisonment 169
Enforcement of maintenance orders 170
Enforcement overseas of maintenance orders made in Scotland 175
Enforcing orders for custody 182
Unauthorised removal of children 184
The Child Abduction and Custody Act 1985 ... 186

Appendices 191

Index 199

TABLE OF STATUTES

	PARA
Administration of Justice (Scotland) Act 1972	
s 1	98
Adoption (Scotland) Act 1978	
s 12(1)	55
18	55
Bankruptcy (Scotland) Act 1985	
s 35	157, 162
Child Abduction Act 1984	
s 6	185
(4)	185
(5)	185
7	185
9	185
10	185
Child Abduction and Custody Act 1985	55, 186
Pt I (ss 1–11)	186, 189
s 5	187
Pt II (ss 12–24)	186, 189
s 14	189
15	188, 189
(2)	189
(a)	189
16	188, 189
17(4)	189
18	188, 189
19	188
20	189
23(2)	189
24A	190
Sch 1	186, 189
art 3	186, 187
5	186
7	186
8	186
11–13	187
15, 16	187
21	187
Child Abduction and Custody Act 1985—contd	
Sch 2	186, 188, 189
art 1, 5	188
9, 10	188, 189
11(2)	189
12	189
13	188
15, 16	188
18	188
Children Act 1975	
s 37	57
47	51
(2)	49
51	57
(1)	57, 119
52	57
53(1)	55
Citation Amendment (Scotland) Act 1882	
s 3	99, 100, 101, 107
6	100, 101
Civil Evidence (Scotland) Act 1988	141, 142, 144
s 1(1)	140
2(1)	140
(b)	144, 149
(3), (4)	149
8	140, 141, 146
(3)	140
(4)	141
9	140
10	141
(1)	146
Schedule	141, 146
Civil Imprisonment (Scotland) Act 1882	
s 4	167, 169, 170

Table of Statutes

	PARA
Civil Jurisdiction and Judgments Act 1982	68, 69, 70, 175
Pt I (ss 1–15)	154
s 5	175
ss 41–46	70
Sch 1	103, 175, 181
art 32	175
Sch 8, r 1	65
2(5)	178
(10)	65
Sch 9, para 1	68, 70

Conjugal Rights (Scotland) Amendment Act 1861
- s 9 .... 50, 54, 71, 123, 165

Contempt of Court Act 1981
- s 15(1) 168
- (2)(a) 168
- 17(5)(a) 169
- (b) 169

Court of Session Act 1830
- s 36 .... 141, 146

Court of Session Act 1988
- s 19 .... 113, 136
- 20 .... 49, 54, 71
- 47(1) 85, 167
- (2) 121, 122

Debtors (Scotland) Act 1880 169
- s 4 167

Debtors (Scotland) Act 1987 .. 170, 171
- ss 51–56 170
- s 52 171
- 54(1) 171
- 55 171
- 59 170
- 62 170
- 73 171
- 87(4) 27, 170
- 102 170
- 106 170

Divorce Jurisdiction, Court Fees and Legal Aid (Scotland) Act 1983
- s 2 140
- Sch 1, para 18 69

Divorce (Scotland) Act 1976 22
- s 1 114
- (1) 130
- (2) 141
- (a) 81
- (b) 81
- (c) 82

Divorce (Scotland) Act 1976—contd
- s 1(2)(d) 82, 147
- (e) 82
- (3) 81, 133
- (4) 147
- (5) 116, 130, 133, 139
- (6) 139
- 2 .... 1, 15
- (1) 81, 82, 107, 136
- (2) 81, 133
- (3) 82
- (4) 82
- 3(1) 140, 144
- (2) 144
- 5 .... 163, 172
- (1) 163
- (2) 163
- (3) 163
- (4) 163
- 13(2) 34, 133

Domicile and Matrimonial Proceedings Act 1973
- s 1 .... 6, 70
- 4 6
- 7(2) 69, 94
- (3) 69
- (5) 68, 69, 94
- 8 69
- (2) 69, 70
- (3) 69, 70
- 10 .... 54, 71, 165
- 11 109
- 12(4) 69, 70
- Sch 2 .... 54, 71, 165
- Pt I 111
- Sch 3 .... 15, 74
- para 2(2) 109
- 7 109
- 8 .... 109, 111
- 9 111
- (1) 110
- (4) 110
- 10(1) 111
- (2) 111
- 11(2)(b) 111
- (c) 111

Education (Scotland) Act 1980 55

Evidence Further Amendment (Scotland) Act 1874
- s 2 145

Evidence (Scotland) Act 1853
   s 3 141
Execution of Diligence (Scotland) Act 1926
   s 1 100
Family Law Act 1986
   Pt I (ss 1–43) 54
   s 1(1)(b).........................55
   4 186
   ss 8–12 54
   8 ....71, 187
   9 165
   10 165
   12 165
   13(2) 54
     (3) 55
     (4) 54, 161
     (5) 161
     (6) 55
   14 120
   15 120
     (1) 161
     (2) 161
   17 ....57, 89, 156
   18(1) 54
   25 182
   26 120
   27 182
   28 183
   29 183
   30 183
   32(1) 56
   33 ....56, 126, 148, 184
   35 119
     (3) 56, 89, 155, 184
     (4) 184
   36 ....56, 184
   37 185
   40(1) 56
   41 185
   42(3) 54
Family Law (Scotland) Act
   1985 ....22, 24, 27, 31, 33,
              36, 40, 41, 46, 84,
                     153, 163
   s 1 ....39, 86, 116
     (1) 8, 10, 25, 27, 28
     (2) 9
     (5) 8, 39
   2 ....24, 25, 26
     (2)(a) 24

Family Law (Scotland) Act
   1985—*contd*
   s 2(3) 24
     (4) 24
       (a) 24
   3 ....24, 25, 26
     (1) 26, 157
   4 ....24, 25, 26, 125
     (1).....................9, 25, 26
     (2) 8
     (3)(a) 9
       (b) 9
   5 ....24, 25, 26
     (1) 156
     (4) 157
   6 ....24, 25, 86, 125
     (2) 24, 152
     (3) 25
     (4) 24, 25
   7(1) 27, 28
     (2) 27, 135
     (4) 27
   ss 8–13 153
   s 8 ....54, 172
     (1) 29, 84, 86, 154, 158
       (a) 29
       (b) 83
     (2) 23, 30, 42, 84, 152,
                  158, 161
       (b) 32, 34
   9 ....30, 32, 42, 43, 45,
               84, 97, 125, 152,
                   158, 163
     (1) 42
       (a) 32, 35, 36
       (b) 36, 37
       (c) 25, 38, 44, 84
       (d) 39, 41, 43, 44, 46,
                    83, 84
       (e) 40, 41, 46, 84, 133
     (2) 37
   10 ....84, 97, 125, 152, 163
     (1) 35, 36
       (b) 36
     (2) 34, 35
     (3) 34
       (b) 34
     (4) 32, 36
       (a) 32
     (5) 33
     (6) 35, 37

	PARA
Family Law (Scotland) Act 1985—contd	
s 10(6)(b)	33
(c)	36
(7)	34
11	84, 97, 125, 152, 163
(2)	38
(3)(a)	38
(4)	39
(c)	41
(5)	40
(6)	38, 40, 41
(7)	35, 37, 39, 40, 46
12	153
(1)	31
(b)	25
(2)	29, 31
(3)	31, 37
(4)	31, 157, 160
13(1)	153
(a)	42
(b)	25, 42
(c)	43
(2)	39, 40, 42, 83, 84, 153
(a)	38, 42, 84
(3)	43, 83
(4)	41, 43, 45, 156, 158, 160
(6)	45, 158
(7)(a)	45
(b)	45
14	20, 38, 42, 162
(1)	86, 161
(2)	23, 29, 30, 39, 86, 157
(d)	29, 30
(e)	29, 30
(3)	23, 30
(4)	30, 157, 159, 160, 161
15	29
(3)	30
16	28, 114, 156, 157, 161, 162
(1)(b)	135
18	21, 161, 162
(1)	66
19	68
(1)(b)	92, 128

	PARA
Family Law (Scotland) Act 1985—contd	
s 20	25, 87
22	116
24(1)	8
(2)	10
25	19, 62, 163
(1)	7
(2)	7
(3)	20
26	7
27	125
(1)	39
(2)	34
28(3)	163
Finance Act 1988	
ss 36–40	46
s 36	46
(4)	47
(6)	47
37	47
38	47
(3)	48
(4)	48
(5)	48
39	47
(3)	48
Guardianship Act 1973	
Pt II (ss 10–14)	165
s 11(1)(b)	120
Income and Corporation Taxes Act 1970	46
Income and Corporation Taxes Act 1988	
s 347A	46
(1)	46
(b)	46
347B	46
(2)	47
(3)	47
348	46
349	46
Judicial Proceedings (Regulation of Reports) Act 1926	
s 1	3
Law Reform (Husband and Wife) (Scotland) Act 1984	
s 2(3)	6
3(1)	6
(2)	6
4	6, 7

Law Reform (Husband and Wife) (Scotland) Act 1984—cont
s 6(1) 6
7(1) 7
(2) 7
(3) 7
Law Reform (Miscellaneous Provisions) (Scotland) Act 1966
s 1 92
8(1) 165
(3) 166
(5) 165
Law Reform (Miscellaneous Provisions) (Scotland) Act 1968
s 9 141
10(1) 145
11 144
Law Reform (Miscellaneous Provisions) (Scotland) Act 1985
s 14 108
Law Reform (Miscellaneous Provisions) (Scotland) Act 1990 82
Law Reform (Parent and Child) (Scotland) Act 1986
s 1(1) 49
2(1) 11
(b) 12, 49
(4) 11
3 . . . . 12, 49, 54, 71, 123
(1) 49, 50, 51
(2) 12, 49, 50, 53, 124
5(1) 7
8 . . . . 11, 12, 49, 50, 53
Sch 1, para 2 . . . . 54, 165
Legal Aid (Scotland) Act 1967
s 2(6)(e) 116
Maintenance Orders Act 1950 173
Pt II (ss 16–25) 171
s 16(1)(b) 171
17 . . . . 174, 175
(7) 175
18(1) 171
(2A) 172
(6) 173, 175
19(2) 173
20(2) 174
21 174

Maintenance Orders Act 1950—contd
s 21(2) 174
22 174
(1) 174
(4) 174
(5) 174
24 173
(1) 175
(2) 175
Maintenance Orders (Reciprocal Enforcement) Act 1972 . . . . . 175, 176, 177
Pt I (ss 1–24) 176, 180, 182
s 2 178
(1) 178
3(5) 179
4 178
(4)(a) 179
(b) 179
5 179
(5) 179
7(2) 179
21(1) 178
Pt II (ss 25–39) 176, 180, 181
s 26 180
(2) 180
31(1) 180
39 180
Pt III (ss 40–49) 176, 181
Matrimonial and Family Proceedings Act 1984
s 28(1) 154
(3) 155
(4) 154
29 172
(1) 155
(4) 155
(5) 155
Matrimonial Homes (Family Protection) (Scotland) Act 1981 . . . . 11, 21, 22, 23, 30, 33, 58, 60, 62, 91, 106, 109, 121, 122, 123
s 1 63
2 23
(5) 62
3 . . . . 20, 23, 92, 121, 134, 157, 162
(1) 58
(a) 58

Matrimonial Homes (Family Protection) (Scotland) Act 1981—*contd*
s 3(1)(b) 59, 91
(c) 59, 91
(d) 59, 91
(e) 59, 91
(2).....................58, 62, 63
(3).....................59, 66, 134
(d)........................134
(4).........23, 58, 63, 121, 122
(5).....................59, 134
(6) 62
(7).....................63, 134
4 ....20, 23, 75, 91, 121, 134, 157, 162
(1) 59, 60
(2) 59, 134
(3) 59, 134
(4) 20, 61, 90, 134
(b).........................63
(c).........................63
(5)...................20, 23, 61
(a) 63, 91
(b).....................20, 62
(c).........................62
(6).....................60, 121, 122
5 ....23, 60, 122
(1) 61, 157
(5)(c).........................90
6.........................24
13 ....31, 154
(1) 66
(3) 66
(4) 66
(7) 20
(9) 66
14.........................21
(2) 65
15.................21, 75, 121, 169
(1) 122
(a).........................63
(b).......23, 63, 77, 79, 121, 134
(2) 64, 122
(4) 64
(5) 64, 122
18(1) 122
(2) 67
(4) 67
19 ....31, 42

Matrimonial Homes (Family Protection) (Scotland) Act 1981—*contd*
22............................63
Matrimonial Proceedings (Children) Act 1958
Pt II (ss 7-15) 161, 165
s 8............................50
(1) 50, 51, 139, 143, 148
(2) 157
9(1).....................54, 161
10 ....51, 93, 126
11 ....125, 126
(4) 147
12 ....51, 93, 127, 183
(1) 120
15 50
42 161
Mental Health (Scotland) Act 1984 ....13, 93, 104, 112
s 1 ....72, 95
(2) 112, 140
Recorded Delivery Service Act 1962
s 1 ....100, 101
Registration of Births, Deaths and Marriages Act 1965
s 41 ....143, 144
Sheriff Courts (Scotland) Act 1907
s 5(2A)........................180
(2B) 13, 68
(2C) 49, 123
6(a) 165
(b) 165
(j)........................165
38B 113, 136
38C 49, 54, 71
Sch 1 (Ordinary Cause Rules)
r 3(5) 15, 75, 78, 120
(7) 131
(8).....................110, 111
(9) 99, 101, 143
4(3) 99
7(1) 102
(2) 102
8(1) 101
(2) 101
9 103
(2) 101
(3) 101

Table of Statutes xvii

Sheriff Courts (Scotland) Act 1907—contd	PARA
r 10	101
(1)	101
11	103
(a)(3)	105
11A	92, 102, 132
(1)	93
(3)	106
(4)	102
(6)	136
12	103
(1)(a)	103
(2)	103
15(1)	101, 103
(4)	101
17	107
19	107
20A	108
21	130
(2)(a)	114
22	49
23	142
(1)	114, 149
(c)	130
(2)	114, 149
(3)	142
28	135
33	128
34	113, 129, 130, 131, 132
(2)	129
(3)	129
(6)	113, 129
43(2)	131
47(1)	131, 135
48	23
51	132
56(1)	132
(3)	113, 129
59(1)	130
59A	136
72	142
(1)	60, 114, 149
(b)	112
(2)	114, 149
(3)	142
(4)	123, 147
(5)	115
72A	149
73(4)	49, 142

Sheriff Courts (Scotland) Act 1907—contd	PARA
r 78	130, 137, 152
(3)	98
80	98, 137
81	137, 152
82	137, 152
84(4)	98
91–96	97
129	87, 135, 162, 164
(1)	24, 160
(2)	156
(c)	154
(3)	162
(4)	87, 120, 160
130	92
(1)(a)	92, 105
(c)	92, 104
(2)(a)	92
(b)	105
(3)	93
(b)	93
(4)	93, 106
(5)	93, 106
(6)	106
(7)	106
(b)	106
(9)	93, 106
(11)(a)	104, 107
(12)	130
(13)	130
131(2)	99, 105
(4)	99, 105
132	107
132A	135
(3)	156
(4)	156
132B	189
132C	78, 87
132E	185
132F	14, 136
133	112
(1)	112
(2)	112
(3)	132
135–143	71, 95
135	13
(2)	71, 195
(3)	95
136	13

	PARA
Sheriff Courts (Scotland) Act 1907—*contd*	
r 137	96
138(6)	96
(10)	105
139(1)	96
140(1)	97
(3)	97
141(2)	97
142	97
143	97
Form B1	99
C1	99, 101, 105
D	101
E	103
E1	103
H1	92, 105
H2	92, 105
H3	92, 106
H4	92, 106
H5	92, 106
H6A	106
H7	106
S1	99, 105
S3	99, 105
T	99, 105, 106
V	102
V1	102, 106
Sheriff Courts (Scotland) Act 1907—*contd*	
Form V2	102, 105
W	102
X	115
SDA1	13, 71, 95
Pt I–III	95
SDA2	13, 71, 95
SDA3	13, 71, 95
SDA4	71, 95, 96
SDA5	71, 95
SDA6	71, 95
SDA7	71, 95, 105
Sheriff Courts (Scotland) Act 1971	
s 37(2A)	108
(3)	108
Sheriff Courts (Scotland) Extracts Act 1892	83, 86
Social Work (Scotland) Act 1968	
Pt II (ss 12–29)	55
ss 16–17A	51
Pt III (ss 30–58)	55
s 44	51
Statutory Declarations Act 1835	149
Writs Execution (Scotland) Act 1877	
s 3	27, 170

TABLE OF ORDERS, RULES AND REGULATIONS

	PARA
Act of Sederunt (Applications under the Matrimonial Homes (Family Protection) (Scotland) Act 1981) 1982, SI 1982/1432	58, 162
para 3	59, 66, 93, 106
9	64
Act of Sederunt (Civil Legal Aid Rules) 1987, SI 1987/492	73
Act of Sederunt (Consistorial Causes) 1984, SI 1984/255 para 3(15)	123
Act of Sederunt (Interest on Sheriff Court Decrees or Extracts) 1975, SI 1975/948	83, 86
Act of Sederunt (Legal Aid Rules) 1958, SI 1958/1872 para 3	73
Act of Sederunt (Maintenance Orders Act 1950, Courts of Summary Jurisdiction Rules) 1951, SI 1951/552	173
Act of Sederunt Maintenance Orders Acts, Rules (Court of Session) 1980, SI 1980/1727	172
r 7	173
9	173
13	173
15	174
17	175
18	175
Act of Sederunt Maintenance Orders Acts, Rules (Sheriff Court) 1980, SI 1980/1732	172
r 4	172
8	173
10	173
Act of Sederunt Maintenance Orders Acts, Rules (Sheriff Court) 1980, SI 1980/1732—*contd*	
r 12	174
14	174
15	174
Act of Sederunt (Proceedings in the Sheriff Court under the Debtors (Scotland) Act 1987) 1988, SI 1988/2013	170
r 42	171
Form 34	171
Act of Sederunt (Reciprocal Enforcement of Maintenance Orders) (Hague Convention Countries) 1980, SI 1980/291	180
Act of Sederunt (Reciprocal Enforcement of Maintenance Orders (Republic of Ireland) Order 1974 Rules) 1975, SI 1975/475	181, 182
para 4	182
7	182
Sch 2, para 4(1)	182
Act of Sederunt (Rules for Registration of Custody Orders of the Sheriff Court) 1988, SI 1988/613	182–3
Act of Sederunt (Rules of Court, Consolidation and Amendment) 1965, SI 1965/321	
RC 66	83, 86
68A	100
72	96, 100, 104
(3)	101
74	99
(b)	99

| PARA | PARA |

Act of Sederunt (Rules of Court, Consolidation and Amendment) 1965, SI 1965/321—*contd*

RC 74(h)	128
(i)	107
74A(2)	102
74B	100, 103
(1)(d)	96
(e)	96
75	102, 103
78	107
(d)	101
79	119
(1)	101
81(1)	128
83(d)	131
84(j)	132
89	130, 135
95–98	137, 152
95	137
(a)	98
95A	98
104A	108
B	108
108A	149
154(2)	112
155	80, 92, 99, 100, 105
(1)	92
(2)	92, 104
(3)	93, 105, 106
(5)	93, 106
156(2)	67, 73
157(1)	80
(2)	83
(3)	120
(a)	75
(b)	15, 75
(c)	131
158	96, 100, 104, 107
159	102, 107
(1)(c)	99
(2)	100
(3)	100
(b)	99, 100
(4)	100
(5)	102
160	105, 106, 107
(1)	105
161	100, 105
(1)	99, 105
(3)	99, 105

Act of Sederunt (Rules of Court, Consolidation and Amendment) 1965, SI 1965/321—*contd*

RC 162	105
(1)	92, 93
(2)	105
(3)	93
164	92, 105
165	130
166	107
(2)	147
167	112
(1)	112
(a)	112
(c)	132
(2)	110, 111
168	115
(1)	142
(b)	112
(2)	114, 149
(3)	142
(4)	142
(5)	140
(6)	123, 147
(9)(a)	116
(10)	142
168A	135
169	136
170B	164
(5)	129
(6)	93
(7)	130, 132, 136
(8)	74, 87, 156, 161
(10)	154, 160, 161, 162
(11)	75, 87
(13)	155, 185
(15)	14, 136
170C(1)	56, 119
(2)	57, 119
170D	129, 164
(c)	93
(2)	131, 132
(3)	154, 159, 161
(5)	132
(7)	135, 161
(8)	161
(9)	106
170E–170L	71, 95
170E(2)	71, 95
(3)	95
170G	96

	PARA
Act of Sederunt (Rules of Court, Consolidation and Amendment) 1965, SI 1965/321—*contd*	
RC 170I	96
(3)	105
170J	97
170K	97
170L	97
170M	154
170P	24, 156, 161
170R	161
188D	58
(3)	122
(4)	122
(7)	66, 93, 106
(c)	59
(9)	64, 122
(13)	64
(15)	60, 123
236	119
260D(10)	136
260EB	184
260EC	185
260J(1)	187
(2)	188
(3)	187
260K	189
(1)	188
(2)	188
(3)	189
(4)	189
260R–260W	182
260U	184
264(a)	97, 136
274	109
275	109
Form 2	81, 87
3	99, 100, 105
15A	99, 105
15C	99, 105
15E	99, 105, 106
16–19	92
16	105
17	102, 105
18	102, 106
18A	106
18B	106
18C	106
18D	106
18E	106
19	105

	PARA
Act of Sederunt (Rules of Court, Consolidation and Amendment) 1965, SI 1965/321—*contd*	
RC Form 19A–19E	13, 71, 95
19A, Part I–III	95
19B	95
20	102
21	102
Act of Sederunt (Variation and Recall of Orders in Consistorial Causes) 1984, SI 1984/667	165
para 3(3)	165
6	166
8	166
Child Abduction and Custody (Parties to Conventions) (Amendment) (No 2) Order 1989, SI 1989/980	188
Child Abduction and Custody (Parties to Conventions) (Amendment) (No 3) Order 1989, SI 1989/1332	186
Evidence in Divorce Actions (Scotland) Order 1989, SI 1989/582	140
Evidence in Undefended Divorce Actions (Scotland) Order 1983, SI 1983/949	140
Family Law (Scotland) Act 1985 (Commencement No 1) Order 1986, SI 1986/1237	163
Family Law (Scotland) Act 1985 (Commencement No 2) Order 1986, SI 1988/1887	163
Maintenance Orders (Reciprocal Enforcement) Act 1972 Rules 1974, SI 1974/939	175
r 3(1)	178
4(1)	178
10(1)	178
17(2)	179
18(a)	179
Reciprocal Enforcement of Maintenance Orders (Designation of Reciprocating Countries Order 1974, SI 1974/556	176, 177

Reciprocal Enforcement of Maintenance Orders (Designation of Reciprocating Countries Order 1975, SI 1975/2187 177
Reciprocal Enforcement of Maintenance Orders (Designation of Reciprocating Countries) Order 1979, SI 1979/115 177
Reciprocal Enforcement of Maintenance Orders (Designation of Reciprocating Countries) Order 1983, SI 1983/1125 .... 176, 177
Reciprocal Enforcement of Maintenance Orders (Hague Convention Countries) Order 1979, SI 1979/1317 177
Reciprocal Enforcement of Maintenance Orders (Hague Convention Countries) (Variation) Order 1981, SI 1981/837 177
Reciprocal Enforcement of Maintenance Orders (Hague Convention Countries) (Variation) (No 2) Order 1981, SI 1981/1545 177
Reciprocal Enforcement of Maintenance Orders (Hague Convention Countries) (Variation) (No 3) Order 1981, SI 1981/1674 177
Reciprocal Enforcement of Maintenance Orders (Hague Convention Countries) (Variation) Order 1983, SI 1983/885 177
Reciprocal Enforcement of Maintenance Orders (Hague Convention Countries) (Variation) (No 2) Order 1983, SI 1983/1523 177
Reciprocal Enforcement of Maintenance Orders (Hague Convention Countries) (Variation) Order 1987, SI 1987/1282 177
Reciprocal Enforcement of Maintenance Orders (Republic of Ireland) Order 1974, SI 1974/2140 181
Sch 2 181
Recovery Abroad of Maintenance (Convention Countries) Order 1975, SI 1975/423 180
Recovery Abroad of Maintenance (Convention Countries) Order 1978, SI 1978/279 180
Recovery Abroad of Maintenance (Convention Countries) Order 1982, SI 1982/1530 180
Recovery Abroad of Maintenance (United States of America) Order 1981, SI 1981/606 181
Recovery of Maintenance (United States of America) Order 1979, SI 1979/1314 181
Recovery of Maintenance (United States of America) (Variation) Order 1984, SI 1984/1824 181

TABLE OF CASES

A, Re (a minor) (Abduction) (1988) 18 Fam Law 54 187
A v B (1858) 20 D 407 139
AB v CB 1937 SC 408 94
AB v Mr and Mrs M 1987 SCLR 389, 1988 SLT 652 (sub nom AB,
 Petitioner) 49
Abrahams v Abrahams 1989 SCLR 102, 1989 SLT (Sh Ct) 113 ....26, 157, 164
Abusaif v Abusaif 1984 SLT 90 54
Aitken v Aitken 1978 SLT 183 51
Allum v Allum 1965 SLT (Sh Ct) 26 174
Anderson v Anderson 1989 GWD 19–814 114
Anderson v Anderson 1990 GWD 29–1677 28
Andrews v Andrews 1961 SLT (Notes) 48 139
Andrews v Andrews 1971 SLT (Notes) 44 ....144, 145
Archibald v Archibald 1989 SLT 199 ....29, 31, 37
Argyll v Argyll 1963 SLT (Notes) 42 146
Armstrong v Armstrong 1970 SLT 247 117
Atkinson v Atkinson 1988 SCLR 396 ....42, 44
B, Re (minors) (1987) The Times, 29 October, 1987 CLY 2467 186
Bain v Bain 1990 GWD 3–136 153
Barbour v Barbour 1965 SC 158 124
Barr v Barr 1939 SC 696 144
Battu v Battu 1979 SLT (Notes) 7 135
Beaton v Beaton's Trs 1935 SC 187 27
Begg v Begg 1987 SCLR 704 26
Bell v Bell 1982 SLT 518 91
Bell v Bell 1983 SLT 224 ....59, 60
Bell v Bell 1988 SCLR 457 44
Bennet Clark v Bennet Clark 1909 SC 591 145
Berry v Berry 1988 SLT 650 30
Berry v Berry 1990 GWD 12–617 152
Beverley v Beverley 1977 SLT (Sh Ct) 3 162
Bird v Bird 1931 SC 731 139
Black v Black 1988 SLT (Sh Ct) 24 160
Black v Black 1990 GWD 30–1777 125
Black Arrow Group v Park 1990 SCLR 99 122
Blance v Blance 1978 SLT 74 53
Bonnar v Bonnar 1911 SC 854 125
Boughen v Scott 1983 SLT (Sh Ct) 94 116
Boyce v Boyce 1986 SLT (Sh Ct) 26 146
Boyd v Boyd 1978 SLT (Notes) 55 130

Boyle v Boyle 1977 SLT (Notes) 69 124
Boyle v Boyle 1986 SLT 656 61
Bradley v Bradley 1987 SCLR 62 50
Brannigan v Brannigan 1979 SLT (Notes) 73 53
British Phonographic Industry v Cohen, Cohen, Kelly, Cohen & Cohen Ltd
    1983 SLT 137 98
Britton v Central Regional Council 1986 SLT 207 51
Brodie v Brodie 1986 GWD 5–100 33
Brown v Brown 1948 SC 5 .... 57, 184
Brown v Brown 1985 SLT 376 .... 58, 60, 61, 91
Browne v Browne 1969 SLT (Notes) 15 51
Brunt v Brunt 1954 SLT (Sh Ct) 74 169
Brunton v Brunton 1986 SLT 49 .... 26, 163
Bryan v Bryan 1985 SLT 444 28
Buczynska v Buczynski 1989 SCLR 224, 1989 SLT 558 ...... 32, 33, 34, 35, 37
Budge v Budge 1990 SCLR (Notes) 144, 1990 SLT 319 36
Burnett v Burnett 1955 SC 183 .... 140, 145
Burnett v Burnett 1958 SC 1 82
Byars v McDonald 1990 GWD 28–1610 123
C, Re (a minor) (1988) The Times, 19 December 186
C v C [1989] 2 All ER 465 187
Cain v McColm (1892) 19 R 813 169
Cairns v McNulty 1989 GWD 37–1688 51
Caldwell v Caldwell 1983 SLT 610 .... 58, 89, 184
Campbell v Campbell (1860) 23 D 99 144
Campbell v Campbell 1977 SLT 125 51
Campins-Coll Petr 1989 SLT 33 189
Carpenter v Carpenter 1990 SLT (Sh Ct) 68 .... 31, 33, 42
Carroll v Carroll 1988 SCLR 104 44
Casey v Casey (1925) 41 Sh Ct Rep 300 108
Casey v Casey 1989 SCLR 761 .... 52, 148
Cassells v Cassells 1955 SLT (Sh Ct) 41 169
Caven v Caven 1987 SLT 761 163
Chalkley v Chalkley 1984 SLT 281 116
Clark v Clark 1983 SLT 371 164
Clark v Clark 1987 SCLR 516 .... 35, 44
Clark v Stirling (1839) 1 D 955 65
Cleghorn v Fairgrieve 1982 SLT (Sh Ct) 17 117
Colagiacomo v Colagiacomo 1983 SLT 559 .... 60, 61
Collins v Collins (1884) 11 R (HL) 19 133
Colville v Colville 1988 SLT (Sh Ct) 23 97
Cook v Wallace & Wilson (1889) 16 R 565 170
Cooper v Cooper 1987 SLT (Sh Ct) 37 .... 145, 150
Cooper v Cooper 1989 SCLR 347 37
Cordiner, Petitioner 1973 JC 16 169
Cosgrove v Cosgrove 1980 SLT (Sh Ct) 105 157
Cosh v Cosh 1979 SLT (Notes) 72 53
Cowan v Cowan 1952 SLT (Sh Ct) 8 174
Coyle v Coyle; Neilly v Neilly 1981 SLT (Notes) 129 26
Craigie v Craigie 1979 SLT (Notes) 60 116
Creasey v Creasey 1931 SC 9 .... 136, 144
Crooks v Crooks 1986 SLT 500 29

Crow v Crow 1986 SLT 270 30
Crowley v Armstrong 1990 SCLR 361 49
Currie v Currie 1950 SC 10 146
Cuthbertson v Cuthbertson 1987 GWD 30–1129......................129
D, Re (A Minor) (Child Abduction) (1988) 18 Fam Law 336, (1989) 1 FLR 97 190
Davidson v Davidson 1989 SLT 466 27
Deans v Deans 1988 SCLR 192 185
Demarco v Demarco (1990) 6 CL 951 138
Dever v Dever 1988 SCLR 352..44
Dickson v Dickson 1982 SLT 128 30
Dickson v Dickson 1990 SCLR 542...................................125
Dickson v Dickson 1990 GWD 23–1265 ....186, 187
Docherty v Docherty 1981 SLT (Notes) 24 100
Don v Don (1848) 10 D 1046 145
Donaldson v Donaldson 1988 SLT 243 24
Donnelly v Donnelly 1990 SCLR 344 ....75, 110, 116
Doughton v Doughton 1958 SLT (Notes) 34 80
Douglas v Douglas 1932 SC 680 125
Douglas v Douglas 1966 SLT (Notes) 43............................137
Driffel v Driffel 1971 SLT (Notes) 60 54
Dunbar v Dunbar 1912 SC 19 108
Dunbar v Dunbar 1977 SLT 169 28
Duncan v Duncan 1986 SLT 17......................................115, 135
Duncan v Gerard (1888) 4 Sh Ct Rep 246...........................10
Dunnett v Dunnett 1990 SCLR 135.....................75, 110, 116
E, Re (A minor) (1989) FLR 35 187
Early v Early 1989 SLT 114, affd on appeal: 1990 SLT 221 50
Ebrahem v Ebrahem 1989 SCLR 540 149
Edgar v Edgar; Porter v Porter 1990 SCLR 96......................115, 135
Edinburgh District Council v Davis 1978 SLT 33....................69
Edmond v Edmond 1971 SLT (Notes) 8 82
Edmonstone v Edmonstone 1987 SCLR 464 37
Edwards v Edwards 1984 SLT 311 ....26, 44
Elder v Elder 1985 SLT 471 28
F v F (minors) [1988] 3 WLR 959 189
Farley v Farley 1990 SCLR 452 132
Findlay v Findlay 1988 GWD 24–1034 141
Finlay v Finlay 1962 SLT (Sh Ct) 43 113
Finlayson v Finlayson's Exrx 1986 SLT 19.........................156, 159
Finnie v Finnie 1984 SLT 439......................................47, 88
Fisher and Donaldson v Steven 1988 SCLR 337...................139
Foreman v Foreman 1989 GWD 14–600 157
Fowler v Fowler 1981 SLT (Notes) 9..............................148
Fowler v Fowler (No 2) 1981 SLT (Notes) 78 ....57, 58
Foy v Foy 1987 GWD 7–206 52
Freel v Freel 1987 SCLR 665 132
Frith v Frith 1990 GWD 5–266 ....9, 26
Fyffe v Fyffe 1954 SC 1 ....124, 125
Gall v Gall 1968 SC 332, 1969 SLT 7.............................54
Gallacher v Gallacher 1934 SC 339................................133
Galloway v Galloway 1973 SLT (Notes) 84........................45, 158

Gardezi v Gardezi 1987 GWD 37–1327 130
Gavin v Gavin 1989 GWD 19–785 170
Geddes v Geddes 1987 SLT 118 44
Gibson v Gibson 1970 SLT (Notes) 60 94
Girvan v Girvan 1985 SLT 92 109
Girvan v Girvan 1988 SCLR 493, 1988 SLT 866 ....71, 159
Glenday v Johnson (1905) 8 F 24 169
Gould v Gould 1966 SLT 130 137
Gover v Gover 1969 SLT (Notes) 78 53
Gow v Gow 1987 SCLR 610, 1987 SLT 798 ....117, 164
Graham v Graham 1984 SLT 89 46
Graham v Robert Younger Ltd 1955 JC 28 66
Gribben v Gribben 1976 SLT 266 ....167, 168
Grindlay v Grindlay 1987 SLT 264 163
Hall v Hall 1958 SC 206 145
Hall v Hall 1979 SLT (Sh Ct) 33 100
Hall v Hall 1987 SLT (Sh Ct) 15 31
Hampsey v Hampsey 1988 GWD 24–1035 61
Hannah v Hannah 1988 SLT 82 164
Hardie v Hardie 1984 SLT (Sh Ct) 49 169
Harris v Harris 1988 SLT 101 66
Hart v Hart 1960 SLT (Notes) 33 24
Hastie v Hastie 1985 SLT 146 147
Hay v Lefelier-Lebos 1989 SCLR 501, 1989 SLT (Sh Ct) 55 167
Hay's Trs v Young (1877) 4 R 398 64
Henderson v Maclellan (1874) 1 R 920 65
Hollywood v Hollywood 1989 SCLR 521 132
Horn v Horn 1935 SLT 589 70
Howarth v Howarth 1990 SLT 289 ....26, 28, 159
Huddart v Huddart 1960 SC 300, 1960 SLT 275 ....51, 53
Huddart v Huddart 1961 SC 393 54
Huggins v Huggins 1981 SLT 179 ....47, 88
Hulme v Hulme 1990 SCLR 181 125
Hunt v Hunt 1987 GWD 14–493 51
Hunter v Hunter (1900) 2 F 771 133
Hunter v Hunter 1979 SLT (Notes) 2 148
Jenkins v Jenkins 1990 GWD 8–425 159
Jenkinson v Jenkinson 1981 SLT 65 ....156, 159
Joffre v Joffre 1989 GWD 536 52
Johnson v Francis 1982 SLT 285 54
Johnston v Carson 1990 SCLR 460 124
Johnstone v Johnstone 1967 SLT 248 120
Johnstone v Johnstone 1990 SLT (Sh Ct) 79 41
Jones v Jones 1990 SCLR 127 71
Jordan v Jordan 1983 SLT 539 51
Jowett v Jowett 1990 SCLR 348 26
Juner v Juner (1908) 15 SLT 732 124
Kavanagh v Kavanagh 1989 SLT 134 ....26, 163
Kelso School Board v Hunter (1874) 2 R 228 65
Kerrigan v Kerrigan 1988 SCLR 603 35
Kilgour v Kilgour 1987 GWD 4–107 187
Killen v Killen 1981 SLT (Sh Ct) 77 179

Kristiansen v Kristiansen 1987 SCLR 462 147
Lacy v Lacy (1869) 7 M 369 143
Lambert v Lambert 1982 SLT 144 46
Lamont v Lamont 1939 SC 484 108
Latter v Latter 1990 SLT 805 .... 33, 137
Leslie v Leslie 1983 SLT 186, 1987 SLT 232 67
Leys v Leys (1886) 13 R 1223 57
Little v Little 1989 SCLR 613 .... 29, 33, 37, 42
Little v Little 1990 SLT 785 .... 33, 34
Love v Love 1983 SLT (Sh Ct) 21 26
Low, Petr 1920 SC 351 57
McAfee v McAfee 1990 GWD 28–1611 28
Macalister v Macalister 1978 SLT (Notes) 78 150
McArthur v Organon Laboratories Ltd 1982 SLT 425 141
McCafferty v McCafferty 1986 SLT 650 .... 59, 60, 61
McCallum v McCallum 1989 GWD 21–890 164
McCann v McCann 1987 SCLR 742 51
MacColl v MacColl 1946 SLT 312 146
McCulloch v McCulloch 1990 SCLR 155, 1990 SLT (Sh Ct) 63 ... 75, 110, 116
McDevitt v McDevitt 1988 SCLR 206 .... 44, 152
MacDonald v MacDonald 1948 SLT 380 34
McDonald v McDonald 1953 SLT (Sh Ct) 36 10
MacDonald v MacDonald 1985 SLT 244 148
McEachan v Young 1988 SCLR 98 .... 49, 50, 54, 124, 139
Macfarlane v Macfarlane 1956 SC 472 .... 141, 144
MacFarlane v MacFarlane (1985) JLSS 126 136
McGeachie v McGeachie 1989 SCLR 99 26
McGowan v Lord Advocate 1972 SC 68 141
McGowan v McGowan 1986 SLT 112 66
McIlhargey v Herron 1972 SLT 185 152
McInnes v McInnes 1954 SC 396 145
MacInnes v MacInnes 1990 GWD 13–690 26
McInnes v McInnes 1990 SCLR 327 149
McIntosh v Macrae (1887) 4 Sh Ct Rep 317 10
MacIntyre v MacIntyre 1962 SLT (Notes) 70 .... 51, 147
Mackay v Mackay 1946 SC 78 146
McKechnie v McKechnie 1990 SCLR 153, 1990 SLT (Sh Ct) 75 ...... 53, 113
MacKenzie v Hendry 1984 SLT 322 53
Mackenzie v Mackenzie 1983 SLT 678 .... 42, 44
McKenzie v McKenzie 1987 SCLR 671 27
McKenna v McKenna 1984 SLT (Sh Ct) 92 .... 63, 65, 90
McKeown v McKeown 1988 SCLR 355 30
McKidd v Manson (1882) 9 R 790 .... 75, 110, 116
Maclellan v Maclellan 1988 SCLR 399 32
MacLennan v MacLennan 1955 SC 105 146
MacLeod v MacLeod 1990 SCLR (Notes) 157 22
MacLeod v MacLeod 1990 GWD 14–767 .... 46, 82, 164
MacLure v MacLure 1911 SC 200 61
McMahon v McMahon 1928 SN 37 133
MacMillan v MacMillan 1989 SCLR 243, 1989 SLT 350 .... 186, 187
McNab v Nelson 1909 2 SLT 68 132
McNeill v McNeill 1960 SC 30 94

Macpherson v Macpherson 1989 SCLR 132, 1989 SLT 231 .... 163, 164, 165
McRae v McRae 1979 SLT (Notes) 45 29
McRae v McRae 1988 SCLR 257 164
McRobbie v McRobbie (1983) 29 JLSS 5 58
McWilliams v McWilliams 1963 SC 259 169
M, Petrs, 1989 SCLR 151 49
Mackin v Mackin 1990 GWD 26–1486 .... 29, 42
Main v Main 1990 SCLR 165 .... 35, 37
Mann v Glendinning 1990 SCLR 137 49
Marchetti v Marchetti (1901) 3 F 888 57
Mather v Mather 1987 SLT 565 .... 62, 134
Matheson v Matheson 1986 SLT (Sh Ct) 2 60
Matheson v Matheson 1988 SLT 238 24
Matthews v Matthews 1985 SLT (Sh Ct) 68 .... 115, 135
Michlek v Michlek 1971 SLT (Notes) 50 142
Mills v Mills 1990 SCLR 213 .... 157, 163
Milne v Milne (1885) 13 R 304 116
Milne v Milne 1987 SLT 45 .... 114, 156, 159
Monkman v Monkman 1988 SLT (Sh Ct) 37 130
Montgomery v Lockwood 1987 SCLR 525 .... 49, 50, 54, 124
Morrison v J Kelly & Sons Ltd 1970 SC 65 141
Morrison v Morrison 1989 SCLR 574 39
Muir v Milligan (1868) 6 M 1125 57
Muir v Muir (1873) 11 M 529 145
Muir v Muir 1989 SCLR 445, 1989, SLT (Sh Ct) 20 .... 34, 42
Munro v Munro 1986 SLT 72 .... 9, 26, 163
Murdoch v Murdoch 1973 SLT (Notes) 13 .... 21, 65, 77, 90, 121
Murphy v Murphy 1981 SLT (Notes) 27 34
Murray v Murray 1990 SCLR 226 97
Neill v Neill 1987 SLT (Sh Ct) 143 .... 25, 43
Nelson v Nelson 1988 SCLR 663 168
Nelson v Nelson 1988 SLT (Sh Ct) 26 .... 23, 58, 60, 122, 130
Nelson v Nelson 1989 SLT (Sh Ct) 18 .... 50, 57, 65, 119
Neville v Neville 1924 SLT (Sh Ct) 43 65
Nicolson v Nicolson (1869) 7 M 1118 57
Nimmo v Nimmo (1983) 29 JLSS 4 58
Nixon v Nixon 1987 SLT 602 157
Nolan v Lindsay 1990 SCLR 56 .... 49, 58
Nolan v Nolan 1979 SLT 293 .... 41, 130
O'Donnell v Murdoch Mackenzie & Co 1967 SLT 229 152
Olds v Olds 1990 SCLR 347 .... 162, 164
Oliver v Oliver 1988 SCLR 285 147
Orr v Orr 1989 GWD 12–506 .... 49, 50, 54
Orr v Orr 27 August 1990, Cupar Sh Ct (unreported) 33
Park v Park 1988 SCLR 584 36
Passmore v Passmore 1972 SLT (Notes) 18 146
Paterson v Paterson 1938 SC 251 .... 133, 139
Paterson v Paterson 1958 SC 141 114
Peploe v Peploe 1964 SLT (Notes) 44 124
Petrie v Petrie 1988 SCLR 390 33
Phillip v Phillip 1988 SCLR 427 .... 44, 152
Philp v Philp 1988 SCLR 313 159

Phonographic Performance Ltd v McKenzie 1982 SLT 272 65
Porchetta v Porchetta 1986 SLT 105 ....50, 53, 139
Pow v Pow 1987 SLT 127..68, 128
Pringle v Pringle 1967 SLT (Notes) 60 132
Rae v Rae 1990 GWD 13-713 108
Raeburn v Raeburn 1990 GWD 8-424 61
Raeside v Raeside 1913 SC 60 136
Ralston v Ralston (1881) 8 R 371.......................................133
Rattray v Rattray (1897) 25 R 315.....................................146
Reid v Reid 1987 GWD 8-308...139
Richardson v Richardson 23 October 1990, Alloa Sh Ct (unreported) 125
Riddell v Riddell 1952 SC 475..133
Risi or Keenan v Keenan 1974 SLT (Notes) 10....................144, 146
Ritchie v Ritchie 1987 SCLR 90, 1987 SLT (Sh Ct) 7......24, 25, 45, 158, 159
Ritchie v Ritchie 1989 SCLR 768 26
Rixson v Rixson 1990 SLT (Sh Ct) 5 125
Robertson v McDonald (1829) 7 S 272....................................65
Robertson v Robertson 1972 SLT (Notes) 64 132
Robertson v Robertson 1981 SLT (Notes) 7 53
Robertson v Robertson 1989 SCLR 71 ....33, 135, 164
Robertson, Petr 1911 SC 1319 57
Robson v Robson 1973 SLT (Notes) 4 114
Ross v Ross 1988 SCLR 267 163
Roy, Nicholson, Becker & Day v Clarke 1984 SLT (Sh Ct) 16 116
Runciman v Runciman 1965 SLT (Notes) 6 51
S v S 1967 SC (HL) 46, 1967 SLT 217 ....51, 53, 54
Sanderson v Sanderson 1979 SLT (Notes) 36 149
Sandison's Exrx v Sandison 1984 SLT 111 ....156, 159
Sands v Sands 1964 SLT 80..133
Savage v Savage 1981 SLT (Notes) 17 137
Scrimgeour v Scrimgeour 1988 SLT 590 170
Scully v Scully 1989 SCLR 757 ....26, 125
Sharp v Sharp 1946 SLT 116...116
Shaw v Henderson 1982 SLT 211 143
Sinclair v Sinclair 1986 SLT (Sh Ct) 54 ....145, 150
Sinclair v Sinclair 1987 GWD 16-587 52
Sinclair v Sinclair 1987 GWD 35-1239 51
Singh v Singh 1988 SCLR 541 71
Sloss v Taylor 1989 SCLR 407..12, 139
Smith v Smith 1964 SC 218, 1964 SLT 309 130
Smith v Smith 1983 SLT 275 ....59, 123
Smith v Smith 1988 SCLR 520, 1988 SLT 840 ....163, 164
Smith v Smith 1989 SCLR 308, 1989 SLT 668 ....33, 136
Sochart v Sochart 1988 SLT 449 ....114, 159
Speedie v Steel 1941 SLT (Sh Ct) 2 11
Stein v Stein 1936 SLT 103..80
Steven v Steven 1919 2 SLT 239 133
Stevens v Stevens 1987 GWD 16-605 130
Stewart v Stewart 1987 SLT (Sh Ct) 48 82
Stewart v Stewart 1987 SLT 246..159
Stewart v Stewart 1990 SCLR 360 27
Stirton v Stirton 1969 SLT (Notes) 48 136

Stott v Stott 1987 GWD 17-645 41
Strain v Strain (1886) 13 R 1029 170
Strain v Strain (1885) 2 Sh Ct Rep 108 10
Sutherland v Sutherland 1988 SCLR 346 ....114, 159, 164
T v T 1987 SLT (Sh Ct) 74 72
Tattersall v Tattersall 1983 SLT 506 ....59, 61, 65
Taylor v Taylor 1988 SCLR 60 106
Thirde v Thirde 1987 SCLR 335 84
Thompson v Thompson (1953) 69 Sh Ct Rep 193 174
Thomson v Thomson (1887) 14 R 634 94
Thomson v Thomson 1908 SC 179 133
Thomson v Thomson 1979 SLT (Sh Ct) 11 ....54, 57
Thomson v Thomson 1982 SLT 521 28
Thomson, Petr 1980 SLT (Notes) 29 ....57, 184
Traill v Traill 1925 SLT (Sh Ct) 54 10
Trolland v Trolland 1987 SLT (Sh Ct) 42 ....23, 58
Tullis v Tullis 1953 SC 312 142
Tyrrell v Tyrrell 1990 SLT 406 ....33, 34, 40, 44
Walker v Walker 1953 SC 297 142
Walker v Walker 1989 SCLR 625 29
Viola v Viola 1987 SCLR 529 187
Wallace v Wallace 1963 SC 256 147
Ward v Ward 1983 SLT 472 ....59, 60, 123
Watt v Watt 1978 SLT (Notes) 55 136
Webster v Lord Advocate 1985 SLT 361 65
Welsh v Welsh 1987 SLT (Sh Ct) 30 ....58, 62, 65, 122
White v White 1947 SLT (Notes) 51 139
White v White 1984 SLT (Sh Ct) 30 169
White v White 1990 GWD 12-612 ....81, 145
Whitecross v Whitecross 1977 SLT 225 ....51, 147
Whiteford v Gibson (1899) 7 SLT 233 169
Whyte v Hardie 1990 SCLR 23 49
Whyte v Whyte 1989 SCLR 375 132
Williamson v Williamson 1989 SLT 866 ....32, 135
Wilson v Wilson (1936) 52 Sh Ct Rep 200 170
Wilson v Wilson 1939 SC 102 144
Wilson v Wilson 1981 SLT 101 ....66, 68
Wilson v Wilson 1987 SCLR 595, 1987 SLT 721 ....163, 164
Winton v Winton 1987 GWD 15-572 ....26, 29
Wiseman v Wiseman 1989 SCLR 757 ....26, 87
Woodcock v Woodcock 1990 SCLR 535 183
Woytaszko v Woytaszko 1988 GWD 11-446 51
Yates v HMA 1977 SLT (Notes) 42 147

CHAPTER 1

A CLIENT COMES IN . . .

In 1987 divorce decrees were granted in 12,133 cases in Scotland. Of these 4,738 were based on two years' non-cohabitation with consent, 4,180 were based on the defender's behaviour, 1,591 were based on five years' non-cohabitation, 1,521 were based on adultery and only 79 on desertion. Over the previous decade the proportions as between the various grounds of divorce changed little. Of the 1987 total 1,468 decrees (12 per cent) were granted in the Court of Session and the remainder in the sheriff court. In 1988 the total figure was 11,472 of which 791 decrees (7 per cent) were granted in the Court of Session. Slightly more than half of all cases involved children under sixteen. About 72 per cent of all actions are at the instance of wives. It is clear that the preferred court for divorce is now overwhelmingly the sheriff court.

Courts are required to encourage reconciliation[1]. But by the time that a divorce action is under way there may be little that the court can usefully do to achieve that end. As the Court of Session Practice Note 1977 No. 3 points out agencies have been established to assist in reconciliation and practitioners should encourage their clients to seek appropriate advice and guidance from persons experienced in marriage guidance.

The above figures suggest, if nothing else, that the problems presented in any particular case are most unlikely to be unique, except in the narrowest sense. Nevertheless for many people the breakdown of a marriage can be a bit like death. A spouse has been lost. For many the trauma arising from that loss is similar to bereavement. For most people it takes as long a time to get over the breakdown of a marriage as it does to get over a bereavement. Divorce differs from death in that the spouse may very well be around, in more senses than one, for a considerable time to come.

How people cope with separation and divorce is often affected to a considerable extent by how they behave towards one another when they first separate. If they behave in a civilised way towards one another they are likely to be able to sort out their difficulties relatively easily. They will have recognised that the other party is a human being with feelings and concerns which, like their own feelings and concerns, should be treated with respect. But if the first reaction is one of hostility to one another, whether that is manifested by solicitors' letters or writs or in some other manner is not important. What does matter is that that reaction will make their problems that much more difficult to solve. Those advising people involved in the breakdown of their marriage have a heavy and in some ways unenviable responsibility to get the

1 See the Divorce (Scotland) Act 1976, s 2.

approach right from the start. If mistakes are made it will affect the children of the marriage and possibly others, perhaps for a very long time indeed.

Before separation there will almost inevitably have been a prolonged period of stress for both husband and wife. Unkind things will have been said and done. Separation may well have come as a shock to at least one of them. It is a very common cause of great resentment that the departing spouse has apparently planned the departure behind the back of the other spouse. It appears to the one left behind that not only has he or she been deceived but that the departing spouse has got a new life all organised. The mistrust caused by a sudden and apparently planned end to cohabitation may prove very difficult to overcome. The final separation can come as a great shock to both of them, even where both were well aware that the marriage was in great difficulty.

Shock is often followed by anger. People become self-centred, depressed and feel much maligned. Self-respect will be at a low ebb. There will be fear, partly of the unknown and an uncertain future. The marriage may have been unhappy but at least the parties knew what life was like. Reassurance will be needed. A good deal of self-justification will be indulged in verbally and, commonly, in writing to anyone who will pay attention. Lawyers are seen as payers of attention. The time which needs to be taken by others to listen to an aggrieved spouse will probably not be so short that a qualified lawyer can be the main listener and still make a living.

Separation usually causes practical problems. A second house or flat may be needed. Yet the income will not have altered. How is the other party to be maintained? What one party thinks would be a reasonable amount of aliment with which to manage the household will greatly exceed what the other party regards it as reasonable to pay. There may be a risk, if the demands are too great, that the payer of aliment will see an advantage in giving up work and going on social security. If that happens the problem of maintaining the family will become more difficult to solve. Who is to have the children? What access is there to be to them? It is very common for parents to fear that, following divorce, they will lose contact with their children. There is a risk, albeit on average slight, that one of them will emigrate thereby making access impossible.

Bitterly contested litigation is expensive. If parties fight over the house, money and the children, it is not unknown for them to become involved in expense which consumes a substantial part of their assets. This expense may result in them being unable to afford to set up two homes. In most cases within not a very long period they will be able to look back on what they did and regret the waste of money. Very few will regard the expenditure which they incurred on litigation as having been worthwhile, even if it seemed to have been necessary at the time.

If a court action is raised the summons or initial writ will contain allegations of fact and a narrative of events as seen in retrospect by one party. It will be expressed in forceful terms. It may come courtesy of a messenger-at-arms or a sheriff officer who will draw attention to any interim interdicts already granted. If so, it will probably mention a power of arrest. It may order the recipient to appear in court in a few days' time. It may seek orders for the exclusion of the defender from the matrimonial home, of which he may be the owner or the tenant, and its transfer to the pursuer. Use of all the furniture and contents of the house may be sought. There will be financial claims which the defender will regard as absurd, though simply because she is aware of the sums sued for the pursuer may expect to receive these sums without having to compromise. It is a useful exercise to ask yourself what your own reaction would be if you were not a lawyer and this was happening to you.

The ground on which a divorce is based may have a material bearing on how easy it is to obtain settlement of custody and finance. Most people are quite content to be divorced on the ground of two years' separation by consent. But unreasonable behaviour is likely to provoke a hostile response. Many people think that all the averments will be in the public domain. In practice it is very unlikely that there will be any report of a divorce in the media unless the parties are public figures. Even then there will not be media coverage of the detailed averments because of the restrictions on reporting contained in the Judicial Proceedings (Regulation of Reports) Act 1926, s 1.

The best approach will usually be to try to settle disputes quickly and quietly. But it is a matter of common experience that some people whose marriage has broken up are so affected by it that they are incapable of bringing themselves to agree to anything for a considerable period. They see the slightest compromise on their part as capitulation and any suggestion that there should be compromise as evidence that their lawyer is really acting for the other party. Many advisers find that their client is out for 'justice', by which is meant revenge.

Particularly if there are children involved, the local Conciliation Service should be given a chance to assist. To get an aggrieved person to go to conciliation may not be easy; to get both to go may be difficult. Solicitors should take the trouble to find out what conciliation services can offer and what cases are and are not likely to be suitable for conciliation. Conciliation is concerned with giving separating or divorcing couples a chance to settle disagreements over future arrangements, especially but not exclusively those for the children. At conciliation a conciliator will usually see both parties together. They will have an opportunity to hear each other's point of view and explore possible solutions to the difficult problems which they face. Children of the marriage may also be involved in the conciliation process. Conciliation is confidential but any agreement reached is put in writing and passed to the solicitor acting for each party.

The settlement of many civil cases at the door of the court often occurs because the parties meet there for the first time. Even if conciliation is unsuccessful in the sense that it does not lead to an agreement, there may be a significantly less hostile attitude thereafter and little will have been lost. Conciliation services in Scotland are currently mainly involved in attempting to resolve disputes concerning children. If a solicitor suggests conciliation it should be suggested positively. Otherwise it may be seen by his or her client as giving in to the other side. It can be pointed out that courts have power to refer parties to the local Conciliation Service. Solicitors can also be conciliatory without in any way damaging their clients' interests. Letters which do not seek to aggravate are likely to be at least as effective as allegations stated at their highest and perceived by their recipient as deliberate lies to which a solicitor has seen fit to add his name.

Courts are not the best forum in which to solve matrimonial differences except as a last resort. If the parties themselves can agree they are more likely to stick to the agreement. Court orders can prove inconvenient and unduly inflexible (as when the court decides what periods of access should be allowed) and may be difficult to enforce when one party refuses to comply with an order, although the threat of contempt of court may provide an incentive. There is less likely to be a need for enforcement when there has been agreement.

Any agreement reached will be more likely to last if it is perceived by both parties to be reasonably fair.

Children are unlikely to have any previous experience of divorce. This will be an unprecedented crisis for them. It is unlikely to be their fault that their parents have not got on well. That will not prevent them from feeling rejected and neglected by the parent who has left them. Yet very rarely are children kept properly and fairly informed of what is going on. Their views are often not asked for, or at least are not sufficiently considered. Lawyers acting for their parents do not see them as their clients. Nor are they. Children's views tend to be conveyed to lawyers and the courts through one of the parties to the divorce. Those views are often distorted, largely unwittingly, by a parent under stress who may have some things to gain, others to lose. But, if it is known by a parent that a child is likely to be asked for his or her view, there is quite a high risk that the child will have been tutored by one of the parents as to what should and should not be said. Nonetheless in many instances it may be of advantage at an early stage when a divorce is in prospect if lawyers were to arrange to see older children as well as the parent who is their client. The purpose would simply be to tell the children what was happening and to give them an opportunity to comment. One thing is indisputable: children do not enjoy being the rope in a matrimonial tug of war. As Lord Justice Butler Sloss said at the Cleveland Child Abuse Inquiry: 'It is unacceptable that the disagreements and failure of communication of adults should be allowed to obscure the needs of children'. It should not be forgotten that some, no doubt a few, parents dislike their children and that some children dislike one or both of their parents.

For children a month is a very long time and a year is an age. A delay which an adult may regard as acceptable will be very unacceptable for a child. For them it is particularly important that differences be resolved as quickly as possible. Many people think that it is better for children to be with one parent in relative peace than with both parents in a state of disharmony. However research shows that children usually want to keep in touch with both parents; it is in their best interests that that should be so; they would in most cases prefer their parents to be back together, albeit unhappily, and they survive separation and divorce much better if they continue to have contact with both parents. At least one-third of children of divorcing parents lose contact with one parent. There is research evidence which shows that some children who feel rejected by one parent will do significantly less well in later life than would have been expected. Such rejection may cause serious psychological problems for some children. That in turn will cause problems for their parents and perhaps their teachers. It can cause avoidable expenditure of private and public funds on a significant scale[1].

It is very common for one person to come to terms with both separation and divorce more quickly than the other, just as some wounds heal more quickly than others. This possibility is rarely appreciated by the particular husband and wife involved. It is often a help to point this out to them. They need to understand that the other party may see things with a quite different perspective and that this is likely to be a reason why one party adapts more quickly than the other. But there are other reasons. One party, usually the wife, may well feel a severe lack of security and justifiably fear the risk of

---

1 For further reading see Ann Mitchell: *Children in the Middle—Living through Divorce* (Tavistock Publications, 1985).

poverty. She may feel that she has to be constantly vigilant and that she has to edge towards a satisfactory outcome over a long period, particularly as regards financial matters, whereas her husband may be more likely to want to have heard and seen the last of their differences as soon as possible. It has been suggested that until there is no bitterness and there are no continuing disputes the parties have not completely untied the knot.

Some lawyers appear consistently to act aggressively and, initially, as little more than a loudspeaker to convey the complaints of the client. Some feel that this phase is necessary to enable the client to vent his or her anger. Letting off steam should be done in such a way that the engine is not wrecked. Others are invariably looking for an agreed solution involving the courts as little as possible. It may be more difficult to persuade a client the latter approach is in his or her best interests but the best solutions are rarely easy. They often appear unacceptable at first sight.

CHAPTER 2

THE SITUATION BEFORE DIVORCE

In order to advise anyone about divorce it is helpful to have in mind the respective rights and duties of spouses to one another arising from the fact that they are married to one another and their rights and duties as parents. There are limits to the extent to which a short book can deal with this. There have been many changes in these rights and duties in recent years with the result that: 'It is perhaps not too cynical to observe that during the marriage the legal consequences of being married are, with some important exceptions such as aliment and the right to occupy the matrimonial home, relatively insignificant compared with being married when the marriage is terminated by divorce or death'[1]. Although in some instances, particularly in connection with a claim for an order for financial provision on divorce, it may be important to compare what the situation would be on the retirement or death of a party with the situation on divorce that is not really within the scope of a book such as this.

It may be helpful before considering the rights and duties of spouses as they now are to list in a negative way some of the many recent legislative changes since reference may be found to these in reported cases or older textbooks. These include the following:

(1) A wife's domicile is not dependent on that of her husband[2]. Where a husband and wife are living apart the domicile of a child will be that of his mother if he then has his home with her and has no home with his father, or had her domicile and has not since had a home with his father[3].

(2) A minor spouse is not subject to the curatory of his parent[4].

(3) A minor wife is not subject to the curatory of her husband.[5]

(4) A husband has no entitlement, because he is the husband, to determine the whereabouts of the matrimonial home[6].

(5) An action of delict can not be raised against a person claiming damages for the enticement of a spouse[7].

(6) A husband is not liable, because he is her husband, for any debts incurred by his wife before marriage[8].

(7) A married woman is not presumed to have been placed in charge of her husband's domestic affairs with a consequent presumed ability to pledge

1 J M Thomson *Family Law in Scotland* (Butterworths, 1987) p 38.
2 Domicile and Matrimonial Proceedings Act 1973, s 1.
3 Ibid, s 4.
4 Law Reform (Husband and Wife) (Scotland) Act 1984, s 3(1).
5 Ibid, s 3(2).
6 Ibid, s 4.
7 Ibid, s 2(3).
8 Ibid, s 6(1).

his credit for household expenses[1]. As a corollary of this it is not competent for a husband to obtain a warrant for inhibition or inhibition to cancel his wife's authority to incur obligations on his behalf[2]. Any inhibition to that effect granted before 24 May 1984 is no longer of any effect[3].

PRESUMPTIONS

Paternity

A man is presumed to be the father of a child if he was married to the mother of the child at any time beginning with conception and ending with the birth of the child or if both he and the mother have acknowledged that he is the father and the child has been registered as such in a Register of Births in the United Kingdom[4].

Household goods

Many items are, on the face of it, bought for households by one party to a marriage. It may be difficult to prove that the other party contributed either directly or indirectly in a financial sense to the purchase and still more difficult to demonstrate that it was only because one party remained at home to care for the children that it was possible for the other to earn the money needed to make a particular purchase.

There is a presumption that, unless the contrary is proved, each party to the marriage has a right to an equal share in any household goods obtained in prospect of or during the marriage other than by way of gift or succession from a third party[5]. Household goods are defined as 'any goods (including decorative or ornamental goods) kept or used at any time during the marriage in any matrimonial home for the joint domestic purposes of the parties to the marriage.' Money or securities, motor cars, caravans, other road vehicles and domestic animals are excluded. The contrary is not proved only because the goods were purchased by one party alone or by both parties in unequal shares[6].

Housekeeping allowance

It is presumed, in the absence of any agreement to the contrary that any money derived from any housekeeping allowance and any property acquired with such money belongs to the parties in equal shares[7].

OBLIGATION TO ADHERE

Since actions of adherence have been abolished[8], it is difficult to say that in law spouses any longer have a duty to adhere to one another. The only effect

1 Ibid, s 7(1).
2 Ibid, s 7(2).
3 Ibid, s 7(3).
4 Law Reform (Parent and Child) (Scotland) Act 1986, s 5(1).
5 See the Family Law (Scotland) Act 1985, s 25(1).
6 Ibid, s 25(2).
7 Ibid, s 26.
8 Law Reform (Husband and Wife) (Scotland) Act 1984, s 4.

in law of their failure to do that is likely to be that a basis may be laid for divorce or separation.

LEGAL CAPACITY

Marriage has no effect on the legal capacity of a spouse. The Family Law (Scotland) Act 1985, s 24(1) provides that, subject to the provisions of any enactment including that Act, marriage shall not of itself affect the rights of the parties to a marriage in relation to their property nor the legal capacity of the parties to the marriage. The legal capacity of parties to a marriage is not affected by divorce. If divorce proceedings are in prospect there are likely to be some contracts in existence which the spouses thought were between one party to the marriage and a third party. But the third party may allege that the spouses contracted jointly or that one spouse was acting as the agent of the other. That other spouse may perhaps be liable on a joint and several basis. The normal law of agency would apply. It would be wise to clarify the position as regards any such contracts.

ALIMENT

Persons to whom an obligation of aliment is owed

An obligation of aliment is owed by, and only by:

(1) a husband to his wife;
(2) a wife to her husband;
(3) a parent to his or her child, and
(4) a person to a child who has been accepted by him as a child of his family[1].

A child in this context means a person under eighteen or a person who is 'over that age and under the age of 25 years who is reasonably and appropriately undergoing instruction at an educational establishment, or training for employment or for a trade, profession or vocation.' Husband and wife in this context include parties to a valid polygamous marriage[2].

Where two or more parties owe an obligation of aliment, there is no order of liability as between them. Both parents may be held liable to aliment a child but it would depend on the circumstances of the case whether each was held to have an equal liability. It could well be that one parent would be held liable to pay all the aliment, as where the father was in well-paid employment and the mother was unable to work because of the need for her to bring up the children. Accordingly the court may make, but is not obliged to make, an award of aliment against these persons. If the court decides to make an award of aliment it may take account of the obligation of aliment owed by any other person[3]. This provision deals with, for example, the situation where a child has been accepted as a child of the marriage and there is a natural parent who also owes that child an obligation of aliment.

1 Family Law (Scotland) Act 1985, s 1(1).
2 Ibid, s 1(5).
3 Ibid, s 4(2).

The test for making an award of aliment

The duty is 'to provide such support as is reasonable in the circumstances'[1], having regard to:

(a) the needs and resources of the parties;
(b) the earning capacities of the parties;
(c) generally to all the circumstances of the case'[2].

Circumstances to be taken into account in making an award of aliment

The court may, if it thinks fit, take account of any support, financial or otherwise, given by the defender to any person whom he maintains as a dependant in his household whether or not he owes an obligation of aliment to that person[3]. This provision gives the court power, but does not oblige the court, to take account of the not uncommon situation where, for example, a husband has set up home with another woman and is maintaining her and to some extent her children. If the court takes account of that, there will be less money available for his wife. Where the husband is employed but has a low income the court may hold that no aliment should be paid by him to the wife. She may be in receipt of social security and may not benefit from an award of aliment. It is not for the court to enable a parent to evade his responsibility to maintain his child, thereby placing that responsibility on the community at large. But if the husband lives with another woman who has significant income, whether from aliment, earnings or savings, that income may be taken into account to the extent that it is used to meet joint expenditure in assessing what he can afford to pay his wife[4]. The court will attempt to make such order as is reasonable in the circumstances. The court has no magic formula which will enable anyone to get more than a pint out of a pint pot. Nor is there any mathematical formula which the court applies in assessing aliment. It is likely that at least one party will regard the decision of the court as unsatisfactory. In very many cases one person's income will not support more than one household or at least will not do so to a sufficient extent to avoid hardship. If one party is on a low wage, too high an award of aliment may make it unattractive to him or her to remain in employment.

Relevance of conduct in relation to aliment

The court is required not to take account of any conduct of a party 'unless it would be manifestly inequitable to leave it out of account'[5]. The wording of this provision should be contrasted with the wording of section 4(3)(a) (which provides that the court may take account of any support given by the defender to any person whom he maintains as a dependant in his household whether or not he owes that person an obligation of aliment). That, in a sense, is conduct. Accordingly the presumption is that any other conduct will not be taken into account except in a few, exceptional, cases. Aliment is not a prize

---

1 Ibid, s 1(2).
2 Ibid, s 4(1).
3 Ibid, s 4(3)(a).
4 *Munro v Munro* 1986 SLT 72; *Frith v Frith* 1990 GWD 5-266.
5 Family Law (Scotland) Act 1985, s 4(3)(b).

to be gained by good behaviour which is subject to proportionate reduction for bad behaviour on some sort of contributory negligence basis. Aliment is inter alia, and as section 1(1) of the 1985 Act makes clear, an obligation by one person to another, eg a husband to a wife and vice versa. Accordingly so long as they remain married the obligation is owed. The court cannot reasonably be expected to hear a blow-by-blow account of the marriage and apportion blame in order to assess aliment. Courts will be very reluctant to permit parties to air grievances about behaviour under the guise of a factor relevant to the assessment of aliment.

RIGHTS BY SUCCESSION

A surviving spouse and the children of a marriage have legal rights in the moveable estate and a surviving spouse may have prior rights in the estate of a deceased spouse[1]. Children have to survive the deceased but for a spouse to claim he or she must also have been married to the deceased at the date of death. On divorce, therefore, a spouse will lose these rights.

WEDDING PRESENTS

Wedding presents may be the joint property of the spouses, or the property of one of them. In the event of a dispute, the first issue would probably be whether a party could prove that the intention of the donor was to give the present to that party. If that cannot be established, there appears to be no binding Scottish authority for the view that there is a presumption in favour of an intention to make a gift to the husband and wife jointly[2]. It has been suggested that a wedding present is to be regarded as being owned by the party from whose friend or relative it was received[3].

It is suggested that the usual solution adopted in such disputes is to regard some gifts as being the exclusive property of one or other of the spouses and some as being at best a matter of doubt. The last-mentioned may then be regarded as joint property. In assessing the category into which a particular gift will fall attention is usually paid to the nature of the gift, the person who gave it and whether that person knew one or both spouses before the wedding. If only the husband is a pigeon fancier the gift of a pigeon loft is likely to be intended as a gift to the husband. A pair of earrings may be taken to be intended to be given to the wife but jewellery given to a husband, if it is an heirloom, may not be presumed to be intended to become the property of the wife. In many cases another practical consideration is what is needed to keep the matrimonial home going and to set up a second home after the separation.

1 And see Family Law (Scotland) Act 1985, s 24(2).
2 For the contrary view see Clive *The Law of Husband and Wife in Scotland* (W Green & Sons), pp 304-5.
3 *McDonald v McDonald* 1953 SLT (Sh Ct) 36; and see *Strain v Strain* (1885) 2 Sh Ct Rep 108; *Duncan v Gerard* (1888) 4 Sh Ct Rep 246; *McIntosh v Macrae* (1887) 4 Sh Ct Rep 317; *Traill v Traill* 1925 SLT (Sh Ct) 54.

GIFTS BETWEEN SPOUSES

Difficulty may arise over alleged gifts between husbands and wives. There will rarely be useful documentary evidence. As well as arguments over whether a gift was or was not made, the creditors of one of the spouses may claim that no gift has been made or that it was made in order to defeat creditors. To achieve a transfer there must be delivery and an intention to donate. There is in law a presumption against donation. But as between husband and wife it is well-known that gifts are common. Some alleged gifts pose few problems. A fur coat bought by a husband just before his wife's birthday which she claims was a birthday present may be likely to have been just that. But 'presents for the house' are more difficult. In order to clarify thoughts in relation to items in dispute it is suggested that the argument be tested by asking which party could prove in a question with a trustee that the particular item did (or did not) form part of his or her estate in the event of sequestration.

MATRIMONIAL HOME

In terms of the Matrimonial Homes (Family Protection) (Scotland) Act 1981 a spouse may, pending divorce and in certain circumstances, be granted by the court rights to occupy the matrimonial home and to have the use of the furniture and plenishings. Comment on relevant provisions of this Act is made in Chapter 5.

IMMIGRANT SPOUSE

Consideration may have to be given to the consequences of separation or divorce where one spouse is an immigrant who has not become a naturalised British citizen. It may be necessary to investigate whether an application for naturalisation should be made by an immigrant spouse before commencing proceedings for divorce.

POLYGAMOUS MARRIAGE

The court may grant divorce to spouses where the marriage was entered into under a law which permits polygamy[1]. There are rules of court which require intimation of any action of divorce which is polygamous to any other spouse.

PARENTAL RIGHTS

Both husband and wife, as the natural parents, have parental rights in relation to any child of theirs[2]. Each of them may exercise such rights without the consent of the other unless any decree or deed conferring the right otherwise provides[3]. 'Parental rights' is defined as meaning 'tutory, curatory, custody or access as the case may require, and any right or authority relating to the welfare or upbringing of a child conferred on a parent by any rule of law'[4].

1 *Speedie v Steel* 1941 SLT (Sh Ct) 2.
2 Law Reform (Parent and Child) (Scotland) Act 1986, s 2(1).
3 Ibid, s 2(4).
4 Ibid, s 8.

A child is defined in relation to custody or access as a child under sixteen; in relation to tutory as a pupil; in relation to curatory as a minor; and in relation to other parental rights as a child under eighteen[1].

A parent may apply to the court for an order relating to parental rights[2]. Neither parent has a right to be awarded either custody or access. Any such award will depend on whether it is in the best interests of the child concerned. The court is required to regard the welfare of the child as the paramount consideration[3]. But if a father is not married to the mother or was not married to her at the time of conception he can be granted parental rights only by authority of the court[4].

---

1 Family Law (Scotland) Act 1985, s 8.
2 Ibid, s 3.
3 Ibid, s 3(2).
4 Ibid, s 2(1)(b); *Sloss v Taylor* 1989 SCLR 407.

CHAPTER 3

TAKING INSTRUCTIONS

SIMPLIFIED PROCEDURE

It will not be necessary to take full instructions if it is possible to proceed by way of the simplified procedure for a divorce. This procedure may be used either in the Court of Session or in a sheriff court having jurisdiction to grant divorce. Simplified procedure may be used where the ground of divorce is either non-cohabitation for two years and the defender consents, or non-cohabitation for five years . There must be no other proceedings pending in any court which could bring the marriage to an end. There must be no children under sixteen. No financial orders may be applied for. Simplified procedure cannot be used when either party suffers from mental disorder within the meaning of the Mental Health (Scotland) Act 1984[1].

When the simplified procedure is appropriate all that need be done is to obtain a copy of the appropriate form and get the client to tick the appropriate boxes and sign the form.

CHOICE OF COURT

Factors which may be relevant to the decision whether to raise the action in the sheriff court or in the Court of Session are set out in chapter 7. As has been noticed the vast majority of divorce actions are raised in the sheriff court. The sheriff court has jurisdiction in respect of actions of divorce by virtue of the Sheriff Courts (Scotland) Act 1907, s 5(2B). The Court of Session and more than one sheriff court may have concurrent jurisdiction in respect of a particular action of divorce. It may be that a court in another part of the United Kingdom or abroad may have jurisdiction concurrently with one or more courts in Scotland. In that event it may be necessary to consider what orders the court in the other jurisdiction may be able to make in addition to granting divorce. This is particularly so of orders for financial provision but it is beyond the scope of this book to compare the remedies which may be available in other jurisdictions with those available in Scotland.

---

1 OCR 135.

OTHER CONSIDERATIONS

The first thing to get clear, if that is possible, is what outcome the client hopes to achieve ultimately, or at least what it is realistic to aim for. The tactical approach most likely to achieve that end, as was pointed out in the first chapter, is not always the one which seems most obvious in the heat of the moment. A lawyer acting for a distraught would-be litigant has a clear responsibility to advise him or her what is likely to be in the best interests of his client and the children, even if that advice is not what the client wants to hear. Consideration should be given to the use of the local Conciliation Service prior to raising an action. It may be possible to resolve some matters, such as custody and access, thereby. That in turn may facilitate the resolution of difficulties over who lives in the matrimonial home and how the family finances are to be rearranged. If parties have not tried conciliation the court may encourage them to do so at an early stage in the course of a divorce action or may refer them to conciliation (with their agreement in a Court of Session case and with or without their agreement in a sheriff court case).[1] When and to the extent that negotiation is unsuccessful it may be necessary to apply to the court for orders such as custody, aliment, transfer of tenancy, exclusion orders, interdicts and powers of arrest and so on. The ancillary orders which may be sought are discussed in chapters 4 and 5.

CASES WHERE SIMPLIFIED PROCEDURE NOT APPROPRIATE

Suggested check list of questions to be asked of a person who wants a divorce, (in this case a wife):

This marriage and the children of it

Your full name? How do you spell it? Your present address?

Your husband's full name? How does he spell it? His present address?

Date and place of marriage? (Obtain extract marriage certificate.)

Names and dates of birth of any children of the marriage? How are their names spelled? (Obtain extract birth certificates for each of those under sixteen.)

Earlier marriages/relationships

Have either of you been married before?

If she was previously married: What was or were your former married surname(s)?

What other children do you and your husband have?

Which of the other children, if any, were accepted as children of your present marriage?

---

1 RC 170B (15); OCR 132F.

What are the full, correctly spelled names and dates of birth of each child accepted as children of the marriage? (Obtain extract birth certificates for each of those still under sixteen.)

Jurisdiction

Were you born in Scotland?

How much of your life have you lived in Scotland?

Was your husband born in Scotland?

How much of his life has he lived in Scotland? What addresses have you and your husband lived at and for how long during the past year? At which addresses have you each lived for the past 40 days?

Are there any court proceedings pending in a court in Scotland or elsewhere which could affect the validity or subsistence of your marriage? If so, details will be required of the nature of these proceedings. These details are:

(1) the court, tribunal or authority before whom they have been commenced.
(2) the date of their commencement.
(3) the names of the parties to these proceedings.
(4) the date or expected date of proof in the proceedings.
(5) such other facts as may be relevant to the question whether this proposed action should be sisted under Schedule 3 of the Domicile and Matrimonial Proceedings Act 1973[1].

Brief history of the marriage

After the marriage at what addresses did you and your husband live?

Was the marriage initially a success?

When and why did it become less successful?

On what date did you finally separate?

Have you lived together or had sexual relations since then? If the answer is yes, between what dates did you live together and where? On such occasions was the resumption of cohabitation with a view to a reconciliation?[2] If not, what was the purpose of the resumption?

Basis of divorce

On how many of the following grounds could you divorce your husband: adultery, unreasonable behaviour, desertion for two years, non-cohabitation for two years and he consents to divorce, non-cohabitation for five years. Extra-marital affairs may be the basis for a divorce based on behaviour as well as adultery.

On which of them do you want to divorce him?

1 RC 157(3)(b); OCR 3(5).
2 As to the effect of any period or periods of reconciliation see Divorce (Scotland) Act 1976, s 2.

Adultery

With whom has your husband committed adultery?

What is her present address?

When did he commit adultery?

Has he admitted adultery to you?

What have you seen or heard yourself which leads you to believe that he has committed adultery?

What are the names, addresses and their relationship to you of any witnesses who can speak to his having committed adultery?

Has he admitted adultery to any of them?

If private detectives are employed is it likely that he will admit adultery to them or will he try to conceal the fact that he is committing it? (If private detectives are employed fairly recent photographs of both husband and wife will be required.)

If, since the marriage, the defender has given birth to a child of whom the pursuer is not the father, a photostat copy of that child's birth certificate should be obtained with a view to identifying the signatures on the certificate. How is it to be shown that the pursuer was not the father? Can it be shown that for the period when conception is likely to have occurred the pursuer had no access to the defender, eg because he was working abroad? What evidence is there that the defender was pregnant prior to date of birth or had the care of a young baby shortly after that date?

Did you connive at the adultery?

Have you cohabited with your husband since the last time he committed adultery and knowing or believing that he had done so?

Where there has been bigamy: who, when and where did the defender 'marry'? (Extract certificate of that 'marriage' is necessary.) What evidence is there available that that 'marriage' took place?

Unreasonable behaviour

What is the nature of the behaviour complained of?

When did it start?

What specific incidents were there?

On what dates?

What happened?

Where did each such incident happen?

Who witnessed each incident happening?

Was he charged by the police and, if so, with what consequences? (Extract convictions should be obtained.)

Who saw its aftermath eg bruises, furniture broken?

What temporary separations took place and between what dates?

What caused the final separation?

What was the effect of the behaviour on you and the children?

Did you go and see a doctor? If so, who and when?

Has your health improved since the separation?

Who can support your allegations about his behaviour and its effect?

Desertion

What precipitated the desertion?

What makes you say that it was desertion and not separation by mutual consent?

Did you give him cause to leave you?

Did you know that he was about to leave and, if so, how did you know?

Has there been any resumption of cohabitation since the initial desertion?

If so, between what dates?

Why did you separate again?

Who can give evidence to support what you have just said about the desertion?

Who can give evidence of the date of separation and that you have not lived with your husband for the two years since the separation?

Has he made any offers to resume cohabitation since the separation?

Were any such offers genuine?

Why do you say they were not genuine?

Did you refuse any such offers and, if so, why?

Two year non-cohabitation and consent of defender

Have you lived apart for the whole of the two years prior to intended date of commencing the action?

Will he sign a form consenting to divorce?

Who can give evidence of when you separated and that you have lived apart for that period?

Five year non-cohabitation

Who can give evidence of when you separated and that you have lived apart for that period?

General

Is there any documentary evidence to support your case eg love letters where there has been adultery?

Has there been any separation agreement? If so, who has a copy of it?

Is there likely to be an argument that a divorce should not be granted because that would cause grave financial hardship?

Children: custody

Who do the children live with?

What accommodation is there for them?

What is that accommodation like?

Who lives there apart from you/him and the children?

Who looks after them while you/he are at work?

What are their interests?

Are they in good health?

What schools do they go to?

How do they get on with you/him?

Which of their relatives do they see and how often?

Are they kept clean and tidy?

What income do you/he have to maintain them?

If the other party has de facto custody and it is proposed that that situation be changed, why is that party unsuitable to continue to have custody?

What arrangements would you make if you got custody? What would the change entail eg change of school? Why would it be in the best interests of the child to make such a change: (a) pending divorce, and (b) on granting decree of divorce?

Is an order for the delivery of the child necessary?

Children: access

Do the children have access to the parent who does not have custody?

If so how often and for what periods?

Does access work well?

If there is no access, why is this?

Has access been sought and if so for what periods?

Why has access been refused?

What is the attitude of the children to access?

Aliment and periodical allowance[1]

What employment do you have? What income do you have from your work gross and net? Do you have wages slips?

What income do you have from social security such as income support and child benefit?

What income do you have from your husband?

Are there any other sources of income such as from a former husband?

What employment does your husband have?

How much will he receive from each source of income gross and net? What are the name and address of his employers?

Do either you or your husband have income from investments, an interest in a business, or other sources? (Details may be required.)

What are your outgoings and those of your husband for rent, community charge, mortgage, hire purchase, insurance, gas, electricity, other regular commitments, outstanding debts, etc?

Does your husband have any other particular commitments such as paying off the loan on the house you live in, aliment for children of a former marriage, supporting a cohabitee? What do these commitments amount to weekly or monthly?

Capital assets

What assets do each of you own or have an interest in either individually or jointly: eg a share in a business, money in bank or building society accounts, investments, insurance policies, pensions, heritable property, furniture, jewellery, other items of value?

What are their approximate current values?

How realisable are they?

How and when were each of these acquired[2]:

    (a) were they acquired by gift?
    (b) were they acquired by succession?
    (c) were they acquired before the marriage and, if so, were they acquired for use as the matrimonial home or its furnishings? If the answer to both parts of this question is in the affirmative, what evidence is there to show that?
    (d) during the marriage and before the date of the final separation?
    (e) later than the final separation?

Which goods are not properly described as 'household goods', ie 'goods (including decorative or ornamental goods) kept or used at any time during the marriage

---

1 Although aliment and periodical allowance are assessed on net income a statement of both gross and net income may be important since some people have considerable deductions in arriving at the net figure; not all of which would be regarded by a court in the same manner as income tax.
2 See Family Law (Scotland) Act 1985, s 25.

in any matrimonial home for joint domestic purposes'? (Money, securities, motor and other road vehicles and caravans and domestic animals are excluded[1].)

To what extent are any of these assets essential for carrying on a business, eg farm land?

If you were awarded a capital sum would your husband be able to pay all of it immediately? If not, how much of it would your husband be able to pay per annum or how long would it take him to pay?

Matrimonial home

Who owns the matrimonial home? If it is tenanted, by whom and from whom? Are either or both of you permitted by a third party to occupy the home? If so with whose permission? The name and address of the landlord or third party permitting occupation should be obtained.

Is transference of a tenancy sought?

If it is let on a long lease or in connection with employment or is or is part of an agricultural holding, croft or the like transfer is incompetent[2]. Is the lease of such a nature?

If transfer of tenancy is not sought are any of the incidental orders set out in the Family Law (Scotland) Act 1985, s 14 such as an order regulating the occupation of the matrimonial home or the use of the furniture and plenishings therein or excluding the other party to the marriage sought? Note that these incidental orders may be made before, on or after granting decree of divorce.

Is it necessary to establish, enforce or restrict the occupancy rights of the spouses in the matrimonial home in terms of the Matrimonial Homes (Family Protection) (Scotland) Act 1981, s 3? If so in what respects and for what reasons? (If the pursuer is an entitled spouse by reason of being sole or joint tenant or owner there is no need to establish that in most instances).

Is an interim exclusion order sought in terms of section 4 of the 1981 Act? How is it to be established that the making of the order is necessary for the protection of the applicant spouse or any child of the family from conduct or threatened or reasonably apprehended conduct which is or would be injurious to the physical or mental health of the applicant or child?

What orders ancillary to an exclusion order are sought: (a) ejection of the defender; (b) interdict prohibiting him from entering the matrimonial home without your express permission; and (c) interdict prohibiting him from removing furniture and plenishings therefrom etc[3]. Are any other orders necessary for the proper enforcement of the orders referred to in (a), (b) and (c) above, and, if so, what orders? Would you agree to the suspension of an order for ejection and/or interdict for a period to enable your husband to find alternative accommodation?

When and if ejection is ordered is it necessary to ask the court to give directions for the preservation of his goods and effects so far as they remain in the matrimonial home?[4] If so in what terms, eg put them in storage?

1 See Family Law (Scotland) Act 1985, s 25(3).
2 Matrimonial Homes (Family Protection) (Scotland) Act 1981, s 13(7).
3 See ibid, s 4(4) and (5), and see chapter 5.
4 Ibid, s 4(5)(b).

Do you wish to interdict the defender from entering or remaining in a specified area in the vicinity of the matrimonial home? If so, what area? Has he been lurking in the vicinity of your house? When? Where?

Interdict

What actions of your husband would you wish the court to prohibit? The most common are:

(a) to prevent molestation of a spouse[1];
(b) to prevent the removal of children from a person's care;
(c) in terms of the Matrimonial Homes (Family Protection) (Scotland) Act 1981 to prevent the defender from entering the matrimonial home without express permission from the pursuer and from removing furniture and plenishings from a matrimonial home, and from entering or remaining in a specified area in the vicinity of the matrimonial home (see paragraph above).

What events would be relied on in support of an application for interdict (if not already dealt with above)? Dates when and places where the incidents complained of together with the names of witnesses to these incidents will be required.

Powers of arrest

Is a power of arrest sought[2]—to be attached to any matrimonial interdict as defined in section 14 of the 1981 Act?

Avoidance transactions

Are any orders sought to set aside or vary any transactions involving property effected by the other spouse within the past five years? Is it necessary to obtain interdict prohibiting the other spouse from entering into any transactions which would defeat in whole or in part a claim for financial provision on divorce?[3]

---

1 See *Murdoch v Murdoch* 1973 SLT (Notes) 13 for the form of such an interdict.
2 Matrimonial Homes (Family Protection) (Scotland) Act 1981, s 15.
3 Family Law (Scotland) Act 1985, s 18.

CHAPTER 4

ANCILLARY ORDERS—ORDERS FOR FINANCIAL PROVISION

ANCILLARY ORDERS—GENERAL

If a divorce action was raised prior to 1 September 1986, on which date the Family Law (Scotland) Act 1985 came into force, any financial claims will be determined by reference to the Divorce (Scotland) Act 1976[1]. Variation or recall of such orders are also determined by reference the latter Act[2].

In the course of a divorce action certain orders can be applied for and granted before divorce. Numerically most of these are interim orders for custody of or aliment for a child or interim aliment for a spouse (see chapter 8). Periodical payments of an alimentary nature payable to a spouse before divorce are known as aliment. Periodical payments of that nature payable to a former spouse after divorce are known as a periodical allowance. Accordingly before divorce a party may be ordered to aliment his spouse but it is not competent to seek an interim periodical allowance pending divorce nor aliment for a spouse following divorce.

Some orders granted before divorce are not interim orders. These include warrants for intimation, for arrestment on the dependence and, in the Court of Session, warrants for inhibition on the dependence. Some orders in a divorce action must be granted before divorce, eg orders for intimation in terms of the relevant rules of court. Some orders can only be granted at the same time as or, in certain circumstances, after divorce is granted, eg an order for payment of a periodical allowance or an order for payment of a capital sum or for the transfer of property. Some orders granted on or after divorce may be varied or recalled after divorce (see chapter 11). Styles of orders which may be sought in the conclusion of a Court of Session summons or in the crave of a sheriff court writ are set out in Chapter 6.

It is common at an early stage after the action has been lodged in court to ask the court to make orders for interim custody of children, interim access to children, interim aliment for the pursuer and for the children of the marriage, interim interdict and orders under the Matrimonial Homes (Family Protection) (Scotland) Act 1981. It may also be necessary to seek orders to prevent the defender from removing the children from the jurisdiction of the court or disposing of assets pending divorce. But unless there are special circumstances it is not common for a court to make interim orders other than orders for common law interdicts prior to service of the writ or, in the Court of Session, prior to calling. That is because it is in the interests of justice that the party against whom the order is directed should be heard before any such order

1 *MacLeod v MacLeod* 1990 SCLR (Notes) 157.
2 As to which see chapter 11.

is made. In connection with certain orders sought in terms of the Matrimonial Homes (Family Protection) (Scotland) Act 1981 the court is expressly prohibited from making such orders unless the the non-applicant spouse has been afforded an opportunity of being heard by or represented before the court[1].

All the orders (including, in the sheriff court, interim orders) which the court will be asked to make at any stage up to and including the granting of divorce should be included in the initial writ or summons from the outset. In a Court of Session summons it is not necessary to make specific reference to interim orders other than those for interdict and those sought in terms of the Matrimonial Homes (Family Protection) (Scotland) Act 1981. That is because the view is generally held that the greater includes the lesser. For example in a Court of Session summons it is not necessary to add: 'and for interim custody' or aliment as the case may be.

The action may be undefended. If it is and it is then decided to seek additional orders, the court will be likely to require amendment of the writ and may require its re-service. That would entail a minute of amendment. This will be an additional expense which, if it is caused through no fault of the defender, is likely to be borne by the pursuer. In a defended sheriff court action which is in course of adjustment one of the adjustments which can be made without a minute of amendment is an alteration of any sum sued for[2].

As a general rule the court will grant an interim order only if it can competently grant the order on a permanent basis. Doubt has been cast on the competence of applying for exclusion orders and other related orders under the Matrimonial Homes (Family Protection) (Scotland) Act 1981 as part of a divorce action[3]. This doubt arose because most orders under that Act, including exclusion orders, fall on divorce being granted. The parties will then have lost the status essential to the grant of such orders, ie that they are married to one another[4].

But orders under sections 2, 3 and 4 of the 1981 Act are commonly applied for in addition to a divorce and are granted in the course of divorce actions on an interim basis. It would be an unnecessary expense to require that a separate action be raised, which is what would be required if *Trolland* were to be followed in every case. To hold that such orders are incompetent as part of a divorce action other than as an alternative to divorce would, it is submitted, negate the clear purpose of the Act. That Act is intended to empower the courts to make orders which the court would have no power to do at common law. The circumstances in which the court will be called upon to make such orders are those circumstances which are commonly to be found between the time when a marriage breaks up and a divorce is granted. Further the court is empowered, on or after granting decree of divorce, to make orders regulating the occupation of the matrimonial home or the use of furniture and plenishings therein or to make an order excluding either party to the marriage from such occupation.[5] It is suggested that in an appropriate case orders be sought both in terms of the 1981 and the 1985 Acts. Orders under the former would cover the situation up to the granting of divorce. Orders under the latter would then supersede the earlier orders in identical or near

1 Eg Matrimonial Homes (Family Protection) (Scotland) Act 1981, ss 3(4), 4(5), 15(1)(b).
2 OCR 48.
3 *Trolland v Trolland* 1987 SLT (Sh Ct) 42.
4 Matrimonial Homes (Family Protection) (Scotland) Act 1981, s 5; for a contrary, and it is submitted, preferable, view to *Trolland* see *Nelson v Nelson* 1988 SLT (Sh Ct) 26 at 28.
5 Family Law (Scotland) Act 1985, s 14(2) and (3) and s 8(2).

identical terms. There is no equivalent of section 6 of the 1981 Act (continued exercise of occupancy rights after dealing) in the Family Law (Scotland) Act 1985 because *ex hypothesi* the marriage has been brought to an end.

ALIMENT

Applications in a divorce action for interim aliment are governed by section 6 of the Family Law (Scotland) Act 1985. That is so because 'aliment,' the word used in sections 2 to 5, is defined in section 27(1) so as not to include aliment *pendente lite* or interim aliment under section 6 of the Act. The court has more limited powers under section 6 than it has under sections 2 to 5. A claim for aliment for children payable after divorce is provided for by sections 2 to 5 of the Act. Accordingly sections 2 to 5 do not apply to applications for interim aliment by one party to the action against the other nor to applications for interim aliment on behalf of children. However the matter is not altogether without difficulty since it would appear from one reading of sections 2(2)(a), (3), (4)(a) that section 2 (and therefore sections 3, 4 and 5) does apply to actions for aliment in proceedings for divorce by a wife against her husband or vice versa. But aliment for a spouse may not be granted after decree of divorce has been granted. Any periodical payments after divorce in favour of a former spouse would be by way of periodical allowance.

The provisions of the 1985 Act apply to applications for aliment for children as from the date when that Act came into force whether the action was raised before or after that date[1].

Section 6 of the 1985 Act provides that a party to the divorce action may claim interim aliment and may also claim it on behalf of any person referred to in section 2(4). That includes a claim by one party as the father or mother of and on behalf of a child under eighteen and a claim by a person entitled to, seeking or having custody or care of a child[2].

The court may make orders for the payment of aliment and interim aliment for the children of the marriage and any children of one party who have been accepted as children of the marriage[3]. Awards of interim aliment may be varied on a material change of circumstances[4]. During the course of a pending action of divorce in either the Court of Session or the sheriff court an application to vary an award of interim aliment is made by motion. But, once the divorce action is concluded, in the case of a sheriff court action a minute is lodged in the divorce process seeking variation[5], and in the Court of Session a motion is enrolled[6]. It is necessary in such a minute to aver what the material change is. It is not enough to say that the previous order was made on the basis of incorrect information[7].

Where the court makes an award by way of interim aliment it may award the sum claimed or any lesser sum or may refuse to make an award of aliment[8]. This is so whether or not the sum is disputed. It is submitted that this provision requires the court to apply its mind to the amount of aliment to be awarded

1 *Matheson v Matheson* 1988 SLT 238; *Donaldson v Donaldson* 1988 SLT 243.
2 Family Law (Scotland) Act 1985, s 2(4).
3 Cf *Hart v Hart* 1960 SLT (Notes) 33.
4 Family Law (Scotland) Act 1985, s 6(4).
5 OCR 129(1).
6 RC 170P.
7 *Ritchie v Ritchie* 1987 SCLR 90, 1987 SLT (Sh Ct) 7.
8 Family Law (Scotland) Act 1985, s 6(2).

in an undefended case. If that is correct the court should not take the simple view that, since the action is undefended as regards that matter, decree should be granted for the sum sued for. That in turn means that those who draft claims for aliment must make sufficient averments, if they can, to enable the court to arrive at a proper figure. The court will require to consider not only what the pursuer needs to maintain herself and the children but also what the defender can afford to pay, ie the means and resources of the parties.

In terms of section 6 the court may award periodical payments payable only until the date of the disposal of the action or such earlier date as the court may specify[1]. The disposal of the financial aspects of the action may be on a date subsequent to divorce because the court has power to delay a decision on certain matters of that sort until after granting decree of divorce[2]. Interim aliment may continue up to the date when such matters have been decided[3]. It is competent but unusual for the court in a divorce action to order interim aliment for a specified period which terminates prior to the date on which divorce is granted or refused. There are cases in which it is known that there will be a change of circumstances. It is submitted that the court should be prepared in a suitable case to make an order that aliment is to cease on a date on which a particular event occurred even though at that time the precise date on which that event will occur may not be known. If events did not occur as anticipated that would amount to a change of circumstances[4]. Such awards may be varied or recalled[5].

The court does not have power to backdate such awards and is restricted, as has been observed, to ordering periodical payments. The court does not have power, in this connection, to order the payment of particular debts which may arise on a regular basis but which may be of uncertain amount, such as mortgage payments due in respect of the house in which the pursuer resides, school or university fees for the children and the like. In order that it may decide what sum to order the court may exercise the power referred to in section 20 of the 1985 Act to order either party to provide details of his or her resources or those of a child or incapax on whose behalf he or she is acting. It is unlikely that a court will make an order under section 20 *ex proprio motu*. Accordingly it is suggested that an application to the court will be needed in most instances before such an order is made.

Aliment for children

Both parents owe an obligation of aliment to their children[6]. Section 9(1)(c) of the 1985 Act provides that the economic burden of caring, after divorce, for a child of the marriage under sixteen should be shared fairly between the parties.

As has been remarked, section 4(1) of the 1985 Act does not apply to awards of interim aliment for children. Accordingly the criteria set out therein do not apply when a decision is taken on the amount of interim aliment. But the provisions of sections 2 to 5 of the 1985 Act apply to orders for aliment for children which are made on divorce. That means that the court has power,

---

1 Ibid, s 6(3).
2 Ibid, ss 12(1)(b), 13(1)(b).
3 *Neill v Neill* 1987 SLT (Sh Ct) 143.
4 *Ritchie v Ritchie* 1987 SCLR 90, 1987 SLT (Sh Ct) 7.
5 Family Law (Scotland) Act 1985, s 6(4).
6 Family Law (Scotland) Act 1985, s 1(1).

in terms of section 3(1) of the Act, to backdate an award of aliment for a child and power, in terms of section 5 of the Act, to vary such an award retrospectively[1]. The court might take the view that it could review the amount of interim aliment for a child by applying sections 2 to 5 retrospectively after divorce was granted.

Nonetheless the criteria set out in section 4(1) are consistent with pre-1985 Act practice so far as interim orders are concerned. The court must consider the needs of the child now and for the immediate future so far as these may be foreseen as well as the earning capacity and resources of the parties and the other circumstances of the case[2].

Quantum of aliment

On divorce the court will require to consider what overall financial provision it is reasonable and appropriate to make having regard to the circumstances of the family as a whole. There is no mathematical formula which can be applied to the determination of the amount of aliment. Little reliance can be placed on reported cases which have been decided solely on their facts unless the facts in the instant case are more or less identical. Where aliment is assessed after divorce the fact that one or both parties have remarried will be taken into account[3]. One of the circumstances which may be taken into account is the fact that the payer is cohabiting with another person[4]. In assessing the amount of aliment payable to a child account may be taken of the amount of aliment previously paid to the mother of that child for the benefit of the child[5] In *Munro* the cohabitee's income was taken into account to the extent that it was used to meet joint outlays[6]. The court will have regard to the style of life of the parties and their respective ability to aliment the children[7] out of their net income[8]. But there may be special cases where it is appropriate to have regard to gross income[9]. Where the payer resides abroad it may be appropriate to have regard to his net rather than his gross income[10]. It may be necessary, where the payer's income fluctuates widely, to average his income over a few years[11]. If the payee commences cohabitation with another man, even though that man does not support her an order for interim aliment may be recalled[12]. Where there are capital assets but no significant income a capital sum has been awarded in lieu of periodical payments of aliment[13]. Where the defender is in receipt of social security there may be no benefit to the children by making an award of aliment[14]. Where a party is in receipt of periodical allowance or aliment it does not follow that there will be no liability to pay aliment for a child who is in the custody of a spouse or former spouse[15].

1 *Abrahams v Abrahams* 1989 SCLR 102, 1989 SLT (Sh Ct) 113.
2 *McGeachie v McGeachie* 1989 SCLR 99.
3 *Ritchie v Ritchie* 1989 SCLR 768.
4 *Munro v Munro* 1986 SLT 72; *Love v Love* 1983 SLT (Sh Ct) 21.
5 *Jowett v Jowett* 1990 SCLR 348.
6 See also *Frith v Frith* 1990 GWD 5-266.
7 *Scully v Scully* 1989 SCLR 757.
8 *Wiseman v Wiseman* 1989 SCLR 757 and see Taxation of Maintenance Payments below.
9 *MacInnes v MacInnes* 1990 GWD 13-690.
10 *Begg v Begg* 1987 SCLR 704.
11 *Edwards v Edwards* 1984 SLT 311.
12 *Brunton v Brunton* 1986 SLT 49, but see *Kavanagh v Kavanagh* 1989 SLT 134.
13 *Winton v Winton* 1987 GWD 15-572.
14 *Coyle v Coyle; Neilly v Neilly* 1981 SLT (Notes) 129.
15 *Howarth v Howarth* 1990 SLT 289.

Prior agreements on aliment

HUSBAND AND WIFE

It is not uncommon for there to be a separation agreement in which the parties set out agreed financial arrangements following on the breakdown of their marriage. Such agreements vary a great deal in their provisions. Some deal only with the situation between separation and divorce. Others deal with the financial arrangements which are to obtain before and after divorce and include a procedure for variation and recall of the agreed arrangements. It is not uncommon for such agreements to be registered in the Books of Council and Session for preservation and for execution. If they have been registered for execution, diligence may be done to enforce the terms of the agreement[1]. As to the situation where the agreement is partly implemented, the parties reconcile but one party later seeks divorce with an order for financial provision see *Davidson v Davidson*[2]. Where there is a subsisting and enforceable agreement and a decree of court which deals with the same matter but does not supersede the terms of the agreement consideration should be given to the risk that a party may be in a position to enforce both when in reality the intention was that only one would be enforceable. The best course may well be to enter into a joint minute whose terms make it clear that both are not to be enforced or agreeing that the agreement is to be superseded in whole or in part by the agreed terms set out in the joint minute or by the decree. It is not appropriate in an action of divorce to vary the alimentary provisions of a separation agreement which would terminate on divorce. A motion for interim variation is incompetent[3].

Any provision in such an agreement which purports to exclude future liability for aliment or to restrict any right to bring an action for aliment has no effect unless the provision was fair and reasonable at the time it was entered into[4]. Prior to the 1985 Act such a provision was thought to be contrary to public policy and to be of no effect.[5] Thus parties may agree to bar themselves from seeking aliment, for example, from one another and the court will be required to give effect to that agreement if it was fair and reasonable at the time it was entered into. That means that if it was fair and reasonable at that time, even though it has subsequently become unfair, it will receive effect. What is fair and reasonable is a question of fact. It will be easier to argue that the agreement is fair and reasonable if its provisions err on the generous side, for it appears that it would be for the payer and not for the payee to satisfy the court that it was fair and reasonable. If there is a material change of circumstances, either party to the agreement may apply to the court for variation or termination of the agreement. Provided that the party to the agreement liable to pay aliment is a person who owes an obligation to pay aliment[6], the court which would have jurisdiction to entertain an action for aliment between the parties may vary the amount payable under the agreement or terminate the agreement[7].

1 Writs Execution (Scotland) Act 1877, s 3 as substituted by Debtors (Scotland) Act 1987, s 87(4).
2 1989 SLT 466.
3 *McKenzie v McKenzie* 1987 SCLR 671; *Stewart v Stewart* 1990 SCLR 360.
4 Family Law (Scotland) Act 1985, s 7(1).
5 Cf eg *Beaton v Beaton's Trs* 1935 SC 187 at 195, per Lord Anderson.
6 See Family Law (Scotland) Act 1985, s 1(1).
7 Ibid, s 7(2) and (4).

PARENT AND CHILD

The same provisions apply to agreements between parents and children as apply between husband and wife[1]. It is therefore possible for a parent to agree with his child to make over a lump sum, say, in exchange for excluding or restricting liability to aliment the child provided that at the time it was entered into the agreement was fair and reasonable. In such a case it would be an obvious and wise precaution to arrange for the child to be separately advised.

SETTING ASIDE OR VARYING AGREEMENTS AS TO FINANCIAL PROVISION TO BE MADE ON DIVORCE

The court may, after divorce, set aside or vary any term of an agreement relating to periodical allowance if the agreement provides for that to be done by the court or may set aside or vary the agreement or any term of it on granting divorce or within a specified period thereafter if the agreement was not fair and reasonable at the time it was entered into[2]. The effect of such an agreement may be to discharge any claims competent to one or both parties to an order for financial provision on divorce or to a periodical allowance. Such agreements are competent and, unless set aside, will be binding[3].

ORDERS FOR FINANCIAL PROVISION

General

Once a husband and wife have been divorced they have no obligation in law to provide support for each other. Section 1(1) of the 1985 Act provides that an obligation to aliment is owed by a husband to his wife and vice versa. Once they cease to have that status the obligation ceases. But as part of the orders for financial provision which may be made in connection with divorce one party may be ordered to pay a periodical allowance to the other, usually for a period of no more than three years. It is unusual, but not incompetent, for the husband to be ordered to pay periodical allowance and for the wife to be ordered to pay aliment for a child in the care of her husband[4]. Both before and after divorce they will have an obligation to aliment their children up to a certain age or stage in the children's lives. The 1985 Act makes provision for the financial dissolution of the marriage and only in very limited circumstances is it contemplated that there will be a long-term financial commitment to or by a former spouse.

The court has been given a wide and at the same time a restricted discretion as to the orders which may be made. That apparent paradox arises because there are few orders which the court might make but lacks the power to make but the discretion to make orders is fettered by various provisions of which the requirement to apply defined principles is one. Nonetheless, as in other fields in which a court of first instance has a discretion, an appeal court will be likely to be reluctant to interfere unless the court of first instance

1 Ibid, s 7(1).
2 Ibid, s 16. Cf *McAfee v McAfee* 1990 GWD 28–1611; *Anderson v Anderson* 1990 GWD 29–1677.
3 *Dunbar v Dunbar* 1977 SLT 169; *Thomson v Thomson* 1982 SLT 521; *Bryan v Bryan* 1985 SLT 444; *Elder v Elder* 1985 SLT 471.
4 *Howarth v Howarth* 1990 SLT 289.

has clearly erred in law, failed to consider a relevant and material factor or reached a result which was clearly inequitable[1]. The court on appeal is likely to refuse to consider information which could have been put before the court of first instance but was not. It is therefore important that all relevant matters be put before that court.

Orders which may be made

The powers of the court are as follows:
Section 8(1) of the Family Law (Scotland) Act 1985 provides:
'In an action of divorce, either party to the marriage can apply for one or more of the following orders—

(a) an order for the payment of a capital sum or the transfer of property to him by the other party to the marriage;
(b) an order for the making of a periodical allowance to him by the other party to the marriage:
(c) an incidental order within the meaning of section 14(2) of this Act.'

The court may stipulate that an order for payment of a capital sum or for transfer of property shall come into effect at a specified future date[2]. The court may also supersede extract in whole or in part for a period or periods[3]. The court is required not to make an order for the transfer of property if (a) the consent of a third party, which it is necessary to obtain, has not been obtained or (b) in relation to property subject to a security without the consent of the creditor unless he has been given an opportunity of being heard[4].

Differences have arisen as to whether a court can make both an order for payment of a capital sum and an order for the transfer of property in view of the wording of section 8(1)(a) of the 1985 Act[5]. It is submitted that Lord Cameron of Lochbroom in *Little* was correct when he decided that both orders could be made. The opinion of Lord Morton of Shuna in *Walker* to the opposite effect was expressed with reluctance and appears to be contrary to the intention of the Act which is to enable the court to make orders which comply with its principles. That intention could be thwarted where the only way in which an appropriate order could be implemented would be partly by payment of a capital sum and partly by transfer of property. It would mean that it was necessary to realise assets which might be disadvantageous at that time for tax reasons or otherwise. It could be argued that the orders referred to in section 8(1) are all listed there but that there is no indication that one was intended to exclude the other, despite the use of the word 'or'.

Incidental orders

Incidental orders of the types set out below may be made before, on or after the granting or refusal of decree of divorce except those orders set out in the Family Law (Scotland) Act 1985, s 14(2)(d) or (e) which may be made

1 *McRae v McRae* 1979 SLT (Notes) 45.
2 Family Law (Scotland) Act 1985, s 12(2). Cf *Mackin v Mackin* 1990 GWD 26–1486.
3 *Crooks v Crooks* 1986 SLT 500; *Winton v Winton* 1987 GWD 15-572 and see particularly *Archibald v Archibald* 1989 SLT 199.
4 Family Law (Scotland) Act 1985, s 15.
5 *Little v Little* 1989 SCLR 613; *Walker v Walker* 1989 SCLR 625.

only on or after the granting of decree of divorce[1]. Subsections 2(d) and (e) take over, as it were, where the Matrimonial Homes (Family Protection) (Scotland) Act 1981 leaves off.

Section 14(2) of the Family Law (Scotland) Act 1985 provides that an 'incidental order' means one or more of the following orders:

(a) an order for the sale of property;
(b) an order for the valuation of property;
(c) an order determining any dispute between the parties to the marriage as to their respective property rights by means of a declarator thereof or otherwise;
(d) an order regulating the occupation of the matrimonial home or the use of furniture and plenishings therein or excluding either party to the marriage from such occupation;
(e) an order regulating liability, as between the parties, for outgoings in respect of the matrimonial home or furniture or plenishings therein;
(f) an order that security shall be given for any financial provision;
(g) an order that payments shall be made or property transferred to any curator bonis or trustee or other person for the benefit of the party to the marriage by whom or on whose behalf application has been made under section 8(1) of this Act for an incidental order;
(h) an order setting aside or varying any term in an antenuptial or post-nuptial marriage settlement;
(j) an order as to the date from which any interest on any amount awarded shall run;
(k) any ancillary order which is expedient to give effect to the principles set out in section 9 of this Act or to any order made under section 8(2) of this Act.

Incidental orders should not be granted to the prejudice of the rights of a third party provided that the third party's rights existed immediately before the incidental order was made[2]. Incidental orders may be varied or recalled on cause shown[3].

When drafting a summons or initial writ it should be borne in mind that it will be necessary to ask the court to make an incidental order in a form suitable to the circumstances of that particular case. It will not be enough to ask the court to order the sale of a particular property. The conclusion should set out exactly what the court is to be asked to do in order to achieve such a sale in the same way as in an action of (division and) sale. The court has a discretion whether to make such orders. Application for orders for the valuation and sale of the matrimonial home before defences are lodged may be refused as premature[4]. An order for division and sale of the matrimonial home, not applied for as an incidental order, will not be delayed unless it is necessary for the defender to have occupation of the matrimonial home at least until divorce[5]. The court may postpone decree in such an action until after divorce[6]. Where there is an application for division and sale it is for

1 See the Family Law (Scotland) Act 1985, s 14(3).
2 Family Law (Scotland) Act 1985, s 15(3).
3 Ibid, s 14(4).
4 *McKeown v McKeown* 1988 SCLR 355.
5 *Berry v Berry* 1988 SLT 650; *Dickson v Dickson* 1982 SLT 128.
6 *Crow v Crow* 1986 SLT 270.

the pursuer to satisfy the court that an offer of suitable alternative accommodation has been made[1].

Orders for payment of a capital sum or the transfer of property

The primary purpose of the 1985 Act is that financial provision should be made, and if possible completely made, as between the spouses by such orders. Property in this context does not include a tenancy transferable under section 13 of the Matrimonial Homes (Family Protection) (Scotland) Act 1981[2]. As that section enables the court to order a transfer on divorce it is not necessary so to enable the court in the 1985 Act also. Otherwise, not surprisingly, there is no definition of property nor of capital sum.

The order may come into immediate effect on granting decree of divorce or the court may stipulate that it shall come into effect at a specified future date. The court may order that the sum be paid or the property be transferred within such period as the court on granting decree of divorce may specify[3]. This provision enables the court to allow time to a party to realise assets or to effect the transfer of property in an orderly way. For instance it may be necessary to sell the matrimonial home. But to do so against a short deadline dictated by the date when the divorce case is to be heard may lead to the property in question being sold at a lower price than it might have been. Where there are shares in a private company their formal valuation and sale to an approved buyer may take some time. In some cases a delay may be sensible because a policy of assurance will mature on a certain future date or a lump sum will be payable on a forthcoming retirement. The sum so paid may be used to pay the capital sum without having to realise assets. There may be capital gains tax implications. There need not be a delay in granting divorce. The court may also order that a capital sum should be paid by instalments[4]. This provision is often used where it is not possible for a party to realise a substantial sum in a short period. But it should not be seen as a roundabout way of obtaining a periodical allowance. The court also has a common law power to supersede extract for a determinate period[5]. As to interest claimed on a capital sum prior to decree see *Carpenter v Carpenter* 1990 SLT (Sh Ct) 68.

Variation of a capital sum

Either party may apply to the court on a material change of circumstances to vary the date or method of payment of the capital sum or the date of the transfer of property.[6] It is to be noted that the nature, extent and method of the transfer of property may not be altered nor may the amount of the capital sum. It may be that a party has inherited assets or has died, with the result that an earlier transfer may be possible, or that the stock market has fallen so that the value of readily realisable assets is insufficient to meet the order (see chapter 11).

1 *Hall v Hall* 1987 SLT (Sh Ct) 15; Matrimonial Homes (Family Protection) (Scotland) Act 1981, s 19.
2 Family Law (Scotland) Act1985, s 27(1).
3 Ibid, s 12(1) and (2).
4 Ibid, s 12(3).
5 Cf *Archibald v Archibald* 1989 SLT 199.
6 Family Law (Scotland) Act 1985, s 12(4).

What is matrimonial property?

Matrimonial property is defined in section 10(4) of the 1985 Act as all property belonging to the parties or either of them at the relevant date which was acquired by one or both of them (otherwise than by gift or succession from a third party):

(1) before the marriage for use by them as a family home or as furniture or plenishings for such home; or

(2) during the marriage but before the relevant date[1]. As to what is the 'relevant date', see below.

The court is enjoined to share the net value of the matrimonial property 'fairly' between the parties to the marriage[2]. The property acquired before the marriage and referred to in section 10(4)(a) is an exception to the rule that the property to be taken into account is that acquired during the marriage, essentially through the efforts of the parties. Subject to the proviso that the court is required to make such order as is reasonable having regard to the resources of the parties[3] it is submitted that the court must ignore assets which do not form part of the matrimonial property in arriving at a figure which is justified by the principles set out in section 9. Thus if a wife has assets acquired by gift or inheritance which are substantial she should be entitled to her fair share of the matrimonial property, modest though that may be. The proviso mentioned above would not justify a deduction from the amount fairly due to her simply to subsidise her husband, eg in his acquisition of a house.

If a person sets up home for himself and furnishes it not contemplating marriage, that property would not become matrimonial property even though the parties later lived in it and regarded it as their home. The property may have been acquired while one of the parties was already married to another person. But if that property was used by a cohabiting couple who subsequently marry, eg as a family home before and after their marriage, it may nonetheless be regarded as matrimonial property[4]. If the property was acquired before marriage when the acquirer was unmarried the fact that it was occupied as a matrimonial home after marriage does not mean that it must be regarded as matrimonial property. Prima facie it would not have been acquired for use 'by them as a family home'. It would be necessary to persuade a court, if that matter was disputed, that that was the purpose of the acquisition. Accordingly a party to an action who wishes to contend that it is matrimonial property must aver that that is so[5]. As to where the onus of proof lies when establishing whether the property was acquired by gift or succession see *Williamson v Williamson*[6].

It is submitted that an important factor, which should be decisive in such cases, is whether, when the property was acquired, ie before marriage, it was intended that it would be used as matrimonial property after an intended marriage[7]. Some dicta in *Buczynska*, above, may go further than was necessary

1 Family Law (Scotland) Act 1985, s 10(4) and see below under 'Date at which matrimonial property is valued'.
2 Ibid, s 9(1)(a).
3 Ibid, s 8(2)(b).
4 *Buczynska v Buczynski* 1989 SCLR 224, 1989 SLT 558.
5 *Maclellan v Maclellan* 1988 SCLR 399.
6 1989 SLT 866.
7 Cf H R M Macdonald *A Guide to the Family Law (Scotland) Act 1985*, p 30 (CCH Editions, 1986).

for the decision of that aspect of that case. What is a matrimonial home for the purposes of the Matrimonial Homes (Family Protection) (Scotland) Act 1981 is irrelevant to the definition of matrimonial property for the purposes of the Family Law (Scotland) Act 1985.

If a parent buys a property for a child, that property will not be regarded as matrimonial property for these purposes and will be left out of account because it has been acquired by gift. But if a parent gives his child money with which the child buys a property that property could be taken into account because the property would not have been acquired by gift. There may be difficult borderline cases where the money was given on the express condition that it was used to buy property[1]. These cases would have to be decided on their facts. The response to an argument that such purchased property should be included would be to refer to section 10(6)(b) of the Act. It may be a 'special circumstance' that the funds were not derived from the income or efforts of the parties during the marriage. Similar considerations apply to acquisitions by way of inheritance. In the course of planning family financial arrangements it may be for consideration whether it may not be better to hand on property rather than money in certain circumstances.

In the case of rights or interests in life policies, pension schemes or similar arrangements the proportion referable to the period of the marriage up to the relevant date forms part of the matrimonial property[2]. There are considerable difficulties in practice valuing an interest in a pension scheme. Some pension schemes are non-contributory but most involve contributions from earnings. Some are very similar to policies of assurance or bonds of annuity. Some can be valued as a capital asset more readily than others. There are as yet insufficient reported cases to enable a statement of the principles of valuation to be formulated. The non-contributing spouse may, on divorce, lose a prospect of income from such a scheme either as the spouse or as the widow of the contributor. She would not have expected to receive a capital sum in her own right in most instances. It is not in accordance with common sense nor would it be reasonable for the court by its order to make it necessary for a party to realise his interest in a pension scheme in a disadvantageous way. An inaccessible pension may be ignored by the court altogether[3].

A redundancy payment acquired after the relevant date is not matrimonial property. That is because it is a payment for loss of employment and not something to which the employee contributed during his employment[4]. It is not a 'similar arrangement' to a life policy or pension scheme. The court may take account of assets in a discretionary trust from which a party has received payments[5]. An award of damages for an injury before marriage received after the parties separated is not matrimonial property[6].

Date at which matrimonial property is valued—the 'relevant date'

The net value of the matrimonial property is assessed as at the 'relevant date' which is the earlier of the date on which the parties ceased to cohabit or

1 See *Latter v Latter* 1990 SLT 805.
2 Family Law (Scotland) Act 1985, s 10(5); *Little v Little* 1989 SCLR 613.
3 *Robertson v Robertson* 1989 SCLR 71 at 73–74. See also *Muir v Muir* 1989 SLT (Sh Ct) 20; *Carpenter v Carpenter* 1990 SLT (Sh Ct) 68; *Orr v Orr* 27 August 1990, Cupar Sh Ct (unreported); *Latter*, supra; *Little v Little* 1990 SLT 785, Inner House.
4 *Smith v Smith* 1989 SCLR 308, 1989 SLT 668; *Tyrrell v Tyrrell* 1990 SLT 406.
5 *Brodie v Brodie* 1986 GWD 5-100.
6 *Petrie v Petrie* 1988 SCLR 390.

the date of service of the summons or initial writ in the action of divorce[1]. In assessing the date on which the parties ceased to cohabit no account is to be taken of any cessation of cohabitation where there was a later resumption of cohabitation unless the cessation of cohabitation was for a continuous period of ninety days or more before they resumed cohabitation for a period or periods of less than ninety days in all[2].

The effect of section 10(2) and (3) is that the value of the assets is in effect frozen at that date. Thus if there is a substantial alteration in value subsequently the party whose asset is affected will gain or lose and the other party will not be affected by that[3]. Nonetheless if there have been significant gains or losses since the relevant date these may be taken into account in assessing what is reasonable having regard to the resources of the parties[4]. The increase in the value of pension rights between 'the relevant date', eg cessation of cohabitation and the proof should be ignored[5]. On appeal new evidence is unlikely to be permitted as to the value of the property[6].

Cessation of cohabitation

Questions may arise as to whether the parties were cohabiting during a particular period. Where a marriage is about to break up, and occasionally when it is not, the extent to which an acquaintance would say that they were living together might be very limited indeed. Section 27(2) of the Family Law (Scotland) Act 1985 provides that parties to a marriage shall be held to cohabit with one another only when they are in fact living together as man and wife[7]. But that does not altogether solve the problem which arises when they are living under the same roof but have little or no other relationship, as where the wife continues to do some cooking and washing but they sleep in separate rooms, do not have sexual relations and do not talk to one another to any significant extent[8]. The approach of the court will be that this is a question of fact to be decided on the evidence led in the particular case. In *Buczynska* above agents for the husband wrote to the wife calling on her to move out of the matrimonial home which she did not do. The date of the letter was taken as the date on which cohabitation ceased though ordinarily where parties continue to reside together cohabitation will be taken to cease on the date of service of the summons or initial writ[9]. It will depend on whether they were living together as husband and wife. The case of *Buczynska* may come to be regarded as exceptional. It is not easy to understand why the writing of a letter should be more than an adminicle of evidence in the establishment of the date when cohabitation ceased.

Net value of matrimonial property

The net value of matrimonial property is the value after deduction of any debts incurred by the parties or either of them before the marriage so far

1 Family Law (Scotland) Act 1985, s 10(2) and (3).
2 Ibid, s 10(7).
3 *Muir v Muir* 1989 SCLR 445; *Buczynska*, above; *Little v Little* 1990 SLT 785.
4 Ibid, s 8(2)(b).
5 *Tyrrell v Tyrrell* 1990 SLT 406.
6 *Murphy v Murphy* 1981 SLT (Notes) 27.
7 See also Divorce (Scotland) Act 1976, s 13(2).
8 See, eg, *MacDonald v MacDonald* 1948 SLT 380.
9 Family Law (Scotland) Act 1985, s 10(3)(b).

as these debts relate to matrimonial property and during the marriage[1] Obviously if a flat was bought before marriage and that flat fell within the definition of matrimonial property any loan from a building society secured over that property would have to be deducted in arriving at the net value. If the flat did not fall within the definition neither would the loan secured over it. Similarly there may be loans or outstanding hire purchase commitments on furniture, a washing machine, a car or the like which would have to be deducted.

Principles to be applied when making orders for financial provision on divorce

DIVISION OF NET VALUE OF MATRIMONIAL PROPERTY

The net value of the matrimonial property should be shared fairly between the parties[2]. The matrimonial property is to be taken to be shared fairly when it is shared equally or in such other proportions as are justified by 'special circumstances'[3]. Despite that provision in some cases courts have arrived at an unequal split without resort to 'special circumstances'[4]. In assessing what is fair it is not relevant that one party was not earning or was earning much less than the other. Where a wife has remained at home to look after domestic matters or has ceased to work to have and bring up children she will not suffer a reduction in her share because she made no or only a limited contribution to the acquisition of the property. But where the principal asset of the parties is their house and the pursuer and the defender have one half *pro indiviso* shares in it, the court may decide not to order that the defender make over his half share to the pursuer so that she can retain the house as a home for herself and the children. Such an order could result in a grossly unfair division[5].

In applying this principle conduct of either party is not to be taken into account unless it has adversely affected the financial resources relevant to a decision on a claim for financial provision[6].

Special Circumstances

'Special circumstances' referred to in section 10(1) which could justify an unequal sharing of the matrimonial property may arise[7] as the result of or where:

(1) The terms of any agreement between the parties on the ownership or division of any of the matrimonial property. The fact that title to the home is in the name of one party only is not of itself an agreement between the parties that it is to be regarded as the sole property of that party.

(2) The source of the funds or assets used to acquire any of the matrimonial property where those funds or assets were not derived from the income or efforts of the parties during the marriage. But if a party acquires heritable property with funds wholly or substantially provided by a parent there may be special circumstances[8]. For

1 Ibid, s 10(2).
2 Ibid, s 9(1)(a).
3 Ibid, s 10(1).
4 See, eg, *Clark v Clark* 1987 SCLR 516.
5 Cf *Main v Main* 1990 SCLR 165.
6 Family Law (Scotland) Act 1985, s 11(7).
7 Ibid, s 10(6).
8 *Buczynska v Buczynski* 1989 SCLR 224, 1989 SLT 558; *Kerrigan v Kerrigan* 1988 SCLR 603.

a case involving a croft where an unequal share was apportioned see *Budge v Budge*[1].

This provision could apply where a house or, for example, a valuable painting was bought during the marriage with funds derived from one party alone who acquired the funds by gift or inheritance or before marriage by his or her own efforts. The more difficult issue could arise where that house had been exchanged for a more expensive one during the marriage. The court may be prepared to make allowance for that contribution by applying the principle in section 9(1)(b). Courts are unlikely to be willing to become involved in attempting to trace funds through what could have been a long marriage. Inflation and changing values over the years would make that a difficult, expensive and probably worthless task. Courts are likely to take a broad approach. It will be easier to persuade a court to exclude an asset where the marriage has been short and the asset has not changed character. This provision and section 10(4) which defines 'matrimonial property' should be considered together. If an asset is acquired by gift or succession it is not matrimonial property. If parents of a spouse give him money which is invested in, for example, the matrimonial home, section 10(1)(b) may have to be relied upon in order to arrive at a fair result.

(3) There has been any destruction, dissipation or alienation of property by either party. The Family Law (Scotland) Act 1985 does not differentiate between debts responsibly incurred or irresponsibly incurred in assessing the net value of the property but the net value of the property is to be shared fairly[2]. However, if one party has spent a significant part of the matrimonial assets on his own unworthy objects that may amount to 'dissipation' which, along with 'destruction' and 'alienation of property' by either party may amount to special circumstances which would warrant an unequal share of the matrimonial property[3]. It has been said that 'dissipation' requires some definite action by a party and cannot occur as a result of passive failure[4]. That was said in a case in which it was argued that failure by the husband to make mortgage payments led to loss of assets as a result of the forced sale of the matrimonial home. Because both parties were obliged to make such payments, it was held that there had not been dissipation of property. It would be difficult to distinguish between active and passive conduct in this field. Why should there not be dissipation if one party stands by and allows others to remove assets without payment? The consequences for a party who has destroyed, dissipated or alienated matrimonial property may be modified by the overriding requirement of the Act that any order be reasonable having regard to the resources of the parties.

(4) The nature of the matrimonial property, the use made of it (including use for business purposes or as a matrimonial home) and the extent to which it is reasonable to expect it to be realised or divided or used as security. There are many marriages in which a substantial proportion of the matrimonial property is tied up in businesses such as farms and shops or part of the matrimonial home is used in connection with a profession or business, for example as a surgery or office. Without most, and in some instances all, of that capital remaining where it is it may not be possible for one party to continue to earn his livelihood. In other marriages the parties may have taken out life insurance in a form which is not readily realisable at the time at which the marriage breaks up. It may not be wise

1 1990 SCLR (Notes) 144 1990 SLT 319.
2 Family Law (Scotland) Act 1985, ss 9(1)(a), 10(1).
3 Ibid, s 10(6)(c).
4 *Park v Park* 1988 SCLR 584 at 587.

to sell the matrimonial home. The result could be that the parties have no house in which one of them could live and could not afford to buy another, let alone two.

The solution to problems in such a case may be for there to be a transfer of the interest of one party in the matrimonial home to the other, possibly with a liability on that other to make a capital payment which could be payable by instalments[1], or which could be, say, half the net proceeds of the home when it is sold. It could be agreed that there would be a sale not later than a certain future date which might be when the youngest child reached a certain age[2]. In *Cooper v Cooper*[3] the defender was ordered to transfer his half share of the matrimonial home to the pursuer. She lived there with the children. He lived in sheltered accommodation. Such an order was refused in *Main v Main*[4].

It is not a special circumstance that the value of the property has increased since the relevant date even though the parties continued to occupy it after that date[5].

(5) The actual or prospective liability for any expenses of valuation or transfer of property in connection with the divorce[6]. This enables the court to make such small adjustment as may seem fair in the circumstances.

ECONOMIC ADVANTAGE AND DISADVANTAGE

Fair account should be taken of any economic advantage derived by either party from contributions by the other, and of any economic disadvantage suffered by either party in the interests of the other party or the family[7]. A claim under this principle is additional to a claim under the preceding principle[8].

'Economic advantage' means advantage gained before or during marriage and includes gains in capital, in income and in earning capacity. Economic disadvantage has a corresponding meaning. 'Contributions' means contributions made before or during the marriage and includes indirect and non-financial contributions such as looking after the family home or caring for the family[9].

Conduct of either party is not to be taken into account unless it has adversely affected the financial resources relevant to a decision on a claim for financial provision[10].

Before or during marriage one party or both may have worked in order to enable the other to obtain a qualification in, say, medicine or at a trade. That would have conferred an economic advantage on the other. Contributions may have been financial in nature either before or after the marriage as where a wife has worked unpaid in a business which was starting up. The husband's work may have required him to live in a part of the world where it was not possible for his wife to obtain work. If she accompanied him there she would suffer a disadvantage. A wife who does not work but is well qualified to do so may have lost a substantial amount of income and may have suffered

1 Family Law (Scotland) Act 1985, s 12(3).
2 Cf *Archibald v Archibald* 1989 SLT 199.
3 1989 SCLR 347.
4 1990 SCLR 165.
5 *Buczynska v Buczynski* 1989 SCLR 224, 1989 SLT 558.
6 Family Law (Scotland) Act 1985, s 10(6).
7 Ibid, s 9(1)(b).
8 *Little v Little* 1989 SCLR 613 at 621.
9 Family Law (Scotland) Act 1985, s 9(2).
10 Ibid, s 11(7); *Edmonstone v Edmonstone* 1987 SCLR 464.

a reduction in her earning potential as a result of losing opportunities for promotion or for increasing, or keeping up to date, her skills. But she will be likely to have contributed to the marriage in other ways. If she had not cared for the children her husband may have had to do so, assuming that his earning power was not sufficient to employ another to look after them. He is likely to have benefited from the fact that his wife was at home engaged on domestic activities and perhaps organising his social life. Many wives, though they may be at home, play an important part in their husband's business, eg by answering the telephone and doing secretarial work and bookkeeping.

In most cases, assuming that there is sufficient matrimonial property to share, the wife, if disadvantaged, will be awarded a fair share of that property. If there is not and the wife is not in a position to earn, for example because there are young children, she may be compensated in some other way. Section 11(2) of the 1985 Act requires the court to have regard to the extent to which—

(1) the economic advantages or disadvantages sustained by either party have been balanced by the economic advantages or disadvantages sustained by the other party, and

(2) any resulting imbalance has been or will be corrected by a sharing of the value of the matrimonial property or otherwise.

A wife may otherwise have the imbalance corrected by, for example, the making of incidental orders in terms of section 14 which permitted her to live on in the matrimonial home with the outgoings in respect of the home and any furniture or plenishings in it (eg in respect of hire purchase) being met by the husband. But that imbalance cannot be corrected by the award of a periodical allowance[1].

ECONOMIC BURDEN OF CARING FOR CHILD

Any economic burden of caring, after divorce, for a child of the marriage under the age of sixteen should be shared fairly between the parties[2]. This principle is not related to a claim for aliment on behalf of a child. It is concerned with the financial provision to be made for a spouse on divorce. But the court is required[3] in applying this principle to have regard to—

(a) any decree or arrangement for aliment for the child;
(b) any expenditure or loss of earning capacity caused by the need to care for the child;
(c) the need to provide suitable accommodation for the child;
(d) the age and health of the child;
(e) the educational, financial and other circumstances of the child;
(f) the availability and cost of suitable child-care facilities or services;
(g) the needs and resources of the parties, and
(h) all the other circumstances of the case.

The court may also take account of any support, financial or otherwise, given by the party who is to make the financial provision to any person whom he maintains as a dependant in his household whether or not he owes an obligation of aliment to that person[4]. This means that if the father has taken on the

---

1 Family Law (Scotland) Act 1985, s 13(2)(a).
2 Ibid, s 9(1)(c).
3 Ibid, s 11(3)(a).
4 Ibid, s 11(6).

responsibility of a second family the court may take account of that. This principle emphasises that both parents are expected to share the economic, as opposed to the physical and spiritual, burden of bringing up children. Section 1 of the 1985 Act provides that both parents owe an obligation of aliment to their child. It does not follow, as some seem to think, that if one has custody of the child the other should pay the full cost of maintaining that child. Nor does it mean that if one parent pays aliment for that child that he thereby acquires a right to have access to that child as a *quid pro quo*.

In the first instance the court is required to apply its mind to the question whether this principle can be met by making an order for financial provision by way of an order for payment of a capital sum or transfer of property. That may be achieved by awarding a substantial proportion of the value of the matrimonial home to the party having care of the children[1]. If it can not be met in that way it does not follow that the solution should be found by making an order for a periodical allowance[2]. The best course of action may be to make use of one or more of the incidental orders specified in section 14(2) or to make an order for aliment for the child at such a level that the burden of caring for that child may be met in that way or by a combination of these. If periodical allowance were to be used for this purpose it may well be that it would be for a period of less than three years whereas having regard to the age of the child the need for support will be likely to last for a much longer period than that.

It should be noted that section 9(1)(c) refers to a child under sixteen. That is the age at which any order of court for custody of the child ceases but, in certain circumstances, the court may award aliment for a child of the marriage up to the age of twenty-five[3]. A child in this context is defined in section 27(1) to include a child (other than a child who has been boarded out with the parties, or one of them, by a local authority or a voluntary organisation) who has been accepted by the parties as a child of the family.

Conduct of either party is not to be taken into account unless it has adversely affected the financial resources relevant to a decision on a claim for financial provision[4].

FINANCIAL SUPPORT FOR DEPENDENT SPOUSE

A party who has been dependent to a substantial degree on the financial support of the other party should be awarded such financial provision as is reasonable to enable him to adjust, over a period of not more than three years from the date of decree of divorce, to the loss of that support on divorce[5].

In applying this principle the court is required[6] to have regard to:

(a) the age, health and earning capacity of the party who is claiming the financial provision;
(b) the duration and extent of the dependence of that party prior to divorce;
(c) any intention of that party to undertake a course of education or training;

1 *Morrison v Morrison* 1989 SCLR 574.
2 Cf Family Law (Scotland) Act 1985, s 13(2).
3 Ibid, s 1(5).
4 Ibid, s 11(7).
5 Ibid, s 9(1)(d).
6 Ibid, s 11(4).

(d) the needs and resources of the parties, and
(e) all the other circumstances of the case.

The court may also take account of any support, financial or otherwise, given by the party who is to make the financial provision to any person whom he maintains as a dependant in his household whether or not he owes an obligation of aliment to that person.[1]

This principle has often been largely ignored by practitioners, particularly where a divorce is undefended. Yet it is central to the whole scheme of the provisions relating to financial provision on divorce. Prior to the 1985 Act an order for a periodical allowance was the only form of order which the court could make to enable the divorced spouse to obtain some benefit from any wealth and enhanced earning capacity which had been acquired as a result of the marriage. The recipient of a periodical allowance was not encouraged by the old provisions to seek employment. Periodical allowance is now intended to play a subordinate role and to be in almost every case an order of short duration.

This principle is intended to enable a spouse to adjust to an unmarried and, more particularly, to a non-dependent state. In every case in which periodical allowance is sought the party seeking it should aver the period for which it is sought and provide information from which the court can determine what is the appropriate period. In an undefended action of divorce the court should not accept that three years is the appropriate period simply because no defence is offered. In particular the court must be satisfied that an order for payment of a capital sum or for transfer of property would be inappropriate or insufficient[2]. It may be necessary for a wife to obtain a qualification or go on a refresher course, eg to resume a career in nursing. Tuition fees and maintenance charges (eg at a college) in that connection should be taken into account. The period of not more than three years runs from the date of decree of divorce even though the award of periodical allowance is made, as in certain circumstances it can be made, after the date on which decree of divorce was granted.

Conduct of either party is not to be taken into account unless it has adversely affected the financial resources relevant to a decision on a claim for financial provision or it would be manifestly inequitable to leave such conduct out of account[3].

FINANCIAL HARDSHIP AS RESULT OF DIVORCE

A party who at the time of the divorce seems likely to suffer serious financial hardship as a result of the divorce should be awarded such financial provision as is reasonable to relieve him of hardship over a reasonable period[4].

In applying this principle the court is required[5] to have regard to;

(a) the age, health and earning capacity of the party who is claiming the financial provision;
(b) the duration of the marriage;
(c) the standard of living of the parties during the marriage;

1 Family Law (Scotland) Act, s 11(6). Cf *Tyrrell v Tyrrell* 1990 SLT 406.
2 Ibid, s 13(2).
3 Ibid, s 11(7).
4 Ibid, s 9(1)(e).
5 Ibid, s 11(5).

(d) the needs and resources of the parties, and
(e) all the other circumstances of the case.

The court may also take account of any support, financial or otherwise, given by the party who is to make the financial provision to any person whom he maintains as a dependant in his household whether or not he owes an obligation of aliment to that person[1]. This permits the court to take account of the *de facto* situation in which a husband has set up home with another woman and is supporting her and possibly children of hers.

As this is clearly intended for the exceptional case a court will be unlikely to be persuaded that there is serious financial hardship in an average case. There are few families which, on separation or divorce do not suffer financial hardship, hardship which at least one of the spouses would regard as serious. It is likely in practice that this provision will be applicable principally where the marriage has been of relatively long duration, where retraining for employment is not an option, for example because the spouse alleging hardship is elderly or not in good health[2], or where there will be significant prospective loss of support from pensions and the like[3]. The seriousness of the hardship is to be assessed at the time of the divorce. That is because the principle refers to hardship 'as a result of the divorce'. If hardship were to occur after divorce, eg as a result of ill health, that would not be regarded as relevant if application were to be made for an order at some time after divorce. Unfair though it may seem, if the position of the payee improves after the divorce, eg as a result of inheritance, the payer may be able to obtain a variation or even recall of an order for periodical allowance. The argument would be that there had been a material change of circumstances[4]. But if the payer's position improved the payee would also be able to apply for a variation on a change of circumstances.

Sections 9(1)(d) and (e) are not alternative to one another. They may be cumulative. It is not enough to establish that a party could undertake education or training.[5] It is necessary to establish that there is an intention to do so.[6]

What is a reasonable period is a question of fact the resolution of which will vary with the circumstances of the case. It is likely to exceed three years. Otherwise the principle set out in section 9(1)(d) would be sufficient to cover 'serious financial hardship.' But this principle should not be seen as necessarily providing a means of obtaining maintenance until remarriage or death unless in the most exceptional case. That is because this is not the only principle which the court is required to apply.

Quantum of financial provision

There is no formula which is or could properly be established or followed in assessing the quantum of an order for financial provision since the court is enjoined to apply the principles set out in the 1985 Act. These principles must be applied to the facts of each case. The value of the matrimonial home will generally be divided equally. That may entail its sale which may be ordered

1 Ibid, s 11(6).
2 Cf *Johnstone v Johnstone* 1990 SLT (Sh Ct) 79.
3 Cf *Nolan v Nolan* 1979 SLT 293.
4 Family Law (Scotland) Act 1985, s 13(4).
5 Ibid, s 11(4)(c).
6 *Stott v Stott* 1987 GWD 17–645.

by the court by way of an incidental order under section 14 of the 1985 Act or a separate action of division and sale may be raised if necessary[1]. Where both parties have pension rights it may be appropriate to divide the difference between the valuations of these rights[2], though not necessarily equally[3]. In assessing the value of such rights it may well be necessary to employ an actuary. It is not for the court to be its own actuary. The court may award less if there is to be immediate payment than if payment is postponed in whole or in part[4]. Among the facts of which account will be taken, in assessing whether or not to make an order for payment of a periodical allowance, would be that one spouse is associating but not cohabiting with a third party in order to avoid loss of income support[5].

Division of capital assets to have priority over periodical allowance

The court 'shall not make an order for a periodical allowance ... unless ... it is satisfied that an order for payment of a capital sum or for transfer of property ... would be inappropriate or insufficient to satisfy the requirements of ... section 8(2)'[6]. Section 8(2) provides that the court shall make such order, if any, as is justified by the principles set out in section 9 of the Act and is reasonable having regard to the resources of the parties.

It is commonly, but wrongly, assumed that it is right and proper for a pursuer to seek orders for payment of a capital sum or for transfer of property and for a periodical allowance without further explanation. But the provision just quoted makes it clear that a periodical allowance may be ordered only if orders for payment of capital or transfer of property are inappropriate or insufficient (eg because there are no such assets or they are of very limited value)[7]. Accordingly it is necessary to aver that such orders are either inappropriate or insufficient and why that is so if it is not self evident.

ORDERS FOR PERIODICAL ALLOWANCE

General

It is submitted that orders for periodical allowance cannot properly be used as a way of meeting the requirements of the first two principles set out in section 9(1) of the 1985 Act (fair sharing of matrimonial property and taking account of economic advantages and disadvantages). But such orders may comprise the whole or part of any order for financial provision in so far as that may be justified by the third, fourth and fifth of these principles[8].

An order for a periodical allowance may be made on granting decree of divorce or within such period as the court may specify on granting decree of divorce[9]. There are likely to be fewer occasions on which it is appropriate

1 In connection with the latter reference should be made to the Matrimonial Homes (Family Protection) (Scotland) Act 1981, s 19.
2 *Little v Little* 1989 SCLR 613 at 615.
3 *Muir v Muir* 1989 SCLR 445, 1989 SLT (Sh Ct) 20. But see *Carpenter v Carpenter* 1990 SLT (Sh Ct) 68.
4 *Little*, supra.
5 *Mackenzie v Mackenzie* 1983 SLT 678.
6 Family Law (Scotland) Act 1985, s 13(2). Cf *Mackin v Mackin* 1990 GWD 26–1486.
7 See, eg, *Atkinson v Atkinson* 1988 SCLR 396.
8 Family Law (Scotland) Act 1985, s 13(2)(a).
9 Ibid, s 13(1)(a) and (b).

to postpone a decision on periodical allowance beyond the date of divorce than there will be when the postponement is in relation to a capital sum or the transfer of property. Such occasions may arise when events are likely to occur which would or might amount to a change of circumstances. The need for a variation of a recent award could be avoided. Such occasions may also arise where there is a good reason to grant a divorce forthwith, perhaps because the parties wish to remarry and there is an unavoidable delay in obtaining information as to their financial resources, eg where the farm on which they live has been put up for sale and new employment is being sought by both of them[1].

Orders for a periodical allowance may be made after decree of divorce where either no such order has been made previously or application has been made after the date of the decree and where since the date of decree there has been a change of circumstances[2]. It is to be noted that for some reason the change of circumstances does not have to be 'material'. That word appears in connection with applications for variation of orders for periodical allowance[3]. Theoretically an application under section 13(1)(c) can be made provided that there has been a change of circumstances which is not material but it is difficult to imagine how a court is to differentiate between a non-material change and no change.

Where an application is made for an order after divorce the court can only make an order for a maximum period of three years from the date of divorce unless the court makes an order for an indefinite period, eg until the death or remarriage of the person in whose favour the order is made[4]. An order for an indefinite period will be made rarely for the reasons set out in the next paragraph.

Quantum and duration of orders for periodical allowance

One of the principles set out in section 9[5] provides that a party who has been dependent to a substantial degree on the financial support of the other party should be awarded such financial provision as is reasonable to enable him to adjust, over a period of not more than three years from the date of divorce to the loss of support on divorce. The next principle provides an exception where there is likely to be 'serious financial hardship' as a result of divorce. In that event the court is to award such financial provision as is reasonable to relieve that hardship over a reasonable period. Section 13(3) provides that a periodical allowance may be for a definite period or until the happening of a specified event. Since a periodical allowance may also be granted on the basis of the principle which deals with the economic burden of caring for a child of the marriage, the definite period might be from the granting of decree of divorce until the date upon which a child of the marriage attains a certain age. The happening of a specified event could be the death or remarriage of the person entitled to the periodical allowance or could be the attainment of a certain age by the youngest child of the marriage. It is submitted that there will be few, if any, instances in which a court, applying the provisions of the Act properly, will make an order for a periodical allowance until the

1 For an example see Neill v Neill 1987 SLT (Sh Ct) 143.
2 Family Law (Scotland) Act 1985, s 13(1)(c).
3 Ibid, s 13(4).
4 Ibid, s 9(1)(d).
5 Ibid, s 9(1)(d).

remarriage or death of the person entitled to that order unless the court has been satisfied that that person is likely to suffer serious financial hardship. If that view is correct it will be necessary to aver and prove such a likelihood. Otherwise the court will either refuse to make an order (which it would probably be bound to do if the only form of order sought was until the happening of one of these indefinite events) or will make an order for a period of not more than three years. As has been remarked above cases where there is likely to be serious financial hardship will be exceptional and any period for which periodical allowance is sought should be justified by averments.

Given that section 9(1)(d) refers to a period of not more than three years, it is to be assumed that the average period will be materially shorter than the maximum applicable to a case in which there is not 'serious financial hardship.' The purpose is to provide transitional financial support to enable a person to adjust from the state of being married to the state of being non-dependent. It will be contended by many that three years in their case is too short a period. But a periodical allowance is additional to such orders for a capital sum or the transfer of property as may be appropriate. Further where there are children under sixteen the economic burden of caring for them is to be shared fairly between the parties.[1] So it may be that while money may not be awarded by way of periodical allowance, it may be available in the form of aliment for the support of children and for a longer period in some cases.

The net income of the parties from all sources and their major outgoings will be the main source of information on which a decision on the amount of periodical allowance will be based. Where a party has a fluctuating income the court may take an average over a few years[2]. Reported decisions based on a particular combination of facts as opposed to the application of principles are of limited relevance to other cases. Many such cases are reported in Scots Law Times, Scottish Civil Case Reports and in Green's Weekly Digest. The following are simply a few examples:

Periodical allowance refused: Association with another falling short of cohabitation, *Mackenzie v Mackenzie* 1983 SLT 678

Periodical allowance granted for six months: six year marriage, husband employed, wife not, *Dever v Dever* 1988 SCLR 352;

Periodical allowance for 3 years: generous capital settlement on wife, husband alimenting child, *Atkinson v Atkinson* 1988 SCLR 396;

Capital sum only: *Geddes v Geddes* 1987 SLT 118 (unequal division, periodical allowance refused); *Clark v Clark* 1987 SCLR 517 (unequal division); *Phillip v Phillip* 1988 SCLR 427 (equal division of net assets acquired by the parties)

Capital sum and periodical allowance: wife poor prospects, husband earning, periodical allowance seven years, capital payment £10,000, *Bell v Bell* 1988 SCLR 457; periodical allowance three years, *McDevitt v McDevitt* 1988 SCLR 206; periodical allowance one year, *Tyrrell v Tyrrell* 1990 SLT 406.

INTEREST ON ORDERS FOR FINANCIAL PROVISION

Interest may be claimed only from the date of citation and not from the date of separation[3].

1 Ibid, s 9(1)(c).
2 *Edwards v Edwards* 1984 SLT 311.
3 *Carroll v Carroll* 1988 SCLR 104.

TERMINATION, VARIATION AND RECALL OF ORDERS FOR PERIODICAL ALLOWANCE

Termination

An order for a periodical allowance in whatever terms it is expressed must terminate on the death of the person entitled to the allowance except in relation to arrears due in terms of it[1]. If the payer dies the order continues to operate against that party's estate[2]. But that death will almost certainly amount to a material change of circumstances. Such orders must also terminate on the remarriage of the person receiving the allowance.

Variation and recall

Where there has been a material change of circumstances since the order was made either party or, where the payer has died, his executor may apply to the court to vary or recall the order. On such an application being made the court may do one or more of the following[3]:

(a) vary or recall the order.
(b) backdate such variation or recall to the date of the application or, on cause shown, to an earlier date. Where backdating is ordered the court may order that an appropriate amount of periodical allowance be repaid[4].
(c) convert the order into an order for payment of a capital sum or for a transfer of property.

It would not be difficult to show cause in relation to backdating where for example there had been concealment of a change of circumstances or where the change was such that it would be unrealistic to expect an application to be lodged immediately. The provision which permits conversion will be of particular value where the payer has died. If periodical allowance has been awarded for a period of three years or longer and particularly where there are considerable assets, it may be necessary or at least advisable to obtain an actuarial valuation of the interest of the payee. That valuation might be expressed as a number of years during which she might be expected to receive the allowance. A calculation of the discount for immediate payment may also be appropriate. It may be difficult (or invidious) to quantify her prospects of remarriage.

As to whether there will be held to be a change of circumstances where there has been no attempt to oppose the order when it was applied for and made or where the order was made on the basis of incorrect information supplied to the court see: *Galloway v Galloway* 1973 SLT (Notes) 84; *Ritchie v Ritchie* 1987 SLT (Sh Ct) 7 and cases cited in *Ritchie*.

RELEVANCE OF THE CONDUCT OF A PARTY

In applying the principles mentioned in section 9 the court is required not to take account of the conduct of either party unless that conduct has adversely

---

1 Family Law (Scotland) Act 1985, s 13(7)(b).
2 Ibid, s 13(7)(a).
3 Ibid, s 13(4).
4 Ibid, s 13(6).

affected the financial resources to be taken into account or, in relation to the principles mentioned in section 9(1)(d) and (e) (adjustment to financial independence over three years and serious financial hardship) it would be manifestly inequitable to leave that conduct out of account[1]. A 10 per cent reduction was made in *MacLeod v MacLeod*[2], but the brief reports of that case would not appear to warrant that reduction. The opinion was expressed that had the wife not succeeded in her action of divorce based on unreasonable behaviour she would not have been awarded a capital sum at all in the action at the instance of her husband because she would have been entirely responsible for the breakdown of the marriage. This decision does not appear to be consistent with the provisions of the 1985 Act.

Litigants are often keen to rehearse the history of their marriage or to air their grievances about each other under the misapprehension that such matters are relevant to a decision as to the quantum of an order for financial provision. But financial provision is not a prize to be earned or lost by conduct, any more than custody is a prize. Such disputes are rarely more than marginally relevant, if that. They occupy much court time and incur considerable expense. Courts have always been very reluctant to allow litigants to pursue such matters[3]. Adultery after separation is irrelevant[4]. That view is now enshrined in the Act. Accordingly in order to persuade a court to take account of conduct it will be necessary to demonstrate that the conduct complained of not only was exceptional but also that it has a material bearing on the appropriate sum which should be awarded.

TAXATION OF MAINTENANCE PAYMENTS

It is outside the scope of this book to provide guidance on taxation as it may affect a separating or divorcing couple. The following is a brief description of the position as at the time of writing. Reference should be made to sections 36 to 40 of the Finance Act 1988. Section 36 adds new sections 347A and 347B to the Income and Corporation Taxes Act 1988 which repealed the Income and Corporation Taxes Act 1970. Brochure entitled *Taxation of Maintenance Payments following Separation and Divorce* (IR 77) and *Income Tax–Separation, Divorce and Maintenance Payments* (IR 93) can be obtained from Inland Revenue offices. Further help is obtainable from Inland Revenue offices and may be obtainable from the Inland Revenue Claims Branch at Bootle where a Maintenance Help Line is maintained (Tel. 051-922 6363).

The scheme of the current arrangements is that the income from which payments are to be made will have been taxed in the hands of the payer. So for all maintenance arrangements made after 15 March 1988 the payee will not pay any tax in respect of any payments made in terms of such arrangements[5]. Accordingly all such payments are made gross, ie not under deduction of tax[6]. The payer will not be eligible for tax relief except that in the case of a maintenance payment to his spouse or former spouse or to such a person for the maintenance of a child of the family aged under 21 he will be able to

1 Family Law (Scotland) Act 1985, s 11(7).
2 1990 GWD 14-767, 768.
3 *Lambert v Lambert* 1982 SLT 144.
4 *Graham v Graham* 1984 SLT 89.
5 Income and Corporation Taxes Act 1988, s 347A (1)(b) (added by the Finance Act 1988, s 36).
6 Income and Corporation Taxes Act 1988, ss 347A(1), 348, 349.

set the first £1,720 (in tax year 1990/91) against tax at his highest marginal rate[1]. The payer qualifies for tax reliefs (at basic and higher rates) for payments up to a limit equal to the married couple's allowance (in tax year 1990/91: £1,720) until the recipient remarries. Tax relief is not available in respect of voluntary payments, payments under a foreign court order or agreement, where the taxpayer already gets tax relief in some other way or for capital or lump sums. If a divorced husband remarries he will be able to claim married allowance as well as maintenance relief for payments to his ex-wife.

Where there is an order made by a court in the United Kingdom or an enforceable written agreement to pay periodical allowance or aliment to or to meet specified expenditure of a separated or divorced spouse (of whom there may be more than one) all payments made in terms thereof count towards the limit of £1,720. The Inland Revenue regards a maintenance agreement registered for preservation and execution in the Books of Council and Session as equivalent to a court order.

It follows that there is no tax relief on payments made direct to the children. Indeed it appears that there is now no tax advantage to be gained by making payments of aliment to children directly. Accordingly the style of crave or conclusion used in, eg, *Huggins v Huggins* 1981 SLT 179 and *Finnie v Finnie* 1984 SLT 439 appears no longer to be advantageous for tax reasons. But there may be other advantages to be gained by arranging for payments to be made to the child rather than the parent. If the income from a court order is aggregated with any other income of the parent for the purpose of assessing benefits or rebates if it is payable to the parent but not if it is payable to the child, there is a clear case for it to be paid to the child. Theoretically however there is no need to make separate orders for payment of maintenance to both a spouse and to or for the benefit of children. But it should be made clear that the sum ordered is to cover maintenance of both spouse and children, if only to avoid complications if a variation is sought.

It also follows that 'small maintenance payments are a thing of the past[2].

Transitional provisions have been made to deal with the following situations:

(a) Court orders made before 15 March 1988.

(b) Court orders applied for on or before 15 March 1988 and made by 30 June 1988.

(c) Maintenance agreements (whether written or oral) made before 15 March 1988 provided that a copy of the agreement or written particulars of an oral agreement was received by the inspector of taxes by 30 June 1988.

(d) Court orders or agreements made on or after 15 March 1988 which vary, replace or supplement such earlier orders or agreements:[3]

Payments under orders or agreements to which the old system applies were made net of tax up to 5 April 1989 but subsequent to that date all payments are to be made gross ie without deduction of tax. The payer gets tax relief on these payments either through PAYE or through his assessment. In respect of payments to children aged eighteen or over basic and not higher rate relief is available unless the payments are made directly to children under a court order. After the child becomes twenty-one basic rate tax relief may be obtained if tax is deducted by the payer on the full amount provided that the agreement or the court order has not been changed since 15 March 1988. If it is payable

---

1 Ibid, s 347B (2) and (3).
2 Finance Act 1988, s 36(6).
3 Ibid, ss 36(4), 37–39.

under a court order higher rate relief will continue to be available but any change may result in loss of relief.

In terms of these transitional arrangements the payer gets relief up to the level for which he got relief in the tax year 1988/89[1]. This limitation will continue to apply in subsequent years. Suppose that an order is varied whereby there is a 50 per cent increase in the amount of periodical allowance. In that event tax relief is obtainable on the original amount but not at all on the extra 50 per cent. But correspondingly the payee will be taxed on an amount which does not exceed the amount which was taxable in his hands in 1988/89[2]. Section 38(5) of the Finance Act 1988 provides that the first £1,720 of the maintenance received by the payee will be exempt from tax. As has been pointed out above the figure of £1,720 is a sum equal to the difference between the single and married person's allowances in the tax year 1990/91 and will be subject to amendment in subsequent years depending upon the figures at which these allowances are fixed.

There is an option to change to the new system. An election to change must be made before, during or within twelve months of the end of a particular tax year. An election must be in respect of all the payments made. As the years go by it may become advantageous to elect but in the first year or two it is unlikely in most cases to be advantageous. Where an election is made the payee must be informed within thirty days of the election[3].

---

1 Finance Act 1988, s 38(3).
2 Ibid, s 38(4).
3 Ibid, s 39(3).

CHAPTER 5

OTHER ANCILLARY ORDERS

PARENTAL RIGHTS

The court may intervene in connection with a child's upbringing in the course of an application for an order relating to parental rights[1]. The sheriff court has jurisdiction in connection with applications for orders relating to parental rights under the Law Reform (Parent and Child) (Scotland) Act 1986, s 3 by virtue of the Sheriff Courts (Scotland) Act 1907, s 5(2C). 'Parental rights' include custody or access and any right or authority relating to the welfare or upbringing of the child conferred on a parent by any rule of law[2]. The 1986 Act applies to parents of a child who are not married to one another but in the case of a father it applies if he is married to the mother or was married to her at the time of conception or subsequently[3]. However, in terms of section 3(1) of the 1986 Act 'any person claiming an interest' may make application to the court for an order relating to parental rights. That section should be read subject to the qualifications set out in the Children Act 1975, s 47(2). That person need not be a parent[4]. Such a person does not require to seek declarator of his parental rights[5].

In terms of Court of Session Act 1988, s 20 and the Sheriff Courts (Scotland) Act 1907, s 38C, it is provided that in any action of, inter alia, divorce the court may make with respect to any child of the marriage (including a child accepted as a child of the marriage), such order (including an interim order) as it thinks fit relating to parental rights and may vary and recall any such order. If in an undefended sheriff court action for parental rights the initial writ has been returned to court the action is called in court. The sheriff may order such inquiry as he thinks necessary[6]. This could involve calling for a report or fixing a proof. The court should not make an order relating to parental rights unless and until it is satisfied that to do so would be in the interests of the child[7]. To do so on an interim basis may require a report to be obtained[8]. Evidence at such a proof in the sheriff court is not recorded[9].

1   Law Reform (Parent and Child) (Scotland) Act 1986, s 3.
2   Law Reform (Parent and Child) (Scotland) Act 1986, s 8.
3   Ibid, ss 1(1), 2(1)(b).
4   *M, Petitioners* 1989 SCLR 151; *Whyte v Hardie* 1990 SCLR 23. For a contrary view see *AB v Mr and Mrs M* 1987 SCLR 389, 1988 SLT 652 (sub nom. *AB, Petitioner*).
5   *Nolan v Lindsay* 1990 SCLR 56.
6   OCR 22.
7   Law Reform (Parent and Child) (Scotland) Act 1986, s 3(2); *Crowley v Armstrong* 1990 SCLR 361.
8   *Montgomery v Lockwood* 1987 SCLR 525; *McEachan v Young* 1988 SCLR 98 (which are commented on in *Mann v Glendinning* 1990 SCLR 137); *Orr v Orr* 1989 GWD 12-506.
9   OCR 73(4).

CUSTODY

For the purposes of custody and access a child means a child under the age of sixteen[1].

Interim custody

At common law the courts may regulate custody and interim custody of children but they also have power in terms of the Conjugal Rights (Scotland) Amendment Act 1861, s 9 to make in the course, inter alia, of an action of divorce such provision as seems just and proper with respect to the custody, maintenance and education of any pupil children of the marriage to which the action relates. Section 3(1) of the Law Reform (Parent and Child) (Scotland) Act 1986 provides that application may be made for an order for parental rights and the court may make such order relating thereto as it thinks fit. Such rights include custody. The court should not make such orders in favour of a pursuer without intimation to the defender[2].

The best interests of the child

The test which is applied is set out in the Matrimonial Proceedings (Children) Act 1958, s 8(1), which provides that in any action of divorce the court shall not grant decree of divorce unless and until it is satisfied as regards every child for whose custody it has power to make provision in that action: that arrangements have been made for the care and upbringing of the child which are satisfactory or are the best that can be devised in the circumstances; or that it is impracticable for the party or parties appearing before the court to make any such arrangements. The Law Reform (Parent and Child) (Scotland) Act 1986, s 3(2) requires the court, in any proceedings relating to parental rights, to regard the welfare of the child as the paramount consideration[3]. An exception to the above rule may be made where it is desirable to grant decree of divorce without delay and an undertaking is given to the court to bring the question of the arrangements for the children before the court within a specified time[4]. 'Child' for this purpose means every child of the marriage and any child of one party who has been accepted as a child of the marriage but does not include a child who is not a child of either party but who has been treated as a child of the marriage[5].

Although custody is a parental right neither party has a 'right' to custody in the sense that he or she may have a right to moveable property[6]. In the past courts tended to assume that the mother was the person best suited to bring up children, particularly young children. That assumption no longer holds and in particular would not hold where the mother has entered into a homosexual relationship[7]. If one party was perceived as having been to blame for the break-

1 Matrimonial Proceedings (Children) Act 1958, s 15; Law Reform (Parent and Child) (Scotland) Act 1986, s 8.
2 *Nelson v Nelson* 1989 SLT (Sh Ct) 18.
3 *Montgomery v Lockwood* 1987 SCLR 525; *McEachan v Young* 1988 SCLR 98; *Orr v Orr* 1989 GWD 12-506.
4 Matrimonial Proceedings (Children) Act 1958, s 8.
5 *Bradley v Bradley* 1987 SCLR 62.
6 *Porchetta v Porchetta* 1986 SLT 105.
7 *Early v Early* 1989 SLT 114, affd on appeal: 1990 SLT 221.

up of the marriage, eg because he had engaged in a course of adultery, the other party might in the past have been seen as the preferred party to care for any children after divorce. The position now is that the overriding principle of the welfare of the child must be approached with no preconceived assumptions. The fact that one party is engaged on a course of adultery may still prove to be an important factor in the decision.

If there is a decree for custody in favour of one party in a foreign court that is a factor to be taken into account[1]. The factor which may prove decisive if the decision is evenly balanced is the avoidance of disturbance to a well-settled child[2].

It is not necessary for the court to make an order for custody on granting divorce provided that the court is satisfied as to the matters referred to in section 8(1) of the 1958 Act. The court may make an order for access without making an order for custody[3]. In an undefended action the defender may have de facto custody of the child and not enter the process. Custody or access may be granted to one parent subject to the supervision of the social work department[4].

In some cases it is in the best interests of the child that he be in the custody of neither parent. He may be better with his grandparents who may apply for an order for custody or access[5]. The child may be in foster care because of the treatment which he has received from his parents or for some other reason. He may be subject to a supervision requirement made by the children's panel which requires him to live in a particular place or with a particular person[6]. The local authority may have assumed parental rights[7]. If there are exceptional circumstances making it impracticable or undesirable for a child to be entrusted to either of the parties to a marriage the court may commit the child to the care of a local authority or to another person[8]. Where there are exceptional circumstances the court may commit the child to the custody of a particular person but place him under the supervision of a local authority[9] .Decisions on custody and access are normally matters within the discretion of the court. An appellate court will interfere only where a wrong principle has been applied or the decision is plainly wrong[10].

CUSTODY TO ONE PARTY

There is much to be said for a reconsideration in Scotland of what is meant by the concept of custody. Current practice, so far as the courts are concerned, is for the court in almost every case to grant unqualified custody to one party, if custody is applied for (which it need not be), and the court may grant access to the other. If the parties reach agreement on custody and access the

1 Campbell v Campbell 1977 SLT 125; Sinclair v Sinclair 1987 GWD 35-1239.
2 Whitecross v Whitecross 1977 SLT 225.
3 Huddart v Huddart 1960 SC 300, 1960 SLT 275; cf. McCann v McCann 1987 SCLR 742.
4 Cairns v McNulty 1989 GWD 37-1688.
5 S v S 1967 SLT 217; Law Reform (Parent and Child) (Scotland) Act 1986, s 3(1).
6 Social Work (Scotland) Act 1968, s 44.
7 Ibid, ss 16 to 17A.
8 Matrimonial Proceedings (Children) Act 1958, s 10; Browne v Browne 1969 SLT (Notes) 15; Aitken v Aitken 1978 SLT 183; Woytaszko v Woytasko 1988 GWD 11-446 (child committed to a 73 year old), and see Children Act 1975, s 47.
9 Matrimonial Proceedings (Children) Act 1958, s 12; MacIntyre v MacIntyre 1962 SLT (Notes) 70; Runciman v Runciman 1965 SLT (Notes) 6; Hunt v Hunt 1987 GWD 14-493.
10 Britton v Central Regional Council 1986 SLT 207 but see Jordan v Jordan 1983 SLT 539.

court will normally give effect to their agreement. But the court must always be satisfied that the arrangements agreed between the parties are the best that can be made in the circumstances. The court may decline to grant divorce until it is satisfied on this point. It may be necessary to obtain an additional affidavit if the matter is not sufficiently dealt with in other affidavits or the court may require to be addressed by counsel or by the agent for the pursuer in the Court of Session or the sheriff court as the case may be.

Where the court is so satisfied it is likely to give effect to the agreement of the parties by interponing authority to a joint minute or by granting decree in terms of that minute. Interponing authority in effect means 'rubber stamping' it. If it is to be enforced it is the agreement, contained in the joint minute, which will be enforced. If the court grants decree in terms of a joint minute it will be the decree of court which will be enforced. Whether the court interpones authority or grants decree will normally depend on the terms of the agreement. If the terms are such that a decree can conveniently be granted and, where appropriate, extracted for enforcement, the court is likely to grant decree. Where the agreement is in vague, complicated or conditional terms the court is likely simply to interpone authority to it.

In current practice if a party is awarded custody he or she can determine most matters relating to the child including where or with whom the child lives subject to any access by the other parent. The court will be likely to intervene only if it can be shown that something is being done or threatened in relation to the child which is not in his best interests. Where a child lives for equal periods with each parent custody may be awarded to one of them[1].

SPLITTING CHILDREN BETWEEN PARENTS

The court does not always give effect to what the parties wish. Before the court will agree to children being split between parents it will require to be persuaded that there are good reasons for such a course[2].

JOINT CUSTODY

The current practice referred to above does not meet the desires of many parents on divorce. It makes custody a prize. Courts, perhaps unwittingly, encourage that idea by using phrases like 'finds the pursuer entitled to custody' or 'awards custody to the pursuer.' Where parties reach agreement about custody and access there are no unreasonable restrictions on the terms in which they may frame their agreement provided that they are reasonably unambiguous and comprehensible. Such an agreement could read in part like this: 'The pursuer and the defender will continue to share their responsibilities as parents of AB and CB. AB and CB will normally live with the pursuer who will have day to day responsibility for their care except when they are living with the defender during such periods as may be agreed or, failing agreement, as may be ordered by the court. The pursuer and the defender will consult each other before either takes any major decisions as regards AB and CB including decisions as to their education, religious upbringing and health and any major changes in the area in which they will live, unless for reasons of emergency it is impracticable to do so.'

1 *Sinclair v Sinclair* 1987 GWD 16-587.
2 *Casey v Casey* 1989 SCLR 761; *Foy v Foy* 1987 GWD 7-206; *Joffre v Joffre* 1989 GWD 536.

Such a formulation or a variation of it may go some way to alleviate common concerns: the loss of all say by one party in the upbringing of his or her children and whether there will be any means of preventing the children being taken to a part of the world which would make access impracticable. Joint custody is occasionally awarded when parties agree that there should be an order for joint custody and sometimes when it is not[1]. The difficulty about such an order is that it can merely postpone the resolution of difficulties unless the parties both agree and specify what they mean by joint custody. The court may refuse to make an order for joint custody unless details are provided of how it would operate[2]. In *Robertson v Robertson*[3] custody was awarded to the father but care and control to the mother. The father was nominally awarded custody but gave an undertaking that he would allow the child to continue to live with the mother except for specified periods and that he would not interfere unnecessarily with the day to day care of the child. The court occasionally awards *de jure* custody to one parent while the other has *de facto* custody subject to substantial access[4].

ACCESS

Access is a 'parental right'[5]. But it is a right only in a limited sense[6], and is subject to the overriding principle that access will be refused where that is in the best interests of the child, since the welfare of the child is the paramount consideration[7]. The court may make an order for access without making an order for custody[8]. As a general proposition it is in the interests of children to keep in touch with both parents after divorce. Both parents, and particularly the parent having custody, are under an obligation to ensure that access is a success[9]. Resumption of access may inevitably involve some temporary upset[10]. If a parent will have an adverse influence on a child, access may be refused or restricted. But it may be difficult to know which parent, if it is only one, is having such influence. In the stress of a failing marriage many parents become very manipulative in order to preserve their position or to gain an advantage over the other spouse. If one spouse considers that he or she has been wronged by the other that other is likely to be treated as a person unsuitable to have anything to do with the children. Situations may be provoked in order to show the other party in a poor light in relation to the children.

Children's attitudes to access can be greatly influenced by the parent who has custody. That parent may wish for reasons unconnected with the welfare of the child to terminate access[11]. Nonetheless the court will give great weight to the wishes of a child if these wishes are genuine and reasonable[12]. In determining

1 *MacKenzie v Hendry* 1984 SLT 322.
2 *McKechnie v McKechnie* 1990 SCLR 153, 1990 SLT (Sh Ct) 75.
3 1981 SLT (Notes) 7.
4 *Robertson*, supra.
5 Law Reform (Parent and Child) (Scotland) Act 1986, s 8.
6 Cf J M Thomson 'Whither the 'Right' of Access' 1989 SLT (News) 109.
7 Law Reform (Parent and Child) (Scotland) Act 1986, s 3(2); *S v S* 1967 SC (HL) 46; *Porchetta v Porchetta* 1986 SLT 105.
8 *Huddart v Huddart* 1960 SC 300, 1960 SLT 275.
9 *Blance v Blance* 1978 SLT 74; *Brannigan v Brannigan* 1979 SLT (Notes) 73; *Cosh v Cosh* 1979 SLT (Notes) 72.
10 *Blance* supra.
11 *Cosh v Cosh* 1979 SLT (Notes) 72.
12 *Gover v Gover* 1969 SLT (Notes) 78.

what access to award on granting divorce the court will take account of the interim access which has been taking place[1]. A court should not award access without sufficient information to enable it to determine that such access would be in the best interests of the child[2]. If a parent emigrates access may for practical purposes cease. The court may grant power to a parent having custody to remove the children from Scotland[3]. Access may be granted to persons who are not parents, eg grandparents[4]. Jurisdiction exists at common law but has been conferred by various statutory provisions[5]

JURISDICTION IN RELATION TO CUSTODY ORDERS

If an action of divorce is before a court in Scotland and that court has jurisdiction to entertain that action then that court will also have jurisdiction in relation to any children of the marriage to which that action relates. A child in this context means a child under sixteen and includes the child of one party who has been accepted as a child of the marriage by the other party[6]. For the purposes of Part I of the Family Law Act 1986 (which is concerned with jurisdiction to make orders relating to custody and the recognition and enforcement of such orders throughout the United Kingdom) matrimonial proceedings in a court in Scotland which has jurisdiction to make a custody order with respect to a child are to be treated as continuing until the child concerned attains sixteen unless the proceedings have been dismissed or decree of absolvitor has been granted[7]. Where there has been dismissal or absolvitor at any stage after proof on the merits of the action has been allowed, there is no power to entertain an application for a custody order under the Matrimonial Proceedings (Children) Act 1958, s 9(1) unless the application predated the dismissal or absolvitor[8]. Nor is there such power if the action is dismissed before proof has been allowed[9].

The court cannot entertain an application for a variation of a custody order under section 9(1) of the Matrimonial Proceedings (Children) Act 1958 if on the date of the application matrimonial proceedings in respect of the marriage are continuing in another court in the United Kingdom[10]. Separate provision is made as regards jurisdiction in relation to custody orders which are applied for other than in matrimonial proceedings[11]. Matrimonial proceedings means proceedings for divorce, nullity of marriage or judicial separation[12]

1 *Thomson v Thomson* 1979 SLT (Sh Ct) 11.
2 *Montgomery v Lockwood* 1987 SCLR 525; *McEachan v Young* 1988 SCLR 98; *Orr v Orr* 1989 GWD 12-506.
3 *Huddart v Huddart* 1961 SC 393; *Johnson v Francis* 1982 SLT 285.
4 Cf *S v S*, 1967 SC (HL) 46.
5 Court of Session Act 1988, s 20; Sheriff Courts (Scotland) Act 1907, s 38C; Conjugal Rights (Scotland) (Amendment) Act 1861, s 9; Domicile and Matrimonial Proceedings Act 1973, s 10 and Sch 2; Law Reform (Parent and Child) (Scotland) Act 1986, s 3. For non-matrimonial proceedings see Family Law Act 1986, s 8.
6 Conjugal Rights (Scotland) Amendment Act 1861, s 9 as substituted by the Law Reform (Parent and Child) (Scotland) Act 1986, Sch 1, para 2.
7 Family Law Act 1986, s 42(3).
8 Family Law Act 1986, s 13(2).
9 *Gall v Gall* 1968 SC 332, 1969 SLT 7; *Driffel v Driffel* 1971 SLT (Notes) 60.
10 Family Law Act 1986, s 13(4).
11 Ibid, ss 8–12.
12 Ibid, s 18(1).

A custody order is an order made by a court of civil jurisdiction in Scotland under any enactment or rule of law with respect to the custody, care or control of a child or access to a child or the education or upbringing of a child excluding—

(1) an order committing the care of a child to a local authority or placing a child under the supervision of a local authority;

(2) an adoption order as defined in the Adoption (Scotland) Act 1978, s 12(1);

(3) an order freeing a child for adoption made under the Adoption (Scotland) Act 1978, s 18;

(4) an order for the custody of a child made in the course of proceedings for the adoption of the child (other than an order made following the making of a direction under the Children Act 1975, s 53(1));

(5) an order made under the Education (Scotland) Act 1980;

(6) an order made under Parts II or III of the Social Work (Scotland) Act 1968;

(7) an order made under the Child Abduction and Custody Act 1985;

(8) an order for the delivery of a child or other order for the enforcement of a custody order;

(9) an order relating to the tutory or curatory of a child[1].

It is apparent from the foregoing definition of a custody order that Parliament contemplates the making of a greater variety of custody orders than has been the practice in Scotland hitherto. It has been the practice in England and Wales to make orders for joint custody or for one party to be awarded care and control of a child while the other party has been awarded custody. That is also now clearly competent in Scotland.

It is also competent for the court in Scotland to make an order regarding the education or upbringing of a child. These orders have to be made under an enactment or rule of law but this provision does not, it is submitted, state that that enactment or rule of law must make provision for the making of an order in that form. It is therefore open to a party to apply for an order restricted to an aspect of what has conventionally been regarded as custody. The traditional view in Scotland has been that one party may be awarded custody. In that event the other party in effect lost the power to exercise his parental functions in relation to that child except during such periods of access as may take place. If this understanding of the foregoing change is correct it is to be welcomed since it provides an opportunity for the parties to continue to act as parents in relation to their children despite separation and divorce. It makes it possible for the parties to reach a mutually acceptable compromise, without too much loss of face, as to who has what responsibility in that connection.

If there are actions of separation and divorce pending the court will have jurisdiction to make a custody order in the divorce action only.[2] A court in Scotland may decline jurisdiction to make a custody order even if there is a divorce action before it, provided that there are proceedings pending before another court in the United Kingdom which would have jurisdiction but for the existence of the divorce action and the Scottish court thinks that the other court would be a more appropriate court to deal with custody[3].

1 Family Law Act 1986, s 1(1)(b).
2 Ibid, s 13(3).
3 Ibid, s 13(6).

DISCLOSURE OF THE CHILD'S WHEREABOUTS

The court may order any person whom it has reason to believe may have relevant information as to the whereabouts of a child to disclose it to the court[1].

RESTRICTING THE REMOVAL OF A CHILD FROM THE JURISDICTION OF THE COURT

A court in Scotland may, at any time after the commencement of proceedings in connection with which the court would have power to make a custody order or in any proceedings in which it would be competent for the court to grant an interdict prohibiting the removal of a child from its jurisdiction, grant interdict or interim interdict prohibiting the removal of the child from the United Kingdom or any part of the United Kingdom or out of the control of any person in whose custody the child is[2]. That provision applies to the sheriff court as well as to the Court of Session. Accordingly a sheriff may grant interdict prohibiting the removal of a child from the United Kingdom or any part of it. He is not restricted to prohibiting removal from the jurisdiction of his court. The application for such an order must come from a party to the proceedings, the tutor or curator of the child concerned or from any other person who has or wishes to obtain the custody or care of the child. Proceedings commence in the Court of Session when the summons is signeted and in the sheriff court when the warrant of citation is signed. Thus, provided that the application is by an appropriate person and that the court has jurisdiction in respect of the application, the Court of Session and any sheriff court may grant an interdict relating to any other part of the United Kingdom. Application in a Court of Session action for interim interdict prohibiting removal of the child is by motion[3].

Where such an order has been made in relation to a child under sixteen it has effect in each part of the United Kingdom as if it had been made by the appropriate court in that other part. 'Appropriate court' in this context means the High Court in England and Wales or Northern Ireland and, as regards a comparable order made in another part of the United Kingdom, the Court of Session in Scotland[4]. Where the order prohibits the removal of the child to that other part of the United Kingdom it has effect as if it included a prohibition on the further removal of the child to any place other than to a place to which he could be removed consistently with the order[5]. This provision has clearly been included to prevent a person, having the child, taking him to various other parts of the country while maintaining that the original order did not prevent him from doing so. Further, either the court which made the original restriction order or the court which in terms of section 36 is treated as having made it may require any person to surrender any United

---

1 Ibid, s 33; *Abusaif v Abusaif* 1984 SLT 90.
2 Family Law Act 1986, s 35(3).
3 Cf RC 170C(1).
4 Family Law Act 1986, ss 40(1), 32(1).
5 Ibid, s 36.

Kingdom passport which has been issued to or which contains particulars of the child.[1]

OBTAINING THE AUTHORITY OF COURT TO REMOVE A CHILD

Where a person, having had care and possession of a child for at least three years in all, has applied for custody of that child it is an offence (in the circumstances set out in the Children Act 1975, s 51(1)) to remove that child from the applicant against the will of the applicant and without the authority of the court. Interdict may be granted prohibiting removal in breach of section 51[2]. Accordingly application may have to be made to the court for such authority. In a Court of Session action application is made by a person other than a party to the action by minute lodged in the process[3]. It is suggested that a similar procedure is appropriate in a sheriff court action.

ORDERS FOR DELIVERY OF A CHILD

A court having jurisdiction to make a custody order in relation to a child also has jurisdiction to make an order for the delivery of that child whether or not the order sought is in implement of a custody order[4], or to order the return of a child removed from the care and possession of an applicant for custody of the child in terms of section 51(1) of the Children Act 1975. Such an order may be made in order to secure the implementation of an order for custody or an order for access. Such an order may be made in order to enable the child to be returned to a jurisdiction in which it is a ward of court[5]. But such an order should not normally be made without prior intimation to the party having the child[6]. There are not likely to be many cases between husband and wife in the present state of the law in which an order for delivery is sought without an order for custody or for access either having been previously granted or being currently applied for[7]. Failure to comply with an order for delivery is contempt of court. On an application to the court, the court may order the person allegedly in contempt to appear before the court. If that person is held to be in contempt, an admonition, a fine or a sentence of imprisonment may be imposed. Further the court may grant warrant to messengers-at-arms or sheriff officers, as the case may be, and other officers of law to search for and seize the child in order to deliver the child to the person entitled to custody (or access)[8]. There is no duty on police officers and procurators fiscal to assist messengers-at-arms and sheriff officers in the

1 Ibid, s 37.
2 Children Act 1975, s 52.
3 RC 170C(2).
4 Family Law Act 1986, s 17.
5 *Thomson, Petr* 1980 SLT (Notes) 29.
6 *Nelson v Nelson* 1989 SLT (Sh Ct) 18.
7 As examples of delivery cases see *Brown v Brown* 1948 SC 5; *Thomson v Thomson* 1979 SLT (Sh Ct) 11; *Thomson, Petr*, supra; *Fowler v Fowler (No 2)* 1981 SLT (Notes) 78.
8 See, eg, *Muir v Milligan* (1868) 6 M 1125; *Leys v Leys* (1886) 13 R 1223; *Nicolson v Nicolson* (1869) 7 M 1118; *Marchetti v Marchetti* (1901) 3 F 888; *Robertson, Petr* 1911 SC 1319; *Low, Petr* 1920 SC 351.

search for children whose delivery has been ordered by the court[1]. An order for delivery of children is a decree *ad factum praestandum* and may be enforced by diligence.[2] Where an appeal has been lodged against an order for custody and delivery, the order is unenforceable pending the outcome of the appeal[3].

ORDERS UNDER THE MATRIMONIAL HOMES (FAMILY PROTECTION) (SCOTLAND) ACT 1981

Rule of Court 188D makes provision for the procedure to be adopted in Court of Session applications under the Act. The Act of Sederunt (Applications under the Matrimonial Homes (Family Protection) (Scotland) Act 1981) 1982, SI 1982/1432) makes similar provision in respect of sheriff court actions.

Regulating rights of occupancy in the matrimonial home

Section 3(1) of the Matrimonial Homes (Family Protection) (Scotland) Act 1981 Act provides:
'Where there is an entitled spouse and a non-entitled spouse, or where both spouses are entitled, or permitted by a third party, to occupy a matrimonial home, either spouse may apply to the court for an order—

(a) declaring the occupancy rights of the applicant spouse;
(b) enforcing the occupancy rights of the applicant spouse;
(c) restricting the occupancy rights of the non-applicant spouse;
(d) regulating the exercise by either spouse of his or her occupancy rights;
(e) protecting the occupancy rights of the applicant spouse in relation to the other spouse.'

An application under section 3(1)(a) above will take the form of a declarator that the pursuer has a right to occupy a specified property. So far as the other orders are concerned the court should be asked to make a specific order which will meet the circumstances of the particular case. It has been said that orders under sections 3(2) and 3(4) of the Act should not be made unless there is a declarator of occupancy rights[4]. But unless there is a dispute over that matter it is difficult to see why the court should be required to determine such an issue unnecessarily. A declarator is not necessary in connection with an application for parental rights in such circumstances[5]. Interim declarators have been granted[6]. It has been suggested that it is inappropriate, if not incompetent, to seek orders relating to occupancy rights in a divorce action[7]. The point was not taken in *Brown v Brown* 1985 SLT 376[8]. It is very doubtful whether the decision in *Trolland* is sound on this point. The court should not be asked to make an order which simply echoes the wording of the section without further specification. If a court granted an order in such a form it would be meaningless and possibly unextractable or unenforceable. The terms of the particular order sought should be set out in the conclusions or craves.

1   *Caldwell v Caldwell* 1983 SLT 610.
2   *Brown*, supra, at 11.
3   *Fowler*, supra.
4   *Welsh v Welsh* 1987 SLT (Sh Ct) 30.
5   *Nolan v Lindsay* 1990 SCLR 56.
6   *McRobbie v McRobbie* (1983) 29 JLSS 5; *Nimmo v Nimmo* (1983) 29 JLSS 4.
7   *Trolland v Trolland* 1987 SLT (Sh Ct) 42.
8   See *Nelson v Nelson* 1988 SLT (Sh Ct) 26.

An application under section 3(1)(b) above may be necessary where, for example, the defender has locked up the property and has the only key. In that event he could be ordered to provide the pursuer with all the keys to the property. Such an order would probably be accompanied by an order under section 3(1)(e) prohibiting the defender from interfering with the pursuer's access to that property, eg by changing or adding to the locks or otherwise. Each of the spouses may be occupying separate parts of a property. But an application under s 3(1)(c) above cannot be used to achieve the effect of an exclusion order[1]. Nor can a matrimonial interdict be used for this purpose[2]. If a person is to be excluded from the whole property an exclusion order is necessary. A party may have his occupancy rights regulated under s 3(1)(d) for periods of time eg when on shore from employment on a North Sea oil rig.

Exclusion orders

Section 4(1) of the 1981 Act provides:
'Where there is an entitled spouse and a non-entitled spouse, or where both spouses are entitled, or permitted by a third party, to occupy a matrimonial home, either spouse, whether or not that spouse is in occupation at the time of the application, may apply to the court for an order suspending the occupancy rights of the other spouse ... in a matrimonial home', ie for an exclusion order.

Applications for exclusion orders, or the terms of the motion by which the application is made, must be intimated to the landlord if the entitled spouse is a tenant of the matrimonial home or to a third party if the entitled spouse is permitted by that third party to occupy the matrimonial home[3].

If the test for the grant of an exclusion order is satisfied the court is required to make an exclusion order unless it appears to the court that the making of an order would be unjustified or unreasonable having regard to the circumstances referred to in section 4(3). That test is whether 'the making of the order is necessary for the protection of the applicant or any child of the family from any conduct or threatened or reasonably apprehended conduct of the non-applicant spouse which is or would be injurious to the physical or mental health of the applicant or child'[4]. That test also applies to interim exclusion orders[5]. The test is not met if all that is said is that an exclusion order should be granted on the basis of balance of convenience[6], or greater need.[7] The Act says injurious to health, not that there must be serious injury to health[8]. Certain dicta in *Bell*, supra, were criticised in *McCafferty*, supra.

Exclusion orders are not intended to deal with the common situation in which the pursuer and the defender cannot live together harmoniously and each loses no opportunity to be nasty to the other. It may well be that if both were to continue to live in such an atmosphere the health of one or

1 See the Matrimonial Homes (Family Protection) (Scotland) Act 1981, s 3(3) and (5).
2 *Tattersall v Tattersall* 1983 SLT 506.
3 RC 188D(7)(c), AS (Applications under the Matrimonial Homes (Family Protection) (Scotland) Act 1981) 1982, para 3 (SI 1982/1432).
4 Matrimonial Homes (Family Protection) (Scotland) Act 1981, s 4(2).
5 *Bell v Bell* 1983 SLT 224 at 227, per Wheatley LJC; *Smith v Smith* 1983 SLT 275; *Ward v Ward* 1983 SLT 472.
6 *Smith*, supra.
7 *Ward*, supra; *McCafferty v McCafferty* 1986 SLT 650 at 655, per Lord Dunpark.
8 *McCafferty*, supra, at 652, per Ross LJC.

the other or both would suffer. Where all that has happened is that there is tension of that sort an exclusion order may be refused[1].

In order that a court can be persuaded to grant an exclusion order it is necessary to aver circumstances sufficient to meet that test and to aver that that test is met. At an early stage in the action the court, on being asked to make an interim order, will be confronted with a summons or initial writ and will have limited other information. For obvious reasons the court will not lightly deprive a party of his or her rights in the matrimonial home unless the circumstances clearly warrant such a course of action. Courts are reluctant to allow a party to found on allegations which have not been included in the writ when they could have been. Apart from very recent events reliance should not be placed in the course of *ex parte* statements or in affidavits on matters not averred.

Exclusion orders have been described as 'draconian'[2]. But such orders can be varied or recalled[3]. Relatively rarely is an application made to vary or recall such an order unless there has been a reconciliation. It was thought in some of the earlier cases that if a spouse had left the matrimonial home, it would be difficult to justify making an exclusion order[4]. But the contrary view has prevailed[5]. Section 4(1) of the 1981 Act now expressly provides for the making of exclusion orders when the applicant spouse is not in occupation of the matrimonial home.

In order to satisfy a court that the test for an exclusion order has been met, it will often be necessary to persuade the court that the granting of a suitable interdict would not be sufficient protection, given that a power of arrest can be attached to such an interdict. But it is thought that, despite some dicta in *Bell v Bell*, supra, it is not appropriate for the court to grant an interim interdict as a first stage, as it were, which could be followed later, if necessary, by an exclusion order. Each case will depend on its own facts[6].

INTERIM EXCLUSION ORDERS

An interim exclusion order may be granted only if the non-applicant spouse has been given an opportunity of being heard[7]. That opportunity must be afforded even if he has not lodged a notice of intention to defend[8].

Where an interim exclusion order is sought it may well be necessary, if it is opposed, to provide the court with affidavits in support of or against the granting of such an order. Affidavit evidence is admissible in place of parole evidence for the purposes of determining an opposed motion for interim orders under the 1981 Act[9]. The court can grant an order only if the test for granting an exclusion order has been met. The test is not which party has the greater need of the matrimonial home[10], nor what is in the best interests

1 *Matheson v Matheson* 1986 SLT (Sh Ct) 2.
2 *Bell v Bell* 1983 SLT 224 at 233, per Lord Grieve.
3 Matrimonial Homes (Family Protection) (Scotland) Act 1981, s 5.
4 *Bell v Bell* 1983 SLT 224.
5 Eg *Colagiacomo v Colagiacomo* 1983 SLT 559; *Brown v Brown* 1985 SLT 376 and particularly *McCafferty v McCafferty* 1986 SLT 650.
6 As examples see *Ward v Ward* 1983 SLT 472; *Matheson v Matheson* 1986 SLT (Sh Ct) 2; *McCafferty*, supra.
7 Matrimonial Homes (Family Protection) (Scotland) Act1981, s 4(6).
8 *Nelson v Nelson* 1988 SLT (Sh Ct) 26.
9 RC 188D(15); OCR 72(1).
10 *Ward v Ward* 1983 SLT 472.

of the children[1]. It may be argued that interim interdict will provide a sufficient remedy[2]. An interdict cannot be competently granted against an entitled spouse which would have the same effect as an exclusion order[3]. Matrimonial tension is not sufficient of itself to warrant granting an exclusion order[4]. The test will not be satisfied if there are competing affidavits which have the effect of cancelling each other out and there is no means of ascertaining which version is true. But if the defender substantially admits the pursuer's allegations an interim order may be granted. An interim exclusion order has been granted on the basis of the pursuer's affidavits before the defender had been able to obtain affidavits[5]. It is unusual not to afford both parties an equal opportunity of presenting information to the court before making such an order but circumstances of special urgency may make such a course appropriate. It was suggested in that case that the defender could apply for recall of the exclusion order on lodging his affidavits[6]. If the pursuer's allegations in her averments or affidavit are unreliable the order may be refused[7]. In that case the pursuer failed to disclose that she was carrying on an adulterous association which was a very obvious reason for marital disharmony. An appeal court will interfere with a decision to grant or refuse an interim exclusion order only if it can be shown that the judge had misdirected himself in law or had reached an unwarranted conclusion[8]. As to the approach of an appellate court in connection with interim exclusion orders see also *Brown v Brown* 1985 SLT 376.

Orders which must or may be granted along with an exclusion order

Section 4(4) of the 1981 Act provides that in making an exclusion order the court shall, on the application of the applicant spouse—

(a) grant a warrant for the summary ejection of the non-applicant spouse from the matrimonial home;

(b) grant an interdict prohibiting the non-applicant spouse from entering the matrimonial home without the express permission of the applicant;

(c) grant an interdict prohibiting the removal by the non-applicant spouse, except with the written consent of the applicant or by a further order of court, of any furniture and plenishings in the matrimonial home;

unless in relation to paragraph (a) or (c) above, the non-applicant spouse satisfies the court that it is unnecessary for it to grant such a remedy. Again it is necessary specifically to seek such orders in the conclusions or craves. Otherwise they will not be granted.

The court is given a discretion in section 4(5) to make any of the following additional orders:

(a) to grant an interdict prohibiting the non-applicant spouse from entering or remaining in a specified area in the vicinity of the matrimonial home;

(b) where the warrant for the summary ejection of the non-applicant spouse has been granted in his or her absence, give directions as to the preservation

1 *Hampsey v Hampsey* 1988 GWD 24-1035.
2 *Colagiacomo v Colagiacomo* 1983 SLT 559.
3 *Tattersall v Tattersall* 1983 SLT 506; but see *MacLure v MacLure* 1911 SC 200.
4 *Matheson*, supra.
5 *Raeburn v Raeburn* 1990 GWD 8-424.
6 Matrimonial Homes (Family Protection) (Scotland) Act 1981, s 5(1).
7 *Boyle v Boyle* 1986 SLT 656.
8 *McCafferty v McCafferty* 1986 SLT 650 at 651, per Ross LCJ.

of the non-applicant spouse's goods and effects which remain in the matrimonial home;

(c) on the application of either spouse, make the exclusion order or the warrant or interdict mentioned in paragraph (a), (b) or (c) of section 4(4) above or paragraph (a) of this subsection subject to such terms and conditions as the court may prescribe;

(d) on application as aforesaid, make such other order as it may consider necessary for the proper enforcement of an order made under subsection (4) above or paragraph (a), (b) or (c) of this subsection.

So far as orders under section 4(5)(b) are concerned it is likely that the court will have to act *ex proprio motu* since it is unlikely that a pursuer will make an application in that regard.

In the exercise of the power granted in terms of section 4(5)(c) interim orders may be granted but suspended for a period to enable a defender to find alternative accommodation.[1] In that event it is not appropriate to grant an immediate order for ejection from the property.

Furniture and plenishings

At common law one spouse has prima facie no right to prevent the other spouse from doing whatever he or she wishes in relation to assets solely owned by him or her. Even when an asset is jointly owned there is no basis for interdict if one of the joint owners does something in relation to it of which the other would not necessarily approve, provided that there is no prejudice to the other owner's interest in it, as there would be if it were to be sold or pledged. In *Welsh v Welsh*[2] it was held that the court has power to prohibit the removal of property which is the subject of litigation. Thus it was necessary for there to be statutory intervention if a right was to be given to one spouse to prevent the other from removing furniture and plenishings from the matrimonial home which he owned either himself or jointly with his spouse. But for such a power the matrimonial home could in some instances be denuded of its contents, lawfully. The 1981 Act allows the court to grant a right to a party to use and possess articles of furniture and plenishings. An order made under the Act does not by itself alter the ownership of the articles though the provisions for apportioning expenditure on articles of furniture and plenishings[3] might eventually have that effect in some instances. These provisions apply to those items which are solely owned as well as those which are jointly owned[4]. Accordingly it is competent in terms of the 1981 Act for a party to seek and for the court to grant interdict prohibiting the removal of any items of furniture and plenishings in the matrimonial home: *Welsh*, supra. If an order is made for the delivery of an article the court may grant warrant to a messenger-at-arms or a sheriff officer to enter the matrimonial home or premises occupied by the other party to search for, take possession of and deliver the article in accordance with the order[5]. It should be noted that in terms of the Family Law (Scotland) Act 1985, s 25 there is a presumption that the parties to a marriage have an equal share in household goods kept or used

1 *Mather v Mather* 1987 SLT 565.
2 1987 SLT (Sh Ct) 30.
3 Matrimonial Homes (Family Protection) (Scotland) Act 1981, s 2(5).
4 See ibid, s 3(2).
5 Matrimonial Homes (Family Protection) (Scotland) Act 1981, s 3(6).

in the matrimonial home for the joint domestic purposes of the parties to the marriage.

Applications for the use and possession of furniture and plenishings in the matrimonial home may[1], but need not be, linked to an application for an exclusion order. If a pursuer has occupancy rights in the matrimonial home, and that might have to be established by way of a declarator, she may apply for an order for possession and use of the furniture and plenishings[2].

Furniture and plenishings are defined in section 22 of the 1981 Act. Broadly they comprise articles owned or being acquired which are reasonably necessary to enable the home to be used as a family residence. But they exclude motor vehicles, caravans and houseboats. Interim orders in relation to them may be made only if the other party has been notified of the application and has been given an opportunity of being heard by or represented before the court[3]. The court is not required to grant an order in respect of all the furniture and plenishings. There is no reason why a court should not grant an order in respect of specified items or all the furniture and plenishings except a list of specified items. The purpose of these provisions is to prevent one spouse removing all or most items from a matrimonial home so that it becomes more or less uninhabitable. But there are cases in which it is reasonable to allow some of the items to be removed in order to enable the other spouse to set up a second home.

EJECTION

Ejection may be granted as an incidental order in connection with an exclusion order in terms of section 3(4). If both spouses are entitled or permitted to occupy a matrimonial home, one spouse cannot bring an action for the ejection of the other from that home[4]. In terms of section 1 of the 1981 Act both spouses will normally be entitled for this purpose.

POWERS OF ARREST

The court is required to attach a power of arrest to a matrimonial interdict ancillary to an exclusion order or an interim exclusion order, if it is applied for[5]. The court has no discretion to attach such a power to such interdicts. These interdicts are those specified in sections 4(4)(b) and (c) and 4(5)(a) (entering the matrimonial home, removing furniture etc and being in the vicinity of the matrimonial home). The court is also required to attach a power of arrest to any other matrimonial interdict where the non-applicant spouse has had the opportunity of being heard by or represented before the court unless the court considers that such a power is unnecessary in the circumstances of that case[6]. Thus the court may have to exercise a discretion as to whether to grant an interdict in relation to the removal of furniture and plenishings where that interdict is granted otherwise than as an order ancillary to an exclusion order. The reason why there is not a requirement for the non-applicant spouse to be given an opportunity to be heard or represented in connection with a power

1 Ibid, s 4(4)(c).
2 ibid, s 3(2).
3 Ibid, s 3(4).
4 Ibid, s 3(7).
5 Ibid, s 15(1)(a).
6 Ibid, s 15(1)(b); *McKenna v McKenna* 1984 SLT (Sh Ct) 92.

of arrest where there is an exclusion order is that no such interim order may competently be granted unless he has had such an opportunity.

Powers of arrest cannot be attached to an interim interdict prohibiting the defender from molesting the pursuer granted at the same time as a warrant for service because the defender will not have been given an opportunity of being heard or represented. Accordingly the earliest stage at which such a power can be attached is the first time that the cause calls in court. The usual practice in the sheriff court is for any interlocutor granting interim interdict along with a warrant for service to include an order for parties to be heard on the interim craves at an appointed time, usually a few days later. The interim interdict is granted until that time. If it is not renewed at that hearing it falls. In the Court of Session at least seven days notice is required of a motion to attach a power of arrest, if application is made after the application for a matrimonial interdict[1].

A power of arrest attached to an interdict is of no effect until the interdict is served on the non-applicant spouse[2]. When an interdict with a power of arrest has been granted it is essential not only to serve it on the non-applicant spouse (by sheriff officer or messenger-at-arms) but also to deliver a copy of the application for interdict and the interlocutor granting it along with a certificate of service to the chief constable of the area in which the matrimonial home is situated and the chief constable of the area where the applicant spouse lives, if different[3]. It can be argued that the requirement to serve an interdict on the non-applicant spouse does not apply where a power of arrest is attached after the interdict has been granted[4]. In the Court of Session the applicant spouse is required to lodge with the court a certificate of delivery to the chief constable. The same practice is to be followed in the sheriff court[5]. The power of arrest terminates on divorce.[6]. It may also terminate when the matrimonial interdict to which it is attached is varied and must do so when it is recalled. Similar intimation and lodging is required when there is a variation or recall[7]. As to the procedure to be followed when there is a need to enforce the power of arrest see chapter 12.

INTERDICT

'Interdict is a remedy, by decree of court, either against a wrong in the course of being done, or against an apprehended violation of a party's rights, only to be awarded on evidence of the wrong, or on reasonable grounds of apprehension that such violation is intended'[8]. The wrong in question may be punishable by the criminal law as in the case of assault or may be the basis of a claim for damages or both. Interdict may not be granted against a com-

1 RC 188D(9).
2 Matrimonial Homes (Family Protection) (Scotland) Act 1981, s 15(2).
3 Matrimonial Homes (Family Protection) (Scotland) Act 1981, s 15(4).
4 D I Nichols and M C Meston, *The Matrimonial Homes (Family Protection) (Scotland) Act 1981* (2nd edn, 1986, Green's) para 5–08.
5 AS (Applications under the Matrimonial Homes (Family Protection) (Scotland) Act 1981) 1982, SI 1982/1432, para 9.
6 Matrimonial Homes (Family Protection) (Scotland) Act 1981, s 15(2).
7 Ibid, s 15(5); RC 188D(13); AS (Applications under the Matrimonial Homes (Family Protection) (Scotland) Act 1981) 1982, para 9.
8 *Hay's Trs v Young* (1877) 4 R 398 at 401.

pleted act, eg the removal of property which has already been removed. But if there is more property which could be removed interdict may be appropriate.

Jurisdiction

In the course of a divorce action where the court has jurisdiction in respect of the divorce it will have jurisdiction to make orders ancillary to the divorce, including orders for interdict although it is most likely that the same court will have jurisdiction in respect of any interdicts sought in any event. Accordingly it is not necessary and it is not the practice to aver a separate basis of jurisdiction for interdict in such circumstances. Where interdict is not ancillary to divorce the basis of jurisdiction is the place where the defender is domiciled or the place where the wrong is likely to be committed[1].

Terms of the interdict

The terms in which interdict is sought must be precise and in such a form that the person interdicted is in no doubt as to what he is prohibited from doing[2]. The court may grant interdicts against acts outwith its territorial jurisdiction. The test is whether the court can make the proposed interdict effective against the defender[3]. If a power of arrest is to be attached to the interdict it must be an interdict within the meaning of a 'matrimonial interdict'[4]. An interdict cannot competently be granted if its terms are such that it would achieve the effect of an exclusion order[5]. As has been noted above it has been held that an interdict can competently be granted at common law to prohibit the removal of property which is the subject of litigation[6].

Interim interdict granted on an *ex parte* basis in a sheriff court action should be granted for no more than a week[7]. Interdict is not effective until the defender is aware of its terms. A certified copy of the interlocutor is commonly served on the defender as soon as possible after interdict is granted, by messenger-at-arms or sheriff officer, so that there can be no argument as to that but informal intimation is sufficient[8]. The date of commencement of an interdict may be postponed[9].

Undertaking in lieu of interdict

An undertaking may be given to the court not to act in a certain way. In such circumstances interdict will not be granted in relation to the same matter simultaneously. The exact terms of any such undertaking given in the Court of Session will be recorded in the minute of proceedings. In the sheriff court it should be recorded either in the interlocutor refusing interdict or in some other manner so that if it is breached contempt of court proceedings may

1 Civil Jurisdiction and Judgments Act 1982, Sch 8, rr 1, 2(10).
2 *Kelso School Board v Hunter* (1874) 2 R 228; *Murdoch v Murdoch* 1973 SLT (Notes) 13; *Webster v Lord Advocate* 1985 SLT 361.
3 *McKenna v McKenna* 1984 SLT (Sh Ct) 92.
4 Matrimonial Homes (Family Protection) (Scotland) Act 1981, s 14(2); *McKenna*, supra.
5 *Tattersall v Tattersall* 1983 SLT 506.
6 *Welsh v Welsh* 1987 SLT (Sh Ct) 30.
7 *Nelson v Nelson* 1989 SLT (Sh Ct) 18.
8 *Robertson v McDonald* (1829) 7 S 272; *Clark v Stirling* (1839) 1 D 955; *Henderson v Maclellan* (1874) 1 R 920; *Neville v Neville* 1924 SLT (Sh Ct) 43.
9 *Phonographic Performance Ltd v McKenzie* 1982 SLT 272.

be taken[1]. When the party on whose behalf an undertaking is given is not personally present in court at the material time or is present but is unaware of its effect, it is the duty of those acting for him forthwith to bring to his attention the terms of the undertaking and the effect of it. The consequences of breach of such an undertaking should be made clear to him. If such an undertaking is breached the court would be likely to grant interdict, in addition to the imposition of an appropriate penalty.

Transfer of tenancy

The court may order that the tenancy of a matrimonial home be transferred into the name of a non-entitled spouse[2], or into the sole name of one spouse where there is a joint tenancy[3]. The application must be intimated to the landlord[4]. The landlord must be given an opportunity of being heard[5].

The court is required to consider all the circumstances of the case including the conduct of the spouses, their needs and resources, the needs of any children of the family, the extent to which the house is used in connection with a trade or business and any offers of suitable alternative accommodation[6]. The issue may be decided on the basis of what is fair and reasonable in the circumstances[7].

Orders relating to avoidance transactions

Where a claim has been made for an order for financial provision on divorce or there is a claim that such an order should be varied or recalled the party making the claim may, not later than one year after the date of disposal of the claim apply to the court for an order:

(a) setting aside or varying any transfer of, or transaction involving, property effected by the other party not more than five years before the date of the making of the claim; or

(b) interdicting the other party from effecting any such transfer or transaction.[8]

Because time is often of the essence it is usually necessary to seek these orders in the divorce summons or initial writ, with an interdict if it is not known whether all the anticipated alienations of property have taken place. It may be necessary to obtain a warrant to arrest on the dependence. Where there may be alienation of significant heritable property consideration should be given to obtaining inhibition on the dependence[9]. Intimation of the orders sought should be made to third parties who may be affected by them[10]. If the court is satisfied that the transfer or the transaction had the effect of, or is likely to have the effect of, defeating in whole or in part any such claim,

1 *Graham v Robert Younger Ltd* 1955 JC 28.
2 Matrimonial Homes (Family Protection) Act 1981, s 13(1).
3 Ibid, s 13(9).
4 Ibid, s 13(4); RC 188D(7); AS (Applications under the Matrimonial Homes (Family Protection) (Scotland) Act 1981) 1982, SI 1982/1432, para 3.
5 Matrimonial Homes (Family Protection) (Scotland) Act 1981, s 13(4).
6 Ibid, ss 13(3), 3(3).
7 *McGowan v McGowan* 1986 SLT 112.
8 Family Law (Scotland) Act 1985, s 18(1).
9 *Wilson v Wilson* 1981 SLT 101; Macphail *Sheriff Court Practice* (Greens) para 22-94.
10 *Harris v Harris* 1988 SLT 101.

it will make the order applied for or such other order as it thinks fit[1]. The court may make the order subject to such terms and conditions as it thinks fit and may make ancillary orders[2]. Such an order must not prejudice the rights in or to the property of any third party who has in good faith acquired the property or any of it or any rights in relation to it for value, or who derives title to such property or rights from any person who has done so. As to the onus of proof on a third party see *Leslie v Leslie*[3].

It would be advisable in drafting a summons or initial writ to include a phrase at the end of the order sought to make it clear that an alternative but unspecified order is sought in the event that the court is not prepared to make the particular order sought eg 'or make such other order as the court may consider appropriate.'[4]

Not infrequently property is transferred to relatives, cohabitees or other persons associated with the transferor either for no financial consideration ('for love, favour and affection' perhaps) or for less than full value. There may be back letters which oblige the associate to return the property at some future date or on the occurrence of some future event. In other cases the assets may be put in trust ostensibly for genuine purposes but in truth in order to defeat a claim in a divorce action. Where that is thought to have occurred suitable averments will have to be made in the summons or initial writ and attempts may have to be made after the action has been raised to recover documents relating to the alleged transaction.

1 Matrimonial Homes (Family Protection) (Scotland) Act 1981, s 18(2).
2 Ibid, s 18(4).
3 1983 SLT 186 and 1987 SLT 232.
4 RC 156(2).

CHAPTER 6

THE WRIT

CHOICE OF COURT

Before raising an action of divorce it is necessary to decide whether to raise the action in the Court of Session or the sheriff court. The decision could be made to commence the action in the Court of Session *inter alia* because:

(1) There was doubt as to whether it could be established that a particular sheriff court had jurisdiction.

(2) It was thought to be necessary to seek inhibition on the dependence of the action in view of the valuable heritable property owned by the defender. Inhibition is not competent in the sheriff court[1], but application may be made to the Court of Session for inhibition in connection with an action for aliment or a claim for financial provision forming part of a sheriff court action of divorce[2]. Inhibition is not restricted to cases in which the defender is about to alienate property, or verging on insolvency[3].

(3) There were substantial assets owned by the parties. Counsel would in any event be involved in dealing with the financial aspects of the case.

(4) There were pending before the Court of Session proceedings which could affect the marriage[4].

Other considerations include whether the action is likely to be defended, cost and convenience for witnesses. The fees for an action of divorce using the simplified procedure in the Court of Session are the same as those in the sheriff court.

JURISDICTION IN SCOTLAND

The Court of Session and the sheriff court have concurrent jurisdiction in actions of divorce[5]. The Civil Jurisdiction and Judgments Act 1982 does not govern jurisdiction in actions of divorce[6].

1 Family Law (Scotland) Act 1985, s 19.
2 For the procedure see Macphail *Sheriff Court Practice* (1988, W Green & Son), paras 11–37, 11–38, 22–04 to 22–18 and as to when inhibition is appropriate see *Wilson v Wilson* 1981 SLT 101.
3 *Wilson*, supra; *Pow v Pow* 1987 SLT 127; Gretton *The Law of Inhibition and Adjudication* (1987, Butterworths) pp 13–14.
4 Domicile and Matrimonial Proceedings Act 1973, s 7(5).
5 Sheriff Courts (Scotland) Act 1907, s 5(2B).
6 Civil Jurisdiction and Judgments Act 1982, Sch 9, para 1.

Court of Session

The Court of Session has jurisdiction by virtue of the Domicile and Matrimonial Proceedings Act 1973, s 7(2) which provides that the court shall have jurisdiction to entertain *inter alia* an action of divorce if (and only if) either of the parties to the marriage in question:

(1) is domiciled in Scotland on the date when the action was begun[1], or

(2) was habitually resident in Scotland throughout the period of one year ending with that date.

Section 7(3) of the 1973 Act sets out the circumstances in which the Court of Session has jurisdiction in respect of actions for declarator of marriage or declarator of nullity of marriage.

Section 7(5) provides that the Court of Session shall, at any time when proceedings are pending in respect of which it has jurisdiction by virtue of subsections 2, 3 or 5 of section 7, also have jurisdiction to entertain other proceedings, in respect of the same marriage, for divorce, separation or declarator of marriage, declarator of nullity of marriage or declarator of freedom and putting to silence (eg a cross action of divorce) even though jurisdiction would not be exerciseable in terms of subsections 2 and 3. As to when proceedings commence see *Edinburgh District Council v Davis*, supra. Proceedings are pending so long as the taking of an appeal is competent or, if an appeal has been taken, so long as the appeal proceedings are pending.[2]

Sheriff court

The jurisdiction of a sheriff court is determined by the Domicile and Matrimonial Proceedings Act 1973, s 8 as amended by the Divorce Jurisdiction, Court Fees and Legal Aid (Scotland) Act 1983, Sch 1, para 18.

Section 8(2) provides that the sheriff court shall have jurisdiction to entertain an action of separation or divorce if (and only if):

(1) either of the parties to the marriage in question-
   (a) is domiciled in Scotland on the date when the action was begun; or
   (b) was habitually resident in Scotland throughout the period of one year ending with that date; and
(2) either party to the marriage-
   (a) was resident in the sheriffdom for a period of forty days ending with that date, or
   (b) had been resident in the sheriffdom for a period of not less than forty days ending not more than forty days before the said date, and has no known residence in Scotland at that date.

Section 8(3) provides that in respect of any marriage the court has jurisdiction to entertain an action of divorce or separation (such as a cross action of divorce even though the court would not have jurisdiction in terms of section 8(2)) provided that such an action is begun at a time when an original action is

---

1 Domicile in this context has the usual meaning and does not mean domicile as defined by the Civil Jurisdiction and Judgments Act 1982. The action is probably begun when the defender is cited: *Edinburgh District Council v Davis* 1978 SLT 33.
2 Domicile and Matrimonial Proceedings Act 1973, s 12(4).

pending in respect of the marriage in regard to which the court does have jurisdiction in terms of subsection 2 or 3. An action is still pending so long as the taking of an appeal is competent or, if an appeal has been taken, so long as the appeal is pending.[1]

Domicile and habitual residence

The essential basis of jurisdiction is thus the domicile or habitual residence of either party to a marriage. Neither of these phrases is statutorily defined. That means that in many cases the Court of Session and one or more than one sheriff court will have jurisdiction or that courts in different parts of the United Kingdom may have concurrent jurisdiction. For that reason rules of court require that averments be made as to any other relevant proceedings (see below). That is also the reason for the requirements and rules relating to the sist of one action when more than one is pending (described in the next chapter).

'Habitually resident' describes the normal place of residence of the person. That place would not cease to be his or her habitual residence simply because the person was absent for periods on holiday, business or attending a course of instruction. But habitual residence would not normally include a holiday cottage. The phrase is largely self-explanatory and must mean the voluntary and usual place of residence[2]. The question is one of fact.

'Domicile' is a concept describing the jurisdiction with which the person has for the time being the strongest connection. There should be specific averments of domicile[3]. It may arise by reason of origin, ie the place where the person was born. Traditionally a child adopted the domicile of his father at birth, unless he was illegitimate or his father had predeceased his birth, in which case he adopted the domicile of his mother. On marriage a wife no longer adopts the domicile of her husband[4]. She can have a different domicile. If she had a dependent domicile before that Act came into force on 1 January 1974, she retains it until she acquires another domicile or an earlier domicile revives. The essential features of domicile in Scotland are residence in Scotland with the intention of remaining there. Domicile will more easily be established where the person was born in Scotland of Scottish parents. If a person is employed abroad he may well retain a Scottish domicile because he will not necessarily have acquired a domicile of choice in that country unless there is evidence of an intention to remain there[5]. Because the Civil Jurisdiction and Judgments Act 1982 does not apply to divorce the definition of domicile in sections 41-46 of that Act is not of assistance in this connection[6].

Jurisdiction—custody, aliment etc

In an action of divorce the court may make, with respect to any child of the marriage to which the action relates, such order as it thinks fit relating

1 Domicile and Matrimonial Proceedings Act 1973, s 12(4).
2 H M Prison, Barlinnie is not likely to be one to which both adjectives apply. As is noted below such an address should not be used in any event.
3 *Horn v Horn* 1935 SLT 589.
4 Domicile and Matrimonial Proceedings Act 1973, s 1.
5 See generally Anton *Private International Law* (1967, W Green & Son), pp 161 et seq.
6 Civil Jurisdiction and Judgments Act 1982, Sch 9, para 1.

to parental rights and may vary or recall any such order[1]. Courts also have jurisdiction at common law and in terms of the Conjugal Rights (Scotland) (Amendment) Act 1861, s 9, and the Law Reform (Parent and Child) (Scotland) Act 1986, s 3. Where the court has jurisdiction in an action of divorce it also has jurisdiction to make such order as may be appropriate in connection with any of the matters referred to in Schedule 2 of the Domicile and Matrimonial Proceedings Act 1973[2]. These include custody, aliment, the variation and recall of such orders, and expenses. These provisions apply to the variation by the sheriff court of Court of Session decrees. Where custody is in issue other than in the course of matrimonial proceedings the basis of jurisdiction is the Family Law Act 1986, s 8.

Prorogation of jurisdiction

The court is required to comply with the rules as to jurisdiction and will almost certainly refuse to hear a case in respect of which it does not have jurisdiction, even where the parties are agreed that that court should hear the case[3]. Although it has been held that where the welfare of a child is in issue and the parties are agreed that the matter be dealt with in a particular way a less technical view may be taken[4], that view is not likely to extend to the court accepting jurisdiction in an action of divorce by agreement of the parties. That case has been described as the most distinguished case of the decade[5].

SIMPLIFIED PROCEDURE

This procedure is available in both the Court of Session and the sheriff court. The procedure is more fully described in chapter 7. In the Court of Session it is governed by Rules of Court 170E to 170L and in the sheriff court by Ordinary Cause Rules 135-143. The appropriate forms are set out in the appendices to these Rules[6]. Prescribed forms rather than an initial writ or summons are used. Printed copies of these forms are available from the Court of Session and Sheriff Clerks' offices and are usually available from Citizens Advice Bureaux.

Simplified procedure may be used only where[7]:

(1) the divorce sought is based on two years non-cohabitation and the defender consents to divorce or on five years non-cohabitation;

(2) no other proceedings are pending in any other court which could have the effect of bringing the marriage to an end;

(3) there are no children of the marriage under sixteen;

(4) neither party seeks any financial provision on divorce, and

---

1 Court of Session Act 1988, s 20; Sheriff Courts (Scotland) Act 1907, s 38C.
2 Domicile and Matrimonial Proceedings Act 1973, s 10.
3 *Singh v Singh* 1988 SCLR 541.
4 See *Girvan v Girvan* 1988 SCLR 493, a case concerned with an inappropriate form of action which has not been followed invariably.
5 *Jones v Jones* 1990 SCLR 127 at 129.
6 RC, forms 19A to 19E in the Court of Session and OCR, forms SDA1 to SDA7 in the sheriff court.
7 RC 170E(2); OCR 135(2).

(5) neither party suffers from mental disorder[1].

If any of these criteria cease to apply at any time before the action of divorce is disposed of, the application must be dismissed if it is a sheriff court application and will be treated as abandoned if it is a Court of Session application. It would be the duty of an applicant or his solicitor to bring such a change of circumstances to the attention of the court.

STYLES OF INITIAL WRITS AND SUMMONSES

It is important to check that initial writs and summonses are correct before they are lodged with the court. Otherwise they will be returned for correction or it will be necessary later to amend the writ and it may be necessary to re-serve them. In the Court of Session it is possible to amend and re-signet a summons prior to service. Errors are often made in the spelling of the names of the parties or their children and in dates and places of marriage and birth. These should be checked against the certificates. The information given in the certificates should be used. If a person is known by a name (other than a nickname) different from that shown in the marriage or birth certificate that should be made clear in the instance or at least in the averments.

The purpose of the instance is to set out who the parties are, where they live and to indicate if any party is legally aided. The purpose of the craves (as they are called in the sheriff court) or conclusions (as they are called in the Court of Session) is to set out the orders which the court is to be asked to make and, with the exception of expenses, in the exact form in which the court is to be asked to make them. Where a sum is sued for, for example, as aliment, that is the maximum sum that may be awarded. If a greater sum is to be sought the crave or conclusion should be amended. The pursuer should not seek orders directed against himself nor in favour of the defender[2].

The purpose of the averments in the condescendence is to give fair notice to the defender of the case which he has to meet. This is done by setting out in a logical sequence those facts which it is intended to establish. These must include all those facts which it is in law necessary to establish in order to obtain the decree or decrees sought. The averments should also include a reference to any statutory provisions on which it is intended to rely. The purpose of averments is not to narrate the evidence to be led.

A plea in law is a legal proposition, which logically follows from the averments and which, unless it is a preliminary plea such as one of relevancy or competency, warrants the making or refusal of the particular order set out in the crave or conclusion to which it relates. It is stated in a form to which the court can give effect. If the court decides to give effect to a plea by a party seeking an order, an order will normally be made in the terms set out in the relevant crave or conclusion. If not the court may make an order in those terms subject to any appropriate modification or may refuse to make such an order. If the court is to refuse to make an order in favour of one party there should be a suitable plea in law for the other party which can be upheld. The court may award a lesser sum than that sought or may award a period of access different from that specified in a crave or conclusion. But the court will not grant divorce on a different ground without amendment. It may be advisable,

---

1 For definition of 'mental disorder see the Mental Health (Scotland) Act 1984, s 1.
2 *T v T* 1987 SLT (Sh Ct) 74.

where the court is likely to make an order but in terms which are difficult to predict, to add some such phrase as 'or to make such other order as the court may consider appropriate'[1].

Legally-aided parties

If either party is legally aided there must be added to that person's name in the instance (whether in the initiating writ or the defences when they are lodged or by amendment if he becomes legally aided at a later stage in the proceedings) the words: 'Assisted Person'. These words should appear on every step of process. On the backing 'A P' is sufficient[2]. A legally-aided party must lodge his legal aid certificate in process along with the initial writ or defences or, if he is granted legal aid at a later stage in the case, as soon as the legal aid certificate is received. If a party ceases to be legally aided during the proceedings he is required to inform all the other parties by registered or recorded delivery letter.

---

1 RC 156(2).
2 AS (Civil Legal Aid Rules) 1987, SI 1987/492 replacing AS (Legal Aid Rules) 1958, para. 3.

Example of a Court of Session summons

COURT OF SESSION, SCOTLAND
SUMMONS
in causa

BARBARA ANNE FERGUSON or BROWN, (Assisted Person), 13 Coal Road, Cupar, Fife,   Pursuer

against

ALEXANDER PATRICK BROWN, 3 Ibrox Road, Cupar, Fife
           Defender

CONCLUSIONS

1. For divorce of the pursuer from the defender on the ground that their marriage has broken down irretrievably by reason of the defender's behaviour.

2. For custody of Elizabeth Anne Brown the child of the marriage under sixteen years of age and for leave to any party claiming an interest to apply to the court thereanent until 23rd June 1998[1]; to find that the said Elizabeth Anne Brown is entitled to payment by the defender of the sum of SIXTY POUNDS (£60) sterling per week in name of aliment; for decree against the defender for payment of the said sum in respect of the said child to the pursuer qua tutrix of the said child or to the said child with the concurrence of the pursuer qua his curatrix, and that for so long as the said child is unable to earn a livelihood; and for leave for any party claiming an interest thereanent to apply to the court until 23rd June 2000.

3. For an exclusion order suspending the defender's occupancy rights in the matrimonial home known as 13 Coal Road, Cupar, Fife; and for such order ad interim; and for warrant for the summary ejection of the defender from the matrimonial home at 13 Coal Road, Cupar, Fife.

4. For interdict against the defender entering the matrimonial home at 13 Coal Road, Cupar, Fife without the express permission of the pursuer; and for interdict ad interim.

5. For interdict against the defender molesting the pursuer by abusing her verbally, threatening her, assaulting her, placing her in a state of fear and alarm or distress; and for interdict ad interim.

6. For the attachment of a power of arrest to the said interdicts.

7. For the expenses of the action.

CONDESCENDENCE

1. The pursuer and the defender were married at Edinburgh on 12th March 1978. There is one child of the marriage, namely Elizabeth Anne Brown who was born on 23rd June 1982. Extract certificates of the relative entries in the Registers of Marriages and Births are produced.

---

1   Cf RC 170B(8).

2. The pursuer and the defender are domiciled in Scotland and have lived at the addresses in the instance for more than twelve months. The pursuer is unaware of any proceedings continuing in any country outside Scotland capable of affecting the validity or subsistence of the marriage[1] The pursuer is unaware of any proceedings in Scotland or elsewhere either pending or concluded which relate to the custody of the said child.[2]

[*Note*. Where proceedings are continuing there should be averments as to:

    (a) the court, tribunal or authority before whom they have been commenced.
    (b) the date of their commencement.
    (c) the names of the parties.
    (d) the date or expected date of proof in the proceedings.
    (e) such other facts as may be relevant to the question whether this action should be sisted under Schedule 3 of the Domicile and Matrimonial Proceedings Act 1973[3].]

Such other proceedings will not be continuing where no procedure has taken place for a year and a day since service of the summons or writ. But if a Court of Session action has been called the proceedings will be continuing[4]. The proceedings will be continuing in a sheriff court action where procedure has taken place subsequent to service[5].

3. The pursuer and the defender lived together at 13 Coal Road, Cupar, Fife, of which property they are joint tenants, from shortly after they were married until the defender left that house on about 31st October 1989. They have neither lived together nor had marital relations since that time.

4. The marriage was never happy. The defender was capable of earning a good wage and did so during periods when he was employed. However he regularly drank to excess, particularly after he received his pay on a Thursday. After heavy drinking over the weekend he frequently failed to go to work on a Monday morning. On some such occasions he was dismissed from his employment. Thereafter the pursuer would suffer financial hardship until he regained employment. The defender assaulted the pursuer on numerous occasions including 1st April 1989 when she sustained a black eye, 23rd May 1989 when she sustained a broken nose and 20th August 1989 when she was bruised on her back and her right arm. The defender has on many occasions claimed that he is employed by the Security Service to keep watch on terrorist suspects. On one such occasion in October 1989 when the pursuer was visiting her brother in England the defender remained at home. On 30th October the pursuer returned home a day earlier than expected. She found the defender in bed with a woman whose identity is unknown to her. The defender told her to get out of the house and threatened to kill her. He got out of bed and pursued her out of the house with an axe which he threw at her while she was going down the garden path. The pursuer cannot reasonably be expected to continue to live with the defender. There is no prospect of reconciliation. The pursuer seeks decree of divorce.

1 Cf RC 157(3)(a).
2 Cf RC 170B(11).
3 RC 157(3)(b); OCR 3(5).
4 *McKidd v Manson* (1882) 9 R 790; *Dunnett v Dunnett* 1990 SCLR 135 *McCulloch v McCulloch* 1990 SCLR 155.
5 *Donnelly v Donnelly* 1990 GWD 9-509.

5. On 31st October 1989 the defender left the matrimonial home. The pursuer returned to live there shortly thereafter and has continued to live there since then. Since the pursuer and the defender separated the defender has frequently arrived at the pursuer's house, usually during the night. He retained a key to that house and has on occasion let himself in. The pursuer changed the locks but the defender broke a window and climbed in. On such occasions he claimed to have come to seek a reconciliation or access to the said child. When the pursuer told him to leave the house or refused to permit him to enter the house he threatened to kill her or to cause her to be disfigured so that no other man would want her. He threatened to remove the said child from the care of the pursuer. As a result of the noise made by and the foul language of the defender on such occasions the said child was woken up and has been much upset by the conduct of the defender. In particular such incidents occurred between about midnight and 1 am on 1st November and 23rd December 1989 and on 1st January and 3rd February 1990. The pursuer is reasonably apprehensive that such conduct will continue. That conduct has been and is likely to continue to be injurious to the health of the pursuer and the said child. In these circumstances the pursuer seeks an exclusion order and warrant for the ejection of the defender from the matrimonial home together with the interdicts concluded for. Reference is made to the Matrimonial Homes (Family Protection) (Scotland) Act 1981, sections 4 and 15.

6. The pursuer seeks custody of the said child. She has all along been in the care of the pursuer and is well cared for by her. The pursuer has ample accommodation for her. It is in her best interests that she be in the custody of the pursuer. The pursuer is employed in a chidren's nursery. She earns about £65 net per week. The defender is now employed on a North Sea oil rig. The pursuer believes that he earns about £13,500 net per annum. The sum sued for as aliment for the said child is reasonable. The pursuer does not seek an order for financial provision for herself.

PLEAS IN LAW

1. The marriage having broken down irretrievably by reason of the defender's behaviour as condescended upon, decree of divorce should be granted as concluded for.

2. It being in the best interests of the said child that she should be in the custody of the pursuer and the sum sued for as aliment being reasonable, decree of custody and aliment should be granted as concluded for.

3. The defender having molested and assaulted the pursuer as condescended upon, and the pursuer being reasonably apprehensive that such conduct will continue, interdict and interim interdict should be granted as concluded for.

4. An exclusion order being in the circumstances necessary for the protection of the pursuer and the said child as condescended upon such order and the orders ancillary thereto, third fourth and sixth concluded for, should be pronounced as concluded for and should be pronounced ad interim.

IN RESPECT WHEREOF

330 Princes Street, Edinburgh
Agent for the Pursuer

Example of an initial writ

<u>SHERIFFDOM OF TAYSIDE, CENTRAL AND FIFE AT CUPAR</u>

INITIAL WRIT

in causa

MRS SUSAN CLARE BROWNLEE or SMITH,
(Assisted Person) 3 Hamlet Road, Cupar, Fife
Pursuer

against

CHARLES AUGUSTUS SMITH, her husband,
39 Buchan Steps, Ladybank, Fife
Defender

The pursuer craves the court:

1. To grant decree of divorce of the defender from the pursuer on the ground that their marriage has broken down irretrievably by reason of the unreasonable behaviour of the defender.

2. To grant warrant to intimate this writ to Miss Lolita Lush, 39 Buchan Steps, Ladybank, Fife as a person with whom the defender is alleged to have committed adultery.

3. To interdict the defender from molesting the pursuer by abusing her verbally, by threatening her, by putting her into a state of fear and alarm or distress, and by using violence towards her; and to grant interim interdict[1]; and to attach a power of arrest to said interdicts.[2]

4. To find the pursuer entitled to custody of Rita Ann Smith and James Henry Brownlee respectively a child of the marriage and a child of the pursuer accepted by the defender as a child of the marriage; and to grant interim custody as aforesaid.

5. To grant decree for payment by the defender to the pursuer of the sum of TWENTY FIVE POUNDS (£25) per week as interim aliment for the pursuer payable weekly and in advance, with interest at the rate of fifteen per cent per annum on each weekly payment from the due date until payment.

1 Cf *Murdoch v Murdoch* 1973 SLT (Notes) 13.
2 That power cannot be attached until the defender has been given a chance to be heard in connection therewith: Matrimonial Homes (Family Protection) (Scotland) 1981 Act, s 15(1)(b).

6. To grant decree for payment by the defender to the pursuer of the sum of TWENTY POUNDS (£20) per week as aliment for each of the said children payable weekly and in advance so long as the said children are in her custody and under 18 years of age, with interest at the rate of fifteen per cent per annum on each weekly payment from the due date until payment.

7. To find the defender liable in the expenses of the action.

CONDESCENDENCE

1. The pursuer and the defender were married at Edinburgh on 6th August 1983. There is one child of the marriage namely Rita Ann Smith, born on 21st November 1984. The defender accepted, as a child of the marriage, a child of the pursuer, namely James Henry Brownlee, born on 4th October 1982. Relative extract certificates of the marriage and the birth of the said children are produced.

2. The pursuer was born in Scotland of Scottish parents. She is domiciled in Scotland. Further she has been habitually resident in Scotland for more than one year immediately preceding the raising of this action. She has resided within the Sheriffdom of Tayside, Central and Fife at 3 Hamlet Road, Cupar, Fife for more than 40 days immediately preceding the raising of this action. She is not aware of any proceedings continuing in Scotland or in any other country in respect of the marriage or which are capable of affecting its validity or subsistence.[1] The pursuer is unaware of any other proceedings either in Scotland or elsewhere either pending or concluded which relate to the said child.[2]

3. After the marriage the pursuer and the defender lived together at 13 Station Road, Peat Inn, Fife until May 1989 and thereafter at 3 Hamlet Road, Cupar, Fife. On 27th June 1989 the defender left the pursuer and went to live at 39 Buchan Steps, Ladybank, Fife. The pursuer and the defender have neither lived together nor had marital relations since then.

4. From a short time after the marriage the defender regularly drank to excess. He regularly returned home drunk on Friday and Saturday evenings. On many occasions after he had gone out for the evening he did not return home until about 2 or 3am. He refused to tell the pursuer where he had been. He refused to allow the pursuer to accompany him on social outings. He kept her short of money although he was in well-paid employment. She had to borrow money on frequent occasions from her parents. On 14th April 1988 at 13 Station Road aforesaid the defender assaulted the pursuer with a telephone while she was in bed. As a result of that assault her head was cut. She received seven stitches. While the pursuer and the defender lived together the defender associated with several women including Miss Lolita Lush whom he invited to stay at 3 Hamlet Road, Cupar in about June 1989. He admitted that he had committed adultery with her on about 23rd June 1989. They now live as husband and wife at their present address. The marriage has broken down irretrievably

---

[1] Cf OCR 3(5). For the averments which should be made if proceedings are continuing see the note to condescendence 2 of the Court of Session summons, supra.
[2] Cf OCR 132C.

by reason of the defender's behaviour. There is no prospect of a reconciliation. The pursuer is entitled to divorce.

5. Since the defender left the pursuer he has called at her house on numerous occasions usually after midnight and in a drunken condition. In particular he did so on 1st, 2nd, 8th, 16th and 30th October 1989 ostensibly seeking access to the said children. On such occasions he shouted and swore loudly at the pursuer and threatened to assault her. On the last of said occasions he was arrested by police officers. He was subsequently convicted at Cupar District Court of breach of the peace. Extract conviction will be produced. The pursuer is afraid of the defender. In these circumstances the pursuer reasonably apprehends that such conduct will continue. Accordingly she requires the protection of an interdict. She wishes a power of arrest to be attached to the said interdict in terms of the Matrimonial Homes (Family Protection) (Scotland) Act 1981, section 15(1)(b).

6. The said children have all along been cared for by the pursuer. She has ample accommodation for them. She is not employed. She can devote all her time to the children. Members of her family live nearby and assist her if required. Both children attend primary school in Cupar and are making good progress. It is in their best interests that they be in the custody of the pursuer. The defender has occasional access to them.

7. The pursuer receives income support. The defender is a self-employed builder. He usually earns at least £200 per week. The pursuer is unaware if the said Miss Lush is employed. The sums sued for as aliment are reasonable.

PLEAS IN LAW

1. The marriage of the pursuer and the defender having broken down irretrievably as condescended upon, decree of divorce should be granted as craved.

2. The defender having molested the pursuer as condescended upon and there being reasonable grounds to apprehend that he will continue to do so, interdict and interim interdict with a power of arrest attached thereto should be granted as craved.

3. It being in the best interests of the said children that they should be in the custody of the pursuer decree of custody and of interim custody should be granted as craved.

4. The defender being a person owing an obligation to aliment the pursuer and the said children and the sums sued for as aliment being reasonable, aliment and interim aliment should be awarded as craved.

IN RESPECT WHEREOF
Solicitor, Omnibus House,
Station Wynd, Cupar
Agent for the pursuer

The names and addresses of the pursuer and the defender

The names and addresses of the purusuer and defender must be set out in the writ unless there are compelling reasons not to do so[1]. One reason is that it must be possible to ascertain that that court has jurisdiction based on residence. Where the pursuer makes suitable averments, eg that she is in fear of further assaults if the defender were to discover her address, she may give her address in the summons or initial writ as care of her solicitors. It is believed that in some sheriff courts a motion on behalf of a party to dispense with the necessity of disclosing the current address of the party concerned may be required. If that address is to remain concealed it should not appear anywhere in the process since the whole process is available to a party for examination. No separate register is kept of such addresses. It is suggested that in appropriate cases the name and address are sealed in an envelope marked 'confidential' and that the clerk does not make it available to the parties or their agents without sanction of the court. Application may be made to the court to compel the disclosure of an address[2]. The defender's address should not appear as 'presently a prisoner in H M Prison ...' even if that is the case at the date of service of the summons or initial writ[3]. That address would continue to appear in the process and could appear on extract decrees of court many years later when the defender may be a reformed character. Nor should summonses and the like design a party as a serviceman by reference to his name, rank and number if his address is a civilian address in Northern Ireland[4].

Address or identity unknown

If the defender's address or the identity or address of a paramour, the children of the marriage over puberty, the next of kin of the defender or the defender's *curator bonis* is unknown, that fact must be averred in the condescendence together with the steps, if any, taken to ascertain that identity or address[5]. The reason for this provision is to enable the court to order intimation to those on whom intimation must be made or to require, if necessary, that steps be taken to attempt to discover the identity or address of any such person.

Examples of conclusions/craves, relative averments and pleas in law

In the sheriff court the craves would be preceded by the words 'The pursuer craves the court: 1. To grant (decree of) ....' In the Court of Session under the Heading: 'Conclusions' the orders usually start with the word 'For' followed eg by 'divorce of ... The following orders are in sheriff court form and would require minor adaptation for the Court of Session.[6]

---

1 *Doughton v Doughton* 1958 SLT (Notes) 34.
2 *Stein v Stein* 1936 SLT 103.
3 Cf Court of Session Practice Note, 23 July 1952.
4 Cf Court of Session Practice Note, 17 December 1974.
5 RC155, 157(1).
6 Court of Session Rules in form 2 set out forms of conclusion.

DIVORCE

Crave/Conclusion

To grant decree of divorce of the defender from the pursuer in respect that the marriage has broken down irretrievably by reason of (the defender's adultery or the defender's behaviour or the defender's desertion of the pursuer or non-cohabitation for two years or more and the defender's consent to decree of divorce or non-cohabitation for five years or more).

There is no reason in principle why divorce should not be sought on more than one ground. But it would be unusual to do so and in most cases would be an unnecessary complication. But if in a defended action there was some doubt as to whether a particular ground could be proved it may be that an alternative ground of divorce should be pleaded eg adultery as an alternative to unreasonable behaviour as was done in *White v White* 1990 GWD 12-612.

Averments

Adultery[1] After stating when the parties last lived together and had marital relations the averments should specify the person with whom, the place(s) where and the dates on which or periods within which adultery is alleged to have been committed; the date and place of any admission of adultery and the person to whom it was admitted, eg 'enquiry agents acting on behalf of the pursuer'. Alternatively some other basis for the proof of adultery may be averred, eg non-paternity of a child born to the defender: pursuer abroad between (dates)—child born to defender on (date)—pursuer is not and could not be the father or, eg the communication of a sexually transmitted disease by the defender to the pursuer. The marriage has broken down irretrievably by reason of the defender's adultery. There is no prospect of a reconciliation. The pursuer is entitled to divorce.

It is not necessary to negative lenocinium (connivance) nor condonation, though if there has been either adultery will not have been established[2]. There will not be condonation where, in the knowledge that adultery has been committed there has been continuation of or a resumption of cohabitation for a period or periods (in total) of not more than three months[3]. But if that cohabitation has been with the encouragement of the court it is not to be taken into account[4]. Any periods during which there was a resumption of cohabitation with a view to a reconciliation should be averred (see below).

Behaviour The test is that the defender has at any time behaved (whether or not as a result of mental abnormality and whether such behaviour has been active or passive) in such a way that the pursuer cannot reasonably be expected to cohabit with the defender[5]. For examples see the specimen summons and initial writ above. Unreasonable behaviour may be established by evidence

1 Divorce (Scotland) Act 1976, s 1(2)(a).
2 Ibid, s 1(3).
3 Ibid, s 2(2).
4 Ibid, s 2(1).
5 Divorce (Scotland) Act 1976, s 1(2)(b).

of associations with others falling short of adultery[1], or unfounded allegations of adultery[2]. Date of final separation should be averred—pursuer and defender have neither lived together nor had marital relations since then—dates and places when particular events took place should be specified, eg assaults. Less detailed specification is required of a course of conduct. Other relevant matters may include the effect on pursuer's health and the reason why the pursuer left the defender. There should be an averment that there is no prospect of a reconciliation, that the marriage has broken down irretrievably and that the pursuer is entitled to divorce.

Resumption of cohabitation (divorce based on desertion) Desertion may be established if there has been no cohabitation for two years following the desertion. But if thereafter there has been cohabitation for more than three months, that basis of divorce will not be established[3].

Desertion Defender left pursuer on (date) of his own free will—no warning—pursuer gave him no reasonable cause to do so—has not returned (minimum is a continuous period of two years after separation)—has made no offer to resume cohabitation—or made an offer on (date)—offer not genuine or not reasonable (state reason why not)[4]—no prospect of a reconciliation—marriage has broken down irretrievably—pursuer entitled to divorce.

Resumption of cohabitation (divorces based on non-cohabitation) Any periods of resumption of cohabitation should be averred[5]. The periods of non-cohabitation do not cease to be 'continuous' if there has been a resumption of cohabitation unless that has been for a period or periods amounting in all to more than six months. That total could be extended where there has been a resumption of cohabitation with the encouragement of the court[6]. Such period(s) of cohabitation do not interrupt the two or five year periods for the purposes of a divorce based on non-cohabitation, but they do not count as part of the period of non-cohabitation[7].

Two years' separation and the defender's consent[8] Parties last lived together on (date)—no cohabitation since then (minimum is a continuous period of two years after the date of the marriage and immediately preceding the bringing of the action)—defender consents to divorce—no prospect of a reconciliation—marriage has broken down irretrievably—pursuer entitled to divorce. As to the situation where there has been a resumption of cohabitation see above.

Five years' separation[9] Parties last lived together on (date)—no cohabitation since then (minimum is a continuous period of five years after the date of the marriage and immediately preceding the bringing of the action)—no prospect

1 *Stewart v Stewart* 1987 SLT (Sh Ct) 48.
2 *MacLeod v MacLeod* 1990 GWD 14–767.
3 Divorce (Scotland) Act 1976, s 2(3).
4 On what is reasonable see *Burnett v Burnett* 1958 SC 1.
5 *Edmond v Edmond* 1971 SLT (Notes) 8.
6 Ibid, s 2(1).
7 Ibid, s 2(4).
8 Ibid, s 1(2)(d).
9 Ibid, s.1(2)(e).

of a reconciliation—marriage has broken down irretrievably—pursuer entitled to divorce. As to the situation where there has been a resumption of cohabitation see above under desertion.

Plea in law for divorce

The marriage between the pursuer and the defender having broken down irretrievably as condescended upon, decree of divorce should be granted as craved/concluded for.

Mental disorder

Where the defender is undergoing treatment for mental disorder in a hospital and divorce is sought on the basis of non-cohabitation, either with or without his consent, averments of the financial position of the pursuer and of any dependent children and, as far as possible of the defender must be made. There must also be averments of the financial arrangements proposed or sought on divorce[1]. Although there is no comparable rule in the sheriff court it is suggested that the requirements of the Court of Session rule should be met in a sheriff court initial writ.

Orders for financial provision

PERIODICAL ALLOWANCE AND CAPITAL SUM

Order

To grant decree for payment by the defender to the pursuer of a capital sum of £   with interest thereon at the rate of (15) per cent per annum from the date of the decree to follow hereon until payment; and (2) a periodical allowance of £   per week (month) payable for a period of three years from the date of decree of divorce or for such shorter period as to the court shall seem proper (or where 'serious financial hardship' is alleged: until, eg, the remarriage or death of the pursuer) with interest at the rate of 15 per cent per annum on each payment from the due date until payment[2]. (The order for payment of a capital sum may be framed so as to provide for payment of instalments, eg so much on divorce and the rest a year later.)

In a Court of Session summons it is not necessary to conclude for payment of interest. RC 66 provides for specific rates of interest and those rates of interest are exigible on every such decree without any requirement that the rate be specified in the interlocutor. The rate of interest varies from time to time[3].

Averments

Capital Sum On (the date when the parties ceased to cohabit (on which date the matrimonial property and its value becomes 'frozen')) the pursuer owned the following (capital) assets with the following values—as at that date defender owned the following (capital) assets with the following values—extent to which

---

1 RC 157(2).
2 See Family Law (Scotland) Act 1985, ss 8(1)(b), 9(1)(d) and 13(2) and (3). For comment on the duration of orders for periodical allowance see chapter 4.
3 It is currently 15 per cent in terms of RC 66 and the Sheriff Courts (Scotland) Extracts Act 1892 as amended by AS (Interest on Sheriff Court Decrees or Extracts) 1975, SI 1975/948.

assets of pursuer and defender were acquired in contemplation of or since the marriage—which assets acquired through gift or succession or otherwise which are not matrimonial property—which of the principles in sections 9 to 11 of the Family Law (Scotland) Act 1985 the pursuer relies on—the facts which support the application of that or these principles should be averred—applying that or these principles the order sought by way of a capital sum/periodical allowance is justified by the said principles and reasonable having regard to the resources of the parties.

Periodical Allowance Set out the sources and amounts of both parties' net income and major expenditure commitments—aver reasons for seeking a periodical allowance eg that payment of a capital sum or transfer of property would not satisfy the requirements of s 8(2) of the 1985 Act[1]—specify which of the principles set out in s 9(1)(c), (d) or (e) are relied on and why[2]—facts which support the making of the periodical allowance sought for the period specified in the crave or conclusion, including serious financial hardship where applicable—the making of an order for that amount and that period is justified by the said principles and reasonable having regard to the resources of the parties. (An application for periodical allowance must be supported by averments, pleas in law and, if necessary, proof of circumstances which would justify such an award[3].)

Pleas in law

The capital sum sued for being justified and reasonable in the circumstances condescended upon decree therefor should be granted as craved/concluded for.

The sum sued for as periodical allowance being justified and reasonable as condescended upon decree therefor should be granted as craved/concluded for.

TRANSFER OF PROPERTY

Order

To grant decree for the transfer from the defender to the pursuer of the whole right, title and interest of the defender in the following property[4]: (here specify the property).

Averments

These should be adapted from those appropriate to a claim for a capital sum above. This order will almost certainly be sought in conjunction with or as an alternative to an order for a capital sum. This is one way in which the court can give practical effect to the provisions of the Family Law (Scotland) Act 1985. For example it can order the transfer of the matrimonial home or of one party's share in it in order to satisfy the sum which might otherwise have been awarded. The averments will vary with the circumstances. It has to be justified by the principles set out in sections 9 to 11 of the 1985 Act.

1 Cf Family Law (Scotland) Act 1985, s 13(2).
2 Ibid, s 13(2)(a).
3 *Thirde v Thirde* 1987 SCLR 335.
4 Family Law (Scotland) Act 1985, s 8(1). The property is not restricted to moveable property nor to the matrimonial home. It could include life assurance policies.

Averments showing that it is so justified are necessary as is an averment that what is asked for is reasonable.

Plea in law

The order for the transfer of property being justified and reasonable as condescended upon decree therefor should be granted as craved/concluded for.

PREVENTING THE ALIENATION OF ASSETS AND RECOVERING THEM

Orders

To set aside the (specify the transaction) entered into by the defender in favour of (name and address) whereby the defender transferred to him/her/them (specify property transferred); (or to make such other order as the court may consider appropriate).

To vary the (specify the transaction) entered into by the defender in favour of (name and address) by (specify the variation sought): or to make such other order as the court thinks fit.

To interdict the defender from effecting any transfer of property owned by him or in which he has an interest which would be likely to affect the claim by the pursuer for financial provision and in particular (specify contemplated transactions, eg the gift of the matrimonial home and the transfer of his controlling interest in the Bass Rock Guano Co PLC to Miss Flossie MacSporran for less than their true value); and for interim interdict.

Averments

When and where transaction(s) entered into—nature of the transaction—particular transaction(s) now contemplated—not for full value—actings showing intention of defender—intention was or at least effect was or is likely to be that the claim by the pursuer will be defeated in whole or in part—detail any variation sought—setting aside/varying the transaction is just and reasonable—pursuer reasonably apprehensive that defender will act to her prejudice in manner averred—interdict necessary.

Pleas in law

1. The said transactions entered into by the defender having the effect or being likely to have the effect of defeating the claim by the pursuer in whole or in part for an order for financial provision as condescended upon decree should be granted in terms of the   and   crave(s)/conclusion(s).

2. The pursuer being reasonably apprehensive that the defender will act to her detriment as condescended upon interdict and interim interdict should be granted as craved/concluded for.

In the Court of Session, in any cause containing a conclusion or crave for interdict, a Division of the Inner House or the Lord Ordinary may, on the motion of any party, grant interim interdict.[1] That would suggest that it is not necessary to have an express conclusion or crave for interim interdict in order to obtain an interim order. Since the Court of Session Act refers

---

1 Court of Session Act 1988, s 47(1).

to a crave it would appear that this provision also applies to a sheriff court action, eg when it is in the Court of Session on appeal. In practice the absence of the words 'and for interim interdict' is usually presumed to be deliberate in the sheriff court and it will be assumed that an interim order is not sought. But in the Court of Session the assumption is that the greater includes the less and that such words are unnecessary.

The Family Law (Scotland) Act 1985, s 14(2) sets out various incidental orders which may be made before, on or after granting decree of divorce.[1] They include orders regulating the occupation of the matrimonial home and its furniture and plenishings as well as exclusion orders. The form in which such orders will be sought will vary with the circumstances of the case. Styles for such orders may be adapted from the Matrimonial Homes Act orders set out below.

INTERIM ALIMENT FOR PURSUER

Order

To grant decree for payment by the defender to the pursuer of interim aliment at the rate of £   per week/month payable weekly/monthly and in advance with interest at the rate of (15) per cent per annum on each payment from the due date until payment.

In a Court of Session summons it is not necessary to conclude for payment of interest. RC 66 provides for specific rates of interest and those rates of interest are exigible on every such decree without any requirement that the rate be specified in the interlocutor. The rate of interest varies from time to time.[2]

Averments

Defender obliged to aliment the pursuer[3]—income and major outgoings of both parties—the needs of the pursuer—sum sued for is reasonable.

Plea in Law

The sum sued for as interim aliment for the pursuer being reasonable as condescended upon decree therefor should be granted as craved/concluded for.

ORDER TO GIVE DETAILS OF RESOURCES

Order

To ordain the defender/pursuer to provide details of his/her capital assets, income and other resources to the pursuer/defender (or by lodging the same in process) and that within fourteen days or such other period as to the court may consider appropriate.

1   Family Law (Scotland) Act 1985, ss 14(1) and 8(1) and see chapter 4.
2   It is currently 15 per cent in terms of RC 66 and the Sheriff Courts (Scotland) Extracts Act 1892 as amended by AS (Interest on Sheriff Court Decrees or Extracts) 1975, SI 1975/948.
3   Family Law (Scotland) Act 1985, ss 1 and 6.

Averments

Defender/pursuer has refused to provide details of his/her resources—such information essential to enable divorce action pending in (specify court) to be concluded—unsuccessful requests made for such information—refusal unwarranted—order sought in terms of Family Law (Scotland) Act 1985, s 20—reasonable that it should be granted.

Plea in law

The defender/pursuer having unwarrantably failed to provide the details sought as condescended upon decree should be granted as craved/concluded for.

Children

CUSTODY

Order

To find the pursuer entitled to custody of [name]
and   [name] the children of the marriage and [name] the child of the pursuer accepted as a child of the marriage under the age of eighteen; and for interim custody.[1]

Averments

See specimen initial writ, supra—test is that it is in the best interests of the child that he should be in the custody of that party.
Averring other proceedings Where a custody order is applied for any party to the action must aver particulars of any other proceedings known to him (whether in Scotland or elsewhere and whether concluded or not) which relate to the child in respect of whom the custody order is sought[2].

Plea in law

It being in the best interests of the said children that they should be in the custody of the pursuer, decree of custody should be granted as craved/ concluded for.

ALIMENT FOR CHILDREN

Order

To ordain the defender to pay to the pursuer the sum of £   per (week/month/quarter) as aliment for each of [name] and [name] the children of the marriage (weekly/monthly/quarterly) in advance so long as each child is in the custody of the pursuer and under the age of eighteen years with interest

---

1 See *Wiseman v Wiseman* 1989 SCLR 757; Court of Session Rules, r 170B(8) and form 2 require the addition of 'and for leave to any party claiming an interest to apply to the court thereanent until (insert the date when the youngest child will attain sixteen years of age).' There is no comparable requirement in a sheriff court case; see OCR 129(4).
2 RC 170B(11); OCR 132C.

on each payment at the rate of (15) per cent per annum from the due date until payment; and for interim aliment.

or

To find that each of the said children is entitled payment by the defender of aliment at the rate of £   per week/month; and to ordain the defender to pay said sum weekly/monthly and in advance in respect of each child to the pursuer as tutrix and (for the purpose of receipt only) curatrix of the said children and that for as long as the children are in her custody and under the age of eighteen years, with interest on each payment at the rate of (15) per cent per annum on each weekly payment from the date the same falls due until payment; and for interim aliment.

In recent years it has been the practice to seek an order in terms of the second of these styles. The reason for the adoption of that form of order was to reduce the incidence of taxation[1]. Under the current rules for the taxation of maintenance payments, it is thought that that form is no longer necessary. See chapter 4 under 'Taxation of maintenance payments.'

Averments

Pursuer unemployed/employed as a (specify employment)—her income per week/month—her major outgoings—defender employed as a (specify employment)—his income from all sources and major outgoings—extent to which the pursuer and the defender fulfil their obligation to aliment the children—any special expenditure required for the children eg as result of disability—sum sued for reasonable.

Plea in law

The defender being liable to aliment the said children of the marriage and the sum sued for being reasonable decree for aliment should be granted as craved/concluded for.

ACCESS

Order

To grant decree for access to [name] and [name] the children of the marriage under sixteen years of age (specify access sought eg every second Saturday between 10am and 6pm and for residential access during the said children's school holidays for one week at each of Christmas and Easter and for two weeks in the summer) or for access for such other periods as to the court may consider appropriate.

Averments

Access unwarrantably refused or restricted by defender—refusal not in best interests of children—pursuer had access every (week between [date] and [date])—no reason for access to be stopped or restricted—pursuer has a good relationship with children—pursuer would make satisfactory arrangements for children while he has access—access sought is reasonable—such access in best interests of the children

1   *Huggins v Huggins* 1981 SLT 179; *Finnie v Finnie* 1984 SLT 439.

Plea in law

It being in the best interests of the said child that the pursuer should have access to him and the access sought being reasonable an order for access should be granted as craved/concluded for

PREVENTING REMOVAL OF CHILDREN

Order

To interdict the defender from removing or attempting to remove (said) children (a) from the care of the pursuer (other than in connection with such periods of access as may be agreed between the pursuer and the defender or ordered by the court)[1] and, (b) from the United Kingdom (or from Scotland) or from (a specified part of the United Kingdom); and for interim interdict.

Averments

Specify threats written or oral made to remove the children with dates and places as appropriate and any threats or attempts successful or otherwise made to remove the children from the pursuer or furth of Scotland or the United Kingdom or the part thereof in respect of which the interdict is sought— children upset by such attempts—removal not in best interests of children— fear of pursuer and of children of such removal—reasonable apprehension that defender will attempt to remove children if interdict not granted. Application is made in terms of Family Law Act 1986, s 35(3).

Plea in law

The pursuer having reasonable grounds to apprehend that the defender will attempt to remove the said children from her care as condescended upon interdict and interim interdict should be granted as craved/concluded for.

DELIVERY OF CHILDREN

Order

To ordain the defender to deliver (name child) the child of the marriage under sixteen years to the pursuer and, failing his doing so within such period as the court may appoint, to grant warrant to officers of court to search for the said child, take him into their possession and deliver him to the pursuer.[2]

Averments

If pursuer already awarded custody specify court and date of award—defender removed child from care of pursuer (specify where and when)—attempts to get defender to return child—refusal of defender unreasonable—in best interests of child that he be returned to pursuer. Application is made in terms of Family Law Act 1986, s 17.

---

1 The words in brackets are optional but, it is submitted, should be included if access is taking place or may take place.
2 The order should not refer to constables—cf *Caldwell v Caldwell* 1983 SLT 610.

Plea in law

It being in the best interests of the said child that he be in the custody/returned to the custody of the pursuer decree of delivery should be granted as craved/concluded for.

INTERDICT

MOLESTATION

Order

To interdict the defender from molesting the pursuer by abusing her verbally, by putting her into a state of fear and alarm or distress, and by using violence towards her; and for interim interdict and for a power of arrest.[1]

Averments

In a divorce based on unreasonable behaviour they will be relevant to the divorce as well as to interdict—otherwise specify the behaviour complained of with the dates on which and the places at which incidents ocurred with particular reference to the most recent—effect on health of pursuer—her fear of defender—pursuer reasonably apprehends that defender's conduct will continue unless interdict granted.

Plea in law

The pursuer having reasonable grounds to apprehend that the defender will act/continue to act towards her in the manner condescended upon interdict and interim interdict should be granted as craved/concluded for.

Orders relating to the matrimonial home

EXCLUSION ORDER AND ORDERS CONSEQUENTIAL TO IT

Orders

To grant an exclusion order suspending the occupancy rights of the defender in (address of matrimonial home); and for such an order ad interim.

To grant warrant for the summary ejection of the defender from (address of matrimonial home).

To interdict the defender from entering (address of matrimonial home) without the express permission of the pursuer.

To interdict the defender or anyone acting on his behalf or under his instructions, from removing, except with the written consent of the pursuer or by further order of court, any furniture and plenishings in (address of matrimonial home)[2]. (Either party may apply to have these orders made subject to such terms and conditions as the court may prescribe[3].)

1 This is the form approved in *Murdoch v Murdoch* 1973 SLT (Notes) 13. Any variation on this form should be 'sharply defined and related specifically to the particular risks which justify its grant.' Cf *McKenna v McKenna* 1984 SLT (Sh Ct) 92.
2 If an exclusion order is made the court is required to make orders in the terms set out above, if so requested, unless the defender satisfies the court that they are unnecessary: Matrimonial Homes (Family Protection) (Scotland) Act 1981, s 4(4).
3 Ibid, s 5(5)(c).

To interdict the defender from entering or remaining within (a specified area in the vicinity of the matrimonial home, eg: 100 metres of (address of matrimonial home))[1].

Averments

House at (address) presently occupied by pursuer and defender is a matrimonial home within the meaning of the Matrimonial Homes (Family Protection) (Scotland) Act 1981—conduct of defender towards pursuer, particularly recent conduct—defender lingering in vicinity of home—threatened future behaviour towards pursuer or, eg to remove furniture etc—pursuer reasonably apprehensive that his conduct will continue—conduct has been or would be injurious to the health of the pursuer and/or any children of the marriage in her custody—interdict not sufficient (explain why)—exclusion order necessary—(matrimonial home is not part of an agricultural holding nor a tied house—only need be averred when that is a likely but unfounded defence)—defender refuses to leave the matrimonial home—pursuer seeks exclusion order, ejection of defender, interdict against defender entering the home, prohibition of removal of the furniture and plenishings therefrom and from remaining in the vicinity of the home. These orders are necessary ad interim and are sought in terms of 1981 Act, s 4.

Pleas in law

The pursuer having reasonable grounds to apprehend that the defender will continue to act towards her in the manner condescended upon to the injury of her health (and/or that of her children) an exclusion order and the ancillary orders referred to in craves/conclusions (numbers) should be granted as craved/concluded for and should be granted ad interim.

RIGHTS OF OCCUPANCY OF MATRIMONIAL HOME

Orders

To grant declarator that the pursuer is entitled to occupy (address of matrimonial home).

Additional orders and interim orders may be required in terms of the 1981 Act, ss 3(1)(b), (c), (d) and (e). The form of such orders will depend on the circumstances of each case[2].

To ordain the defender to permit the pursuer to enter and occupy the said property/that part of said property consisting of (specify); (to ordain the defender to provide the pursuer with a key to the said property and that within three days or such other period as to the court shall seem proper); to grant to the pursuer the possession and use of those items of furniture and plenishings situated within the said property and listed in the schedule hereto; and for such orders ad interim.

Averments

Address of the home—who owns the home—status of pursuer in regard to it, eg joint heritable proprietor, sole or joint tenant or wife of sole tenant/

---

1 This remedy is discretionary when an exclusion order is granted: ibid, s 4(5)(a).
2 See, eg, *Bell v Bell* 1982 SLT 518; *Brown v Brown* 1985 SLT 376.

heritable proprietor—extent of pursuer's occupation of it (with dates)—defender's occupation of it (with dates)—pursuer an entitled/non-entitled spouse—it is a matrimonial home in terms of the Act—pursuer entitled to declarator—defender locked pursuer out of house and changed the locks—pursuer needs a key—pursuer requires to occupy main part of house with children—cannot continue in battered wives refuge—needs furniture etc to provide a home for children. Orders are sought in terms of the Matrimonial Homes (Family Protection) (Scotland) Act 1981, s 3.

Pleas in law

1. The said house being a matrimonial home as condescended upon the pursuer is entitled to decree of declarator as (first) craved/concluded for.
2. In the circumstances it being just and reasonable that the (other orders craved/concluded for—refer to crave/conclusion eg 'fourth craved') should be granted decree therefor should be granted as craved/concluded for.

EXPENSES

Order

For the expenses of the cause[1].

WARRANTS FOR ARRESTMENT ON THE DEPENDENCE AND INTIMATION[2]

Warrants for arrestment

It is not competent to arrest any earnings or any pension on the dependence of the action[3]. In the craves of an initial writ and in a summons in an action of divorce in the Court of Session it is necessary to apply for warrants in certain circumstances. The form of such warrants is set out below. The words 'to grant' would appear in a sheriff court writ but not in a Court of Session summons.

Warrant for arrestment on the dependence of the action. Such a warrant can be granted in the Court of Session or in the sheriff court in connection with an action for aliment or a claim for financial provision[4]. The form of warrant sought is: '(To grant) warrant for arrestment on the dependence.'

Warrant for intimation

In the Court of Session the court may in any action order intimation to be made to such person as it thinks fit[5]. Where adultery is alleged the form of warrant will be:

'(To grant) warrant to intimate to (name and address) as a person with whom the defender is alleged to have committed adultery'[6].

Where incest or rape is alleged there is no intimation[7]. Where an improper relationship such as sodomy or homosexuality, is alleged the court has a discretion as to intimation[8]. The pursuer in a sheriff court action must enrol a motion

1 This should be included in every case in which expenses will or may be asked for. If it is not, the court is unlikely to grant expenses unless the writ is amended to include it. There does not need to be a plea in law as regards expenses.
2 See RC155 and forms 16 to 19; OCR 11A, 130 and forms H1 to H5.
3 Law Reform (Miscellaneous Provisions) (Scotland) Act 1966, s 1.
4 Family Law (Scotland) Act 1985, s 19(1)(b).
5 RC 164.
6 RC 155(1); OCR 130(1)(a).
7 RC 155(2); OCR 130(1)(c).
8 RC 162(1); OCR 130(2)(a).

for intimation immediately after expiry of the period of notice. The court must then decide whether to order intimation or to dispense with intimation. But in the Court of Session such a motion should be enrolled immediately after the calling of the summons[1]. Where the court dispenses with intimation it may order that the name of the person be deleted from the condescendence[2].

'(To grant) warrant to intimate to (name and address) as the local authority/ as the body having the care of (name of child) a child of the marriage'[3].

'(To grant) warrant to intimate to (name and address) as (the local authority having care of (name and address of child) *or* (a person who is liable to maintain (name and address of child) *or* (the person who in fact has parental rights of (name and address of child)'[4].

'(To grant) warrant to intimate to (name and address of polygamous wife) as an additional spouse of the pursuer/defender'[5].

'(To grant) warrant to intimate to (name and address) as (the person in whose favour the transfer of (or transaction involving) property referred to in the condescendence of this Summons/Initial Writ was made (or is to be made) or (a person having an interest in the transfer of (or transaction involving) property referred to in the condescendence of this summons/initial writ'[6].

Where the address of the defender is unknown or he suffers from a mental disorder within the meaning of the Mental Health (Scotland) Act 1984:
'(To grant) warrant to intimate to AB and CB as the children of the marriage[7], to Mrs DB as (eg) the mother and one of the next of kin of the defender and to XY the *curator bonis* of the defender'[8].

Intimation may be ordered when the court proposes to make an order under section 10 or has made an order for supervision of a child under section 12 of the Matrimonial Proceedings (Children) Act 1958. However in a Court of Session action such intimation is likely to be made only when an order under either section 10 or section 12 of the 1958 Act has been made. In that event the interlocutor making the order and not the summons will be intimated. The Court of Session summons would normally be intimated if there was a care order in force.

'(To grant) warrant to intimate to (name and address) as the landlord of or as a party permitting the occupation of the (house/flat ie the matrimonial home) at address.'[9]

1 RC 162(1).
2 RC 162(3); OCR 130(3).
3 RC 170B(6); OCR 130(4).
4 A child for this purpose includes a child of the marriage or of one party (including an illegitimate or adopted child) accepted as a child of the marriage: RC 170B(6); OCR 130(3)(b).
5 RC 155(5); OCR 130(5).
6 RC 170D(c); OCR 130(9).
7 All the children over twelve in the case of girls and over fourteen in the case of boys should receive intimation: RC 155(3); OCR 11A(1).
8 If any. The writ should contain averments that the defender is suffering from a mental disorder or has a curator bonis when that is the case.
9 RC 188D(7); AS (Applications under the Matrimonial Homes (Family Protection) (Scotland) Act 1981) 1982 para 3.

CHAPTER 7

RAISING THE ACTION

The choice of court in which to raise the action and jurisdiction are more particularly discussed in chapter 6. In brief: to establish jurisdiction in the Court of Session one of the parties must be domiciled in Scotland on the date when the action commenced or have been habitually resident in Scotland throughout the period of one year ending on that date[1]. To raise an action in a particular sheriff court, it is necessary also to establish that:

(1) one of the parties was resident in the sheriffdom for forty days ending on that date, or

(2) had been resident in the sheriffdom for not less than forty days ending not more than forty days before the said date and has no known residence in Scotland at that date[2].

The common practice where an action is to be raised in the sheriff court is to raise it in the sheriff court district in which the pursuer has resided for the requisite period.

MENTAL CAPACITY OF THE PARTIES

Before a pursuer can raise an action of divorce, she must have the mental capacity to sue. A person who is insane cannot competently sue for divorce[3]. However, where the pursuer suffers from mental disorder falling short of insanity she can sue, at least when she can understand the meaning, effect and consequences of divorce[4]. The defender may plead that the pursuer is barred from raising the action on the ground of her incapacity which renders her incapable of giving instructions. The court may order a preliminary proof on this matter but the defender may find it difficult to satisfy the court that the action should not be permitted to proceed[5]. It appears to be undecided whether, assuming that a divorce would be clearly in the interests of the pursuer, the court would appoint a *curator ad litem* with power to conduct such an action on her behalf.

An action may be raised against a defender who does not have the mental capacity to defend it. Where it appears to the court that he is suffering from mental disorder a *curator ad litem* is appointed by the court.

1 Domicile and Matrimonial Proceedings Act 1973, s 7(2) but see also s 7(5).
2 See *McNeill v McNeill* 1960 SC 30.
3 *Thomson v Thomson* (1887) 14 R 634.
4 *Gibson v Gibson* 1970 SLT (Notes) 60.
5 *AB v CB* 1937 SC 408 at 418.

SIMPLIFIED PROCEDURE

Simplified procedure is available in the Court of Session and the sheriff court. In the former it is governed by Rules of Court 170E to 170L and forms 19A to 19E; in the latter by Ordinary Cause Rules 135 to 143 and forms SDA1 to SDA7. Prescribed forms rather than a summons or initial writ are used. Printed copies of these forms may be obtained from the Court of Session, sheriff clerks' offices and usually from citizens advice bureaux. The appropriate form is completed and signed by the applicant.

Cases to which simplified procedure applies

The procedure may only be used where:

(1) the divorce sought is based on two years' non-cohabitation and the defender consents to divorce or on five years' non-cohabitation;
(2) no other proceedings are pending in any other court which could have the effect of bringing the marriage to an end;
(3) there are no children of the marriage under sixteen;
(4) neither party seeks any financial provision on divorce; and
(5) neither party suffers from mental disorder[1].

If any of these criteria cease to apply at any time before the action of divorce is disposed of the application will be treated as abandoned in the Court of Session and will be dismissed in the sheriff court[2]. It is the duty of an applicant or his solicitor to bring such a change of circumstances to the attention of the court.

Two year case

In a two year case the applicant first completes part 1 of form 19A/SDA1. Part 2 of form 19A/SDA1, is a consent form which requires to be completed by the respondent. Part 3 of that form is an affidavit which must be completed by the applicant and be sworn before a justice of the peace, notary public or commissioner of oaths or other duly authorised person. After the applicant has completed part 1 of the application, she should send the application and, if it is a sheriff court application, a copy of form SDA3 to the respondent. Form SDA3 *inter alia* asks the defender to check that part 1 is correctly completed. There appears to be no form equivalent to form SDA3 in the Court of Session. When the consent is returned to her the applicant should take the whole of form 19A/SDA 1 to a justice of the peace, notary public, commissioner of oaths or other duly authorised person to have the affidavit completed and sworn.

Five year case

The applicant completes form 19B/SDA2. If the address of the respondent is unknown, intimation will have to be made by the court to every child of the marriage and one of the next of kin of the respondent over the age of

---

1 RC 170E(2); OCR 135(2). As to the definition of 'mental disorder' see section 1 of the Mental Health (Scotland) Act 1984.
2 RC 170E(3); OCR 135(3).

puberty. In that event the forms require their names and addresses and, in the case of children of the marriage, their dates of birth.

Lodging the application

The whole application so completed is lodged with the Principal Clerk of Session or the appropriate sheriff clerk, along with an extract of the marriage certificate and the correct fee. It may be posted or delivered by hand[1].

Although the practice about to be described is not universally required in an action of divorce using the simplified procedure, it is thought that if it is appropriate in other actions of divorce, it is also appropriate in an action using the simplified procedure. In other actions of divorce the court takes precautions to prevent decree of divorce being granted to parties who are already divorced. This can happen where parties have lost contact with one another[2]. The precautions are taken where the defender's address is unknown. In that event a letter should be lodged in court from the General Register Office, New Register House, Edinburgh. That letter will state whether as a result of a search any trace has been found of a divorce relating to the parties. In order to carry out such a search the names of the parties and the date and place of the marriage should be provided. The letter should be dated within one month of the application being lodged[3]. Alternatively an up to date marriage certificate should be lodged with the application.

Exemption from court fees

It is possible for applicants of limited means to obtain exemption from paying court fees by completing a form obtainable from the Court of Session or from sheriff clerks' offices.

Legal aid

Legal aid is not available in connection with a simplified divorce but free legal advice and assistance may be although not for the purpose of completing the form.

Citation

The Principal Clerk of Session or his authorised officer or the sheriff clerk, as the case may be, carry out citation of the respondent and intimate any document (in five year cases in the sheriff court in accordance with form SDA4)[4]. The periods of notice are the same as in ordinary actions and are set out in Rule of Court 158 and 72 and Ordinary Cause Rule 138(6)—21 days when the respondent is resident or has a place of business within Europe; 42 days when the addressee is resident or has a place of business outside Europe, but in a Court of Session action where there has been personal service on a respondent outside Europe in accordance with the provisions of rule 74B(1)(d) or (e) the period is twenty-one days after the date of execution of service.

1 RC 170G; OCR 137.
2 The writer has seen the pleasure on the face of a lady who discovered, while in the witness box and for the first time, that she had already been divorced.
3 See Court of Session Practice Note, 10 March 1966, 1984 SLT (News) 100.
4 RC 170I; OCR 139(1).

If a person who has been cited or to whom intimation has been made wishes to challenge the jurisdiction of the court or to oppose the granting of an application under the simplified procedure, he may write a letter to the court[1]. In that event the application will be dismissed by the court unless the opposition is frivolous. Intimation of dismissal will be sent to all parties by the sheriff clerk[2]. If an application is dismissed an action of divorce in the usual form may be raised instead. Dismissal occurs in practice when, for example, the respondent intimates that she wishes to make a financial claim or where it appears that the applicant and respondent continue to live in the same house and the court is not satisfied that cohabitation has ceased.

Extract

Extract of a decree granted in a simplified divorce by the Court of Session is granted immediately[3]. In the sheriff court extract is issued not less than fourteen days after decree has been granted[4].

Appeal

In the sheriff court an appeal may be made by the respondent within fourteen days of the grant of decree of divorce[5]. This is done by letter to the court giving reasons for the appeal[6]. Rule 142 does not require the respondent to specify whether the appeal is to the Sheriff Principal or to the Court of Session, but that should be done. It is thought that the Ordinary Cause Rules dealing with appeals (OCR 91 to 96) would apply to such an appeal so far as not inconsistent with rule 142. In the Court of Session the period for appeal is twenty-one days[7]. The normal rules for a reclaiming motion would apply.

Applications after a simplified divorce has been granted

After divorce has been granted either party to a simplified divorce may lodge a minute in those proceedings specifying that there has been a material change of circumstances and the nature of such change and asking the court to make the order sought[8]. But it may be necessary to proceed by way of an initial writ in a sheriff court action[9]. The orders which may be sought are likely to relate to those financial matters which the court has power to make subsequent to divorce. There must be appropriate averments to warrant the making of the order sought particularly when periodical allowance is sought for the first time. These should include reference to the particular principles set out in the Family Law (Scotland) Act 1985, ss 9–11 on which reliance is to be placed[10].

---

1 RC 170J (which appears to be restricted to those to whom intimation has been made, ie not respondents); OCR 140(1).
2 OCR 140(3); there appears to be no Court of Session equivalent.
3 RC 170K.
4 OCR 141(2).
5 OCR 142.
6 *Colville v Colville* 1988 SLT (Sh Ct) 23.
7 RC 264(a).
8 RC 170L; OCR 143.
9 *Murray v Murray* 1990 SCLR 226 (application for periodical allowance).
10 *Murray*, supra.

RECOVERY OF DOCUMENTS BEFORE AN ACTION IS RAISED

Application for commission and diligence in a sheriff court action may be made at any time after tabling[1], but the sheriff may order production of documents at any stage of the cause[2]. But application may be made for commission and diligence for the recovery of documents before or after the calling of a summons in a Court of Session action[3]. Where such application is made before calling the application is made by letter addressed to the Deputy Principal Clerk of Session, enclosing a copy of the specification of documents in respect of which commission and diligence is sought. The letter must at the same time be intimated to the other party and, if necessary, to the Lord Advocate. The application is put before a Lord Ordinary in chambers at a time which will have been intimated to the parties. The solicitor for the applicant must appear and have with him the principal copy of the summons duly signetted. For more detailed discussion of the procedure reference should be made to works on court practice: eg MacLaren, *Court of Session Practice* pp 1058 et seq; Maxwell *The Practice of the Court of Session* pp 281 et seq; Macphail *Sheriff Court Practice* 15-49 et seq.

APPLICATIONS FOR AN ORDER UNDER THE ADMINISTRATION OF JUSTICE (SCOTLAND) ACT 1972, s 1

It is competent to obtain orders inter alia for the inspection, photographing, preservation, custody and detention of documents and other property prior or subsequent to the raising of the action in terms of the Administration of Justice (Scotland) Act 1972, s 1. For the procedure in the Court of Session, which is similar to the above, see RC 95A. In the sheriff court application prior to the raising of the action must be made by initial writ[4]. Such an application may be granted on an ex parte basis provided that sufficient information is provided to the court to warrant the court concluding that (a) the documents or other property will be essential to the pursuer's case and if so, (b) there would be a risk that the documents or property would be destroyed if the application were to be intimated to the defender[5]. Application subsequent to calling in the Court of Session is made by motion lodged along with a detailed and articulate specification of the documents or other property in relation to which the order is sought. Copies of the specification are sent to the solicitor acting for the other party and to the haver and, where appropriate, the Lord Advocate. In the sheriff court application is made by minute specifying the order sought. The sheriff fixes a diet at which the application is heard and orders intimation to the other party to the proceedings and any person who appears to have an interest in the application.

1 OCR 78(3).
2 OCR 80.
3 RC 95(a).
4 OCR 84(4).
5 *British Phonograpphhic Industry v Cohen, Cohen, Kelly, Cohen & Cohen Ltd* 1983 SLT 137.

COMMENCING AN ORDINARY ACTION

The summons or initial writ in an action of divorce (which must contain an application for any necessary warrants for intimation, cf RC 155, 74) is lodged along with an extract marriage certificate and extract birth certificates relating to any children of the marriage and of children of one party to the marriage who have been accepted as children of the marriage[1] and with the appropriate fee. Abbreviated birth certificates are not accepted. When the whereabouts of the defender are unknown, there should also be lodged a letter from the General Register Office, New Register House, Edinburgh. stating that the parties are not already divorced. In order to search for a trace of any prior divorce the parties' names and the date and place of the marriage must be provided. The letter should be dated within one month of the lodging of the writ if the pursuer is not legally aided and within three months if legally aided[2]. An up to date marriage certificate may be accepted as an alternative.

Assuming that the writ is in order, in the Court of Session it will pass the Signet, and in either court a warrant of citation[3] and where appropriate, warrants for intimation or arrestment will be granted by the court.

Acceptance of service

Where the defender is willing to accept service himself or has a known solicitor, who is prepared to accept service on his behalf, the defender or his solicitor should endorse on the summons or initial writ a holograph docquet, which should be signed, in the following or similar terms: 'I ((or) On behalf of the within named defender I) accept service of the foregoing writ.' He may add: 'and dispense with the induc. period of notice' if appropriate. If he does, formal citation, with its attendant cost is avoided, and the inducae or period of notice, are deemed to expire on acceptance of service[4].

Citation in divorce actions (other than by simplified procedure)

Documents which are served on the defender along with the service copy summons/initial writ:
Two year non-cohabitation and defender consents; forms 3, 15A and 15E or (in the sheriff court) form C1, form S1 and form T [5].
Five year non-cohabitation: forms 3 and 15C or (in the sheriff court) form C1, form S3[6].

CITATION IN A COURT OF SESSION ACTION

Citation may be executed by post[7]. Only a messenger-at-arms or a solicitor entitled to practise in the Court of Session may carry out postal citation. It

---

1 OCR 3(9).
2 Court of Session Practice Note, 10 March 1966, 1984 SLT (News) 100. Strictly this is a Court of Session Practice Note but it should be followed in the sheriff court.
3 In the Court of Session the form of warrant is form 3: cf RC 159(3)(b); in the sheriff court form B1: cf OCR 4(3).
4 RC 74(b).
5 RC 161(1); OCR 131(2).
6 RC 161(3); OCR 131(4).
7 Citation Amendment (Scotland) Act 1882, s 3; RC 159(1)(c).

may be by recorded delivery[1], or by registered post[2]. If service is by recorded delivery it will be by first class post[3]. The envelope must contain the required notice on the face of it[4]. Citation by recorded delivery is the more commonly used method. The form used is form 3 along with the notices referred to in RC 161 if applicable[5]. Unless there are good reasons for not attempting postal citation, that method should be used. Courts will refuse to allow the greater cost of service by messenger-at-arms where that was not necessary[6].

Alternatively service may be personal in which event it will usually be carried out by a messenger-at-arms. Service of a Court of Session summons may be carried out by sheriff officer where there is no resident messenger-at-arms[7]. It is not personal service to leave a summons at the defender's house[8]. If the messenger-at-arms after due inquiry has reasonable grounds for believing that the defender is residing at a particular dwelling place service may be by leaving the citation in the hands of a resident or by depositing it in the dwelling place. Putting it in the lock hole does not comply with the last mentioned method[9]. If none of these methods (or the method referred to in RC 74B, which provides for citation and service furth of the United Kingdom) are successful, citation is to be made edictally on an induciae of twenty-one days[10].

In the Court of Session a summons which has passed the signet is warrant for service on the defender, for any competent diligence by way of inhibition or arrestment on the dependence and for any of the intimations referred to in RC 155, if any warrant for intimation, inhibition or arrestment has been applied for in the summons. RC 78(d) requires that all documents founded on in the summons shall be lodged with the summons for calling.

INDUCIAE

The induciae for the citation of a defender and for intimation to any person in respect of whom a warrant for intimation requires to be endorsed are to be in accordance with RC 72[11]. That rule provides that:

(1) for citation within Europe twenty-one days after the date of execution of service;

(2) where there has been personal citation outside Europe (by an huissier, other judicial officer or competent official in the country where the defender is, at the request of a messenger-at-arms, or personal citation by the pursuer or his agent) twenty-one days after the date of execution of service, and

(3) otherwise forty-two days after the date of execution of service.

1 Recorded Delivery Service Act 1962, s 1
2 Citation Amendment (Scotland) Act 1882, s 3.
3 RC 68A.
4 RC 159(3) and (4).
5 RC 159(3)(b). For rule 161, see below.
6 Citation Amendment (Scotland) Act 1882, s 6.
7 Execution of Diligence (Scotland) Act 1926, s 1.
8 *Hall v Hall* 1979 SLT (Sh Ct) 33.
9 *Docherty v Docherty* 1981 SLT (Notes) 24.
10 RC 159(2).
11 RC 158.

SHORTENING OR EXTENDING THE INDUCIAE

Application may be made by motion to a Lord Ordinary in chambers[1]. The Lord Ordinary may shorten the induciae where an interim order is applied for prior to service of the summons[2].

Citation in a sheriff court action

A warrant for citation, which may include a warrant for arrestment on the dependence and a warrant or warrants to intimate, may be signed by the sheriff clerk[3]. But where the warrant of citation appoints parties to be heard on a specified date in connection with interim craves the warrant may be signed by the sheriff clerk or the sheriff. It must be signed by the sheriff only if the period of notice is shortened or lengthened[4]. Citation will be refused, except in an emergency, if the relevant marriage and birth certificates are not lodged with the initial writ[5].

Citation is to be given in accordance with form C1. Such a form must be prefixed to a copy of the initial writ and warrant of citation[6].

If the defender is in Scotland the citation may be executed by post[7], or by officer of court[8]. Unless there are good reasons for not attempting postal citation, that method should be used. Courts will refuse to allow the greater cost of service by sheriff officer where that was not necessary[9]. Citation by post may be by recorded delivery first class[10], or by registered post[11] The former is the more commonly used.

If citation is by sheriff officer the service will be personal or, if the defender cannot be found, by means of a copy of the initial writ and any necessary accompanying documents being left in the hands of an inmate of or employee at the person's dwelling place or place of business. If that fails the officer of court may deposit these documents at that person's dwelling place or place of business by means of a letter box or other lawful means or by affixing it to the door of his dwelling place or place of business. If the last mentioned method is used, the officer of court must also post a copy to the most likely address of the defender[12]. When citation has been executed a certificate of citation must be completed and lodged with the sheriff clerk[13]. If it is by recorded delivery or by registered post, postal receipts as evidence of such posting must be attached to it[14].

1 RC 72(3).
2 RC 79(1).
3 OCR 8(1).
4 OCR 8(1) and (2).
5 OCR 3(9).
6 OCR 9(2).
7 Citation Amendment (Scotland) Act 1882, s 3.
8 OCR 10(1).
9 Citation Amendment (Scotland) Act 1882, s 6.
10 Recorded Delivery Service Act 1962, s 1; OCR 15(1).
11 Citation Amendment (Scotland) Act 1882, s 3.
12 OCR 10.
13 OCR 9(3), form D.
14 OCR 15(4).

PERIOD OF NOTICE

In the sheriff court the period of notice is:

(1) twenty-one days where the defender is resident or has a place of business within Europe, and

(2) forty-two days when the defender is resident or has a place of business outside Europe[1].

SHORTENING OR EXTENDING THE PERIOD OF NOTICE

The sheriff may shorten or extend the period of notice either as regards service on the defender but at least two days notice must be given[2].

Court of Session and sheriff court actions

WHEREABOUTS OF DEFENDER UNKNOWN OR DEFENDER SUFFERING FROM MENTAL DISORDER[3]

Where the address of the defender cannot be ascertained it is necessary to aver his last known address and domicile. Similarly it is necessary to aver that the defender is suffering from mental disorder if that is the case. Where either of these apply to a defender the warrant of citation in an action of divorce will include an order for intimation to every child of the marriage over the age of puberty, one of the next of kin of the defender and the defender's *curator bonis*, if he has one. The appropriate forms in a Court of Session case and in a sheriff court case are respectively form 18 or form V1 for mental disorder and form 17 or form V2 for an unknown address. Intimation is not required if the address of the person to whom intimation would be made is unknown and if there is an averment to that effect in the summons or initial writ. In a mental disorder case where the defender is in hospital or a similar institution, the citation is sent to the medical officer in charge along with a request (in form 20 or form W as the case may be) that he either deliver the writ personally along with the notice and explain the contents to the defender or certify that such delivery or explanation would be dangerous to the health or mental condition of the defender. There is also enclosed a certificate (in form 21 or form V) for him to fill in and return to the solicitor for the pursuer. This states which of these courses of action he has taken[4]. That certificate must then be attached to the summons or initial writ when it is lodged for calling in court.

The Court of Session may order edictal citation[5]. A motion is enrolled when the summons is presented for signet for warrant to cite the defender edictally, for an order for citation of the defender by advertisement in a newspaper circulating in the area of his last-known address or elsewhere or for dispensation with advertisement, and, where there are no averments in the summons to that effect, stating what steps have been taken to trace the defender. The motion, if made before calling, is heard in chambers. The solicitor for the pursuer must appear and speak to it. The advertisement will be in form 4A.

1 OCR 7(1).
2 OCR 7(2).
3 RC 159; OCR 11A.
4 RC 159(5); OCR 11A(4).
5 RC 74A(2), 75.

Edictal citation is carried out by service of a copy of the summons at the office of the Extractor of the Court of Session along with a copy of form 4 duly completed. The induciae, where citation is edictal, is six months[1].

In the sheriff court the sheriff will either order advertisement (in form E) in a newspaper circulating in the area of the last-known address of the defender or will order that a copy of the instance and crave of the initial writ, the warrant of citation and a notice in form E1 be displayed on the walls of court. Where either method is employed the pursuer must supply a service copy of the initial writ and warrant of citation to the sheriff clerk from whom they may be uplifted; where the latter method is employed, a certified copy of the instance, crave and warrant of citation, which are for display purposes, must be supplied to the sheriff clerk[2].

DEFENDER AT A KNOWN RESIDENCE IN ENGLAND, WALES, NORTHERN IRELAND, THE ISLE OF MAN, THE CHANNEL ISLANDS OR ANY NON-CONVENTION COUNTRY

Service may be effected either in accordance with the rules for personal service under the domestic law of the place where service is to be effected or by posting in Scotland by the solicitor for the pursuer or by an officer of court[3]. Service may be effected by sending a copy of the initial writ by registered post, recorded delivery (first class)[4], or the nearest available equivalent addressed to the defender at his residence or place of business[5]. For service upon a person resident within another part of the United Kingdom, the Channel Islands and the Isle of Man, in a straightforward case, postal service should be used. It should also be used at least as a first resort where the defender is resident in a non-convention country, if only because where personal service is used in such a country the pursuer is required to lodge a certificate by a person conversant with the law of that country and who practises or has practised as an advocate or solicitor in that country or is a duly accredited representative of the government of that country stating that the form of service employed is in accordance with the law of the place where service was effected.

Advice on the service of writs whether in convention or non-convention countries may be obtained from The Director, Scottish Courts Administration, 26/27 Royal Terrace, Edinburgh EH7 5AH.

CONVENTION COUNTRIES

The rules are somewhat involved. The conventions which apply are the Hague Convention on the Service Abroad of Judicial and Extra-Judicial Documents in Civil or Commercial Matters dated 15 November 1965 and the European Convention on Jurisdiction and the Enforcement of Judgments in Civil and Commercial Matters (which is set out as Schedule 1 to the Civil Jurisdiction and Judgments Act 1982). For the means of citation in terms of these conventions, see the detailed provisions of Rule of Court 74B or Ordinary Cause Rule 12 as the case may be. For an explanation of these rules and a list of convention countries see Macphail *Sheriff Court Practice*, paras 6-29 et seq. The convention countries currently are Antigua and Barbuda, Barbados, Belgium, Botswana, Cyprus, Czechoslovakia, Denmark, Egypt, Finland, France, West Germany,

1 RC 75.
2 OCR 11.
3 OCR 12(2). The forms to be used are those referred to in OCR 9, supra.
4 OCR 15(1).
5 OCR 12(1)(a).

Greece, Israel, Italy, Japan, Luxembourg, Malawi, The Netherlands, Norway, Spain, Pakistan, Portugal, Seychelles, Sweden, Switzerland, Turkey, United Kingdom, and the USA. Advice may be obtained as above.

Intimation

Persons to whom intimation should be made are discussed in chapter 6. In a Court of Session action the induciae for intimation are the same as for service and are set out in Rule of Court 72[1]. In a sheriff court action the period of notice is 21 days unless the sheriff otherwise directs but in no circumstances may the period be less than 48 hours[2].

In certain circumstances a person who is not a party to a divorce action may have an interest in it. The divorce action may contain allegations as to that person's conduct with one of the parties to the marriage. That conduct may be adulterous or may be of a homosexual nature. Sodomy may be alleged. The person named may wish to refute the allegations. But intimation is not made where the allegation is that the defender committed incest or rape[3]. There may be issues raised as to the future ownership or occupation of the matrimonial home, over which there may be a standard security, or there may be a tenancy. The lender or the landlord may wish to appear to safeguard their interest. Even if they do not it is right that they should know what is going on in that regard. A child may be in the de facto custody of another. There may be another person or a local authority who has a liability to maintain a child as to the arrangements for whom the court is required to be concerned. The court may have it in mind to make a supervision order in relation to such a child. The marriage may be polygamous. Another wife may have an interest in the divorce or at least in the financial provisions which may be made. One of the parties to the marriage may have a *curator bonis*. It is suggested that even though a party is not suffering from a mental disorder within the meaning of the Mental Health (Scotland) Act 1984 at the date of commencement of the action, if he has a *curator bonis*, intimation should be made to the curator if there is a claim for an order for financial provision.

All these either should or must be given an opportunity to appear and make representations to the court so far as they have an interest to do so. The rules make provision for intimation of a copy of the summons or initial writ to them at an early stage in the case. It may be that their interest does not become known or that their whereabouts become known after the case has made some progress. In that event the court will be likely to order intimation of the pleadings in their then state rather than the summons or initial writ which may by then be out of date.

The other type of situation in which intimation will be ordered is where the address of the defender is unknown or where the defender is suffering from mental disorder. The rules require that intimation be made to one of the next of kin of the defender and to all the children over the age of puberty and, if the defender is suffering from mental disorder within the meaning of the Mental Health (Scotland) Act 1984, to his *curator bonis*, if any.

---

1 See supra, RC 158.
2 OCR 130(11)(a).
3 RC 155(2); OCR 130(1)(c).

Documents which must accompany the service or intimation copy of a divorce summons or initial writ

Any appropriate warrants to intimate should have been included in the copy summons or initial writ. Attached to the copy summons or initial writ should be a copy of the appropriate form or forms referred to below[1].

These documents may have to be served or intimated at any stage in a divorce action when an order for service or intimation is made. Service on the defender may be required after the commencement of an action where his address becomes known. Intimation at a later stage may be required where, for example a paramour is named for the first time. Intimation is required whatever the ground of divorce. If in a divorce based on the behaviour of the defender there is an allegation of adultery with a named person that person should receive intimation. The requirements as regards intimation are not identical in the Court of Session and the sheriff court. The Court of Session may order intimation to such person as it thinks fit[2]. There is no comparable provision in the sheriff court Ordinary Cause Rules but those rules include a requirement to intimate to a greater number of specified persons than do the Rules of Court. In any event the sheriff has a discretion at common law to make such orders as seem necessary to do justice in a cause. If it appears to him that intimation should be made to a particular person intimation could be ordered.

The procedure for execution of a warrant for intimation in a Court of Session case is, subject to appropriate modifications, similar to that for citation[3].

SERVICE ON THE DEFENDER

Two year non-cohabitation and defender consents; forms 3, 15A and 15E (in the Court of Session) or (in the sheriff court) form C1, form S1 and form T[4].

Five year non-cohabitation: forms 3 and 15C (in the Court of Session) or (in the sheriff court) form C1, form S3[5].

INTIMATION

Intimation to alleged paramour: form 16 (in the Court of Session) or (in the sheriff court) form H1[6].

Intimation to person with whom an improper association is alleged: form 19 (in the Court of Session) or (in the sheriff court) form H2[7]

Intimation to children and next of kin where defender's address is unknown: form 17 (in the Court of Session) or (in the sheriff court) form V2[8].

1 See generally RC 160 and 161.
2 RC 164.
3 RC 160(1); cf RC 162(2).
4 RC 161(1); OCR 131(2).
5 RC 161(3); OCR 131(4).
6 RC 155, 160; OCR 130(1)(a).
7 RC 162; OCR 130(2)(b).
8 RC 155(3), 160, 170I(3); OCR 11(a)(3), 138(10).

Where the defender is suffering from a mental disorder: form 18 (in the Court of Session) or (in the sheriff court) form V1[1].

Intimation to additional spouse of either party: form 18A (in the Court of Session) or (in the sheriff court) form H4[2].

Intimation to local authority or third party liable to maintain a child: form 18B (in the Court of Session) or (in the sheriff court) form H3[3].

Intimation to person having de facto custody of a child: form H5[4]. There is no equivalent form in the Court of Session but Form 18B should be used.

Intimation to local authority or third party to whom the court proposes to give the care of a child: form H6[5]. There is no equivalent form in the Court of Session.

Intimation to local authority that court has made a supervision order: form H6A[6]. There is no equivalent form in the Court of Session.

Intimation to person having an interest in a settlement: form 18C[7]. No equivalent forms are specified in the Ordinary Cause Rules.

Intimation to a person having an interest in an application under the Matrimonial Homes (Family Protection)(Scotland) Act 1981 (eg in a house or other property): form 18D[8].

Intimation to a person having an interest as a creditor in the transfer of property subject to a security: form 18E (in the Court of Session) or (in the sheriff court) form H7[9].

Intimation must also be made to a landlord of inter alia applications for an exclusion order and a transfer of tenancy if the entitled spouse is a tenant of the matrimonial home, and to a third party who has permitted an entitled spouse to occupy the matrimonial home of inter alia claims for occupancy rights or for an exclusion order[10].

Consent to decree

In a two year non-cohabitation case the defender, in order to indicate his consent should do so by notice in writing to that effect to the Deputy Principal Clerk of Session or the sheriff clerk of the court referred to in the initial writ, as the case may be. But the defender may deliver the consent form personally or via an intermediary, who may be the pursuer's solicitor[11]. Form 15E or Form T if signed by the defender will be treated as such notice. One witness is sufficient to establish that the signature is that of the defender.

1 RC 155(3), 160; OCR 11A(3).
2 RC 155(5), 160; OCR 130(5).
3 RC 160; OCR 130(4).
4 OCR 130(6).
5 OCR 130(7).
6 OCR 130(7)(b).
7 RC 160.
8 RC160. No similar sheriff court form has been prescribed.
9 RC 170D(9); OCR 130(9).
10 RC 188D(7); AS (Applications under the Matrimonial Homes (Family Protection) (Scotland) Act 1981) 1982 (SI 1982/1432), para 3.
11 *Taylor v Taylor* 1988 SCLR 60.

A defender may give notice in writing to the court that he does not consent or that he has withdrawn his consent. In either event that fact will be notified to the pursuer or his agent. If the defender denies or withdraws his consent, the pursuer is required to enrol a motion to sist the cause. In the event of the court sisting the cause, and the sist neither being recalled nor renewed within six months, the pursuer is deemed to have abandoned the action[1].

Carrying out service and intimation of the writ

As has been remarked, service will normally be by recorded delivery and will be carried out by the solicitor for the pursuer. In the Court of Session and the sheriff court the procedure for intimation is broadly the same as for service of the summons (but the periods of notice are not identical in the sheriff court[2], though they are in the Court of Session[3]. Execution of a warrant for intimation is certified by attaching to the summons a copy of the intimation and a certificate of execution.

If service or intimation is to be by messenger-at-arms or sheriff officer he must be provided with either the original or, preferably, a copy of the summons or initial writ which has been certified correct by the solicitor for the pursuer, in addition to the service copy[4]. It is not unknown for the principal copy to be provided to and served on a defender by a process server where the defender is outwith Scotland. In all probability there will then be no principal copy available for return to the court. Whether or not the attempted service is successful, the principal copy is returned to court. If it has been unsuccessful or if it has been irregular, in an action in the sheriff court, a new warrant for service will be granted[5]. If service has been successful an execution of the citation must be written on or attached to it along with evidence of service, eg a recorded delivery slip.

In the Court of Session the summons is called. It appears on the calling list. It cannot be called before the day on which the inducaie expire[6].

TRANSFER, REMIT AND SIST OF ACTIONS

Sist for reconciliation

If it appears to the court that there is a reasonable prospect of reconciliation it is required to continue the case to enable an attempted reconciliation to take place[7]. This is most likely to be done by sisting the cause either on the motion of a party or by the court *ex proprio motu*.

Transfer between sheriff courts

Actions raised in one sheriff court may, in certain circumstances, be transferred to another sheriff court[8]. There must be jurisdiction against the defender in

1 RC 166; OCR 132.
2 OCR 130(11a).
3 RC 158 and see the Citation Amendment (Scotland) Act 1882, s 3; RC 160, 159.
4 RC 74(i).
5 OCR 17.
6 RC 78.
7 Divorce (Scotland) Act 1976, s 2(1).
8 OCR 19.

the court to which the transfer is made. Of the three situations to which that rule applies two could apply to an action of divorce—(1) where a plea of no jurisdiction has been sustained and there is a motion before the court to transfer the cause (in which event it may be transferred to the sheriff court before which it appears it should have been brought), and (2) where the sheriff on sufficient cause decides to remit the cause to another court. In the former case the sheriff is required not to transfer unless he considers it expedient to do so having regard to the convenience of parties or witnesses. Sufficient cause might arise where there is already an action, perhaps more procedurally advanced and which could affect the status of the parties to the action of divorce, or where the subject matter in both actions is at least partly the same. The sheriff is required to state the reason(s) for the transfer in the interlocutor. The court to which the transfer is made is required to accept the transfer.

Remit to the Court of Session from the sheriff court

In terms of the Sheriff Courts (Scotland) Act 1971, s 37(2A) the sheriff or the sheriff principal may, of his own accord, remit inter alia any action of divorce or action relating to the custody of a child to the Court of Session. A decision to remit under that subsection is not subject to review[1]. This is likely to occur when there is a related action pending in the Court of Session which either affects the status of the parties or affects the children of the marriage. There should not be a remit unless there is a matter of special difficulty or delicacy involved[2].

Remit to the sheriff court from the Court of Session

The Court of Session may remit any action which could have been brought in a sheriff court, either at its own instance or on the application of any of the parties, to the sheriff of the court within whose jurisdiction the action could have been brought where the nature of the action makes it appropriate to do so[3]. A remit of an action of divorce may be refused where there is an action of division and sale of matrimonial property pending in a sheriff court[4]. On receipt of the process the sheriff clerk records the date of receipt on the interlocutor sheet and enrols the cause for further procedure on the first court day not less than 14 days after receipt[5]. The action then proceeds as an ordinary action using the existing process.

Transmission of a process to the Court of Session

The Court of Session may order that a sheriff court process be transmitted to it. This may be done where there is contingency or necessity[6]. There will

1 Sheriff Courts (Scotland) Act 1971, s 37(3).
2 *Dunbar v Dunbar* 1912 SC 19; *Casey v Casey* (1925) 41 Sh Ct Reps 300; *Lamont v Lamont* 1939 SC 484.
3 Law Reform (Miscellaneous Provisions) (Scotland) Act 1985, s 14; RC 104B.
4 *Rae v Rae* 1990 GWD 13–713.
5 OCR 20A.
6 For a more detailed explanation of the criteria and procedure see Macphail *Sheriff Court Practice*, paras 13–67–13–69; Maxwell *The Practice of the Court of Session*, p 240; RC 104A.

be contingency where a decision in one action would decide the other action in whole or in part. If on a motion made to it the Court of Session accepts that it is necessary that a process depending before a sheriff court be transmitted to that court, an order will be made requiring that to be done by the appropriate sheriff clerk. The sheriff makes no order. Court of Session procedure on transmission taking place is governed by RC 274 and 275.

Sist of action

Any action may be sisted at any time prior to granting of the final decree disposing of the action either on the motion of one or both parties or by the court *ex proprio motu*. Sists are common where a party wishes to apply for legal aid. The court will normally be sympathetic to an application for a sist on this ground. But where there are issues of interim custody, access or aliment, or interim orders under the Matrimonial Homes (Family Protection) (Scotland) Act 1981 are sought, the court may wish to dispose of any interim motions in that connection prior to granting a sist for for legal aid. In an occasional sheriff court case the court may order defences to be lodged prior to sisting the case. This is not likely to occur except where interim orders of an urgent nature should first be disposed of. Defences may be of assistance to a reporter to be appointed by the court to investigate the arrangements for the children or may clarify the issues where an interim exclusion order is sought and the allegations are extensive. Where there are actions pending in more than one court whether or not one of these cases is pending in a court in another part of the United Kingdom the court may sist a cause in order to allow the cause in the other court to proceed[1].

One of the reasons for the requirement on both parties to provide details in their pleadings of concurrent proceedings is to enable the court to decide whether there should be a sist in order to avoid a conflict between courts[2]. The court may, if it thinks fit, sist the action up to the commencement of the proof, and may do so thereafter if it is satisfied that a party has not made the required averments. There are corresponding provisions to those aftermentioned in other parts of the United Kingdom.

Mandatory sists

The Domicile and Matrimonial Proceedings Act 1973, Sch 3, para 8 provides that it is mandatory to sist an action where, before the beginning of a proof in any action of divorce, it appears to the court on the application of a party to the marriage that:

(1) in respect of the same marriage proceedings for divorce or nullity of marriage are continuing in a related jurisdiction[3], and

(2) the parties to the marriage resided together after the marriage was contracted, and

(3) the place where they resided together when the action in the court concerned was begun or, if they did not then reside together, the place where

---

1 *Girvan v Girvan* 1985 SLT 92.
2 Domicile and Matrimonial Proceedings Act 1973, s 11 and Sch 3, para 7.
3 A 'related jurisdiction' means England and Wales, Northern Ireland, Jersey, Guernsey, Alderney, Sark and the Isle of Man: Domicile and Matrimonial Proceedings Act 1973, Sch 3, para 2(2).

they last resided together before the date on which that action was begun is in that jurisdiction, and

(4) either of the parties was habitually resident in that jurisdiction throughout the year ending with the date on which they last resided together before the date on which the action was begun.

The key to this provision is to discover in which jurisdiction the parties resided. If that was not in Scotland and at least one of them was habitually resident in that jurisdiction then that jurisdiction will be assumed to be the one which should entertain and dispose of the action. Any action in Scotland will be sisted pending the outcome of the action in the other related jurisdiction. Assume that Mr and Mrs Smith get married and live in England. Mrs Smith lived in the family home in England throughout their cohabitation. She was habitually resident there. Prior to their separation Mr Smith worked for most of the year in Saudi Arabia. He was not habitually resident in England throughout the year prior to the separation. Mr and Mrs Smith separate and thereafter Mrs Smith comes to live in Edinburgh where she lives for more than a year before she raises an action of divorce. Prima facie there will be jurisdiction in both England and Scotland. If a divorce action is raised in London by Mr Smith and a similar action is raised in Edinburgh by Mrs Smith, Mrs Smith's action must be sisted. Application for a sist is by way of motion[1].

Discretionary sists

The court has a discretion to sist an action where, prior to the beginning of the proof, it appears to the court that:

(1) any other proceedings in respect of the marriage in question or affecting its validity are continuing in another jurisdiction, and

(2) the balance of fairness (including convenience) as between the parties to the marriage is such that it is appropriate for those proceedings to be disposed of before further steps are taken in the action in the said court[2].

In these events the court may sist that action if it thinks fit. This applies to proceedings in any jurisdiction outside Scotland and not just to proceedings in a 'related jurisdiction'. It has wider application than the provisions relating to mandatory sists which are restricted to proceedings for divorce or nullity of marriage. As to whether proceedings are continuing in a court in Scotland where no steps have been taken for a year and a day since service see *McKidd v Manson* (1882) 9 R 790; *Dunnett v Dunnett* 1990 SCLR 135; *McCulloch v McCulloch* 1990 SCLR 155. The effect of such inactivity is that the instance will have fallen and accordingly proceedings are not continuing. A sist would then be unnecessary. The position is otherwise in a sheriff court action where there has been procedure subsequent to service[3].

The convenience of witnesses, delay and expense are among the factors to be considered[4].

1 RC 167(2); OCR 3(8).
2 Domicile and Matrimonial Proceedings Act 1973, Sch 3, para 9(1).
3 *Donnelly v Donnelly* 1990 GWD 9–509.
4 Domicile and Matrimonial Proceedings Act 1973, Sch 3, para 9(4) requires that the phrase 'before the beginning of the proof' be disregarded in circumstances in which there has been a failure to comply with the duty to inform the court about concurrent proceedings.

Recall of sists

A mandatory or a discretionary sist granted in terms of paras 8 or 9 of Schedule 3 of the Domicile and Matrimonial Proceedings Act 1973 may be recalled if either the other proceedings are sisted or concluded or if it appears that a party to those proceedings has unduly delayed in prosecuting those proceedings[1]. Once a sist has been granted in terms of para 8 and recalled, there will be no further sist in terms of para 8[2]. Application to recall a sist is made by motion[3].

The effect of a sist on interim orders

Where an action is sisted by reference to proceedings in a 'related jurisdiction' (for the definition of which, see supra) the court does not have power to make a 'relevant order' in connection with the sisted action unless as a matter of necessity or urgency it is necessary to make or extend an order[4]. 'Relevant orders' are defined in Part 1 of Schedule 2 to the 1973 Act. They comprise orders relating to aliment, custody of and access to a child, prohibition of the removal of a child, the commission of the care of the child to an individual and the variation or recall of any such order.

Relevant orders made in connection with the sisted action cease to have effect on the expiry of three months starting on the date when the sist comes into operation unless the sist or relevant order has previously been recalled.[5] But any relevant order will be superseded immediately when the court in the related jurisdiction makes an order in the course of the continuing action (or where that court has already made such an order, on the granting of the sist) in relation to any of the following matters:

(1) periodical payments for a spouse of the marriage in question;
(2) periodical payments for a child;
(3) the custody of or access to a child;
(4) the education of a child.

Once the order of a court has been superseded that court whose order has been superseded cannot make an order relating to the same spouse or child and dealing with the same subject matter, eg aliment. Nor where there has been supersession can it make such orders on the basis that there is necessity or urgency. Once the sist has been recalled the powers of the court in regard to the action which was sisted are no longer restricted. Nor is the court prevented from varying or recalling a relevant order so far as it is for the time being in force nor from enforcing a relevant order as respects a period when it is or was in force.

Where the action is undefended

An action may be undefended in whole or in part. For example it may be defended on some financial aspect but not on the merits of the divorce. Even if it is defended on the merits initially, that defence may be withdrawn as

1 Ibid, para 10(1).
2 Ibid, para 10(2).
3 RC 167(2); OCR 3(8).
4 Domicile and Matrimonial Proceedings Act 1973, Sch 3, para 11(2)(c).
5 Ibid, para 11(2)(b).

sometimes occurs when the parties have reached agreement on other matters. In that event a motion is enrolled to repel the defences and to appoint the cause to proceed as an undefended action. It then proceeds as such. So long as it is defended on the merits affidavits should not be lodged.

An action cannot be treated as undefended until either the time for lodging a notice of intention to defend, a minute contesting financial matters or a counterclaim for custody, access or maintenance has expired or, where a curator *ad litem* has been appointed, until he has lodged a minute intimating that he does not intend to lodge defences.

Appointment of a curator *ad litem*

Where it appears to the court that the defender is suffering from mental disorder within the meaning of the Mental Health (Scotland) Act 1984, the court will appoint a curator *ad litem*[1]. A curator *ad litem* is not appointed in an action proceeding by way of the simplified procedure because one of the necessary requirements for that procedure will be absent if the defender is suffering from a mental disorder. In those circumstances the court would dismiss the action raised by using that simplified procedure. It would be open to the pursuer to raise an ordinary action for divorce.

In the Court of Session the appointment of a curator is made on the expiry of the time for lodging defences. Where the basis of the divorce is two years' separation and the consent of the defender, the court, on the appointment of a curator *ad litem*, informs the Mental Welfare Commission for Scotland and requests a report as to whether in the Commission's opinion the defender is capable of giving such consent[2].

When a curator has been appointed the pursuer or his agent must send to the curator within seven days in the case of a sheriff court action, and as soon as reasonably practicable in the case of an action in the Court of Session, a certified copy of the initial writ or summons, as the case may be, and the defences, if any.

The curator may, within fourteen days of the Commission providing the report, or within twenty-one days of his appointment in any other case, lodge a notice of appearance, defences to the action, a minute adopting the defences already lodged or a minute stating that he does not intend to lodge defences. He may appear in the action at any time to protect the interests of the defender[3]. Despite the permissive terms of these rules, the curator should lodge with the court a minute of his intentions, if he decides not to lodge defences. This is because, until he does, the action cannot proceed further by way of affidavit evidence[4]. When he has lodged a minute stating that he does not intend to lodge defences, the practice is that proof by affidavit evidence is allowed and an order is made directing that the fee and expenses of the curator *ad litem* are payable by the pursuer[5]. In a defended action the curator *ad litem* should satisfy himself that the defence has been properly conducted so far and should

1 RC 167; OCR 133.
2 RC 167(1)(a); OCR 133(1); RC 154(2) and the Mental Health (Scotland) Act 1984, s 1(2), referred to in OCR 133(1), define mental disorder as 'mental illness or mental deficiency however caused or manifested'.
3 RC 167(1); OCR 133(2).
4 RC168(1)(b); OCR 72(1)(b).
5 Court of Session Practice Note, 10 February 1983.

be continued or that it should not be insisted in and report to the court accordingly. If it is to be insisted in he should satisfy himself that it continues to be properly conducted in the interests of the *incapax*, and make such reports as he considers necessary or as the court may require[1].

There is no reason in principle why the court should not appoint a curator *ad litem* in other cases, particularly to safeguard the interests of children. Orders for their alleged benefit are made in the course of a divorce action. Actions of aliment for them are raised but the principal areas of contention are their custody, access to them and their upbringing generally. It is perhaps remarkable that curators *ad litem* are not commonly appointed to look after the interests of children which will not otherwise be represented independently in relation to matters which may affect them for the rest of their lives, and particularly for the rest of their childhood.

Involvement of the Lord Advocate

The Lord Advocate may enter appearance as a party to an action of divorce and may lead such proof and maintain such pleas as he thinks fit. The court may direct that any such action be brought to the notice of the Lord Advocate in order that he may determine whether to enter appearance. If he does so no expenses may be claimed by or against him[2].

Joint minute

A joint minute may be entered into in which the parties agree custody, access, aliment, maintenance of a child, periodical allowance, payment of a capital sum or transfer of property. In a sheriff court action the court may grant decree in terms of the joint minute whether or not these have been craved in the summons, initial writ or counterclaim[3]. This applies also to orders for financial provision in cases in which a minute has been lodged disputing the liability for, the amount of or other matters relating to such orders[4].

A joint minute is subject to the approval of the court particularly in so far as it deals with matters such as custody and access. The court may not approve of the agreement of the parties. It has been suggested that the minute should contain an agreement, where defences are to be withdrawn, that the action will proceed as undefended as regards the divorce so that if the court takes a different view from the parties on, say, custody the defender may continue to make representations on such a matter[5]. But that seems unnecessary. Where the court intends to depart from arrangements set out in a joint minute it is suggested that the interests of justice will be best served if the court gives the party who has withdrawn an opportunity to make representations before the court makes an order on its own initiative. That may entail an adjournment of the case.

Once a joint minute has been entered into it may not be possible to resile from it even though there may have been a change of circumstances since

---

1 *Finlay v Finlay* 1962 SLT (Sh Ct) 43.
2 Court of Session Act 1988, s 19; Sheriff Courts (Scotland) Act 1907, s 38B.
3 OCR 34, 56(3).
4 OCR 34(6).
5 *McKechnie v McKechnie* 1990 SCLR 153.

it was entered into and decree of divorce has not been granted[1]. It may be possible to seek variation of a joint minute under the Family Law (Scotland) Act 1985, s 16 if it can be shown that it was not fair and reasonable when it was entered into[2]. A joint minute may oust the jurisdiction of the court so that if, in the joint minute, a party agrees that there should be no capital sum, an application for such a sum on a change of circumstances would be refused[3]. If a joint minute is entered into on a particular basis consideration should be given to setting out that basis in writing. If the understanding is that the wife will get employment but that is not recorded, it may be argued that there has been a change of circumstances if she gets employment[4]. If jurisdiction is not ousted, as it cannot be in respect of the arrangements for custody or access, a joint minute is not binding on the court[5].

Allowance of proof

In the Court of Session a proof before answer is allowed automatically in a straightforward undefended divorce, as soon after the lapse of 7 days from the date of calling as may be practicable[6].

Proof of the merits of the divorce

Decree in an action of divorce cannot be granted in absence. Irretrievable breakdown must be established[7]. In an undefended action affidavit evidence is admissible in place of parole evidence and may be sufficient evidence[8]. Indeed these rules provide that proof in all undefended actions of divorce shall be by way of affidavit evidence unless in that particular action the court directs otherwise. The court is likely to give such a direction where affidavits have been lodged but appear to be unsatisfactory for some reason, such as that there does not appear to be sufficient evidence to establish irretrievable breakdown of the marriage or that the arrangements for the care of the children do not appear to be in their best interests, and may do so where there are inconsistencies between the affidavits or between the affidavits and the averments. Occasionally such a direction may be given where it appears that the maker of the affidavit is speaking to events of which he patently has no knowledge. Where the court perceives a defect it will normally be drawn to the attention of the agent concerned who will be given an opportunity to remedy the defect whether by leading further evidence or otherwise[9]. If the defect is not remedied in a Court of Session action the case will be put out by order. If the court is not satisfied and if the defect arises in affidavits the court may refuse to grant decree on the basis of such evidence but may allow parole evidence to be led, or it may refuse decree.

1 *Sochart v Sochart* 1988 SLT 449(Outer House) and 799(Inner House).
2 *Anderson v Anderson* 1989 GWD 19-814.
3 *Milne v Milne* 1987 SLT 45.
4 *Sutherland v Sutherland* 1988 SCLR 346.
5 *Robson v Robson* 1973 SLT (Notes) 4.
6 Court of Session Practice Note 1976 No 1.
7 Divorce (Scotland) Act 1976, s 1; OCR 21(2)(a).
8 RC 168(2); OCR 23(1), (2), 72(1), (2).
9 *Paterson v Paterson* 1958 SC 141.

Amendment of the ground of divorce

It is competent to amend the ground of divorce in the course of a divorce action. Where a divorce is plainly incompetent, for example because the requisite period of non-cohabitation has not elapsed, the action will be dismissed unless the ground is amended[1]. Amendment may be made to found on a ground of divorce which would not have been competent at the date on which the action was raised[2]. The court may allow amendment of an action of separation so that it becomes an action of divorce but may refuse to allow a similar amendment of an action of aliment[3].

Lodging of affidavits

While affidavits may have been prepared prior to the commencement of the action when it is known that it is not to be defended, they should not be sworn any significant time before they are lodged in court. Circumstances may change, particularly as regards any children of the marriage or the financial position of the parties[4]. Along with the affidavits may be lodged any consent by the defender, productions such as photographs of the parties in an adultery action, extract convictions, reports by a medical practitioner and any joint minute which may have been entered into. The marriage and birth certificates which should have been lodged with the writ will have been borrowed from process. They will have been docquetted by the pursuer when swearing her affidavit. They must be re-lodged along with the other productions.

Minute for decree

The agent for the pursuer endorses or lodges separately a minute for decree. The form of this minute is specified[5]. The minute is to be as follows:

> 'AB for the pursuer having considered the evidence contained in the affidavits and the other documents all as specified in the Schedule hereto and being satisfied that upon this evidence a motion for decree (in terms of the conclusions of the summons[6] or crave of the initial writ) or (in such restricted terms as may be appropriate) may properly be made, moves the court accordingly.'
>
> In respect whereof
>
> (Signed)
>
> (Designation)
>
> Schedule
>
> (number and specify the documents considered)

1 *Matthews v Matthews* 1985 SLT (Sh Ct) 68.
2 *Duncan v Duncan* 1986 SLT 17.
3 *Edgar v Edgar*; *Porter v Porter* 1990 SCLR 96.
4 Cf Court of Session Practice Note, 11 April 1978, para 10; Sheriff Principals' Practice Note para 9.
5 RC 168; OCR 72(5) and Form X.
6 Where the defender's means are unknown there may be added 'or such other sum (or sums) as the court may think proper'—Notes by Dean of Faculty etc, para 13, printed as an Appendix hereto.

In the Court of Session this minute is signed by counsel[1], and in the sheriff court by the agent (or counsel) for the pursuer.

Thereafter the court may at any time and without any appearance for the pursuer grant decree in terms of the minute or may put the case out for further procedure, including proof by parole evidence. In most sheriff courts, once affidavits have been lodged the papers will be put before a sheriff along with any comments which the sheriff clerk may have to make. Decree may then be granted. In an action based on non-cohabitation for five years the court is not bound to grant decree if in the opinion of the court grave financial hardship would result from doing so[2]. But, as has been noted, if there are apparent errors, deficiencies or defects, decree may not be granted or the court may afford an opportunity to remedy any errors or lodge additional or supplementary affidavit evidence.

If the pursuer does not minute for decree within a year and a day of service the instance falls unless in a Court of Session action the summons has called in court or in a sheriff court action some other procedure has taken place[3].

Expenses

The old rule was that unless the wife had separate estate her husband was liable to pay the expenses of a divorce action. The basis of that rule was that he was under an obligation to maintain his wife[4]. There were occasional exceptions to this rule[5]. That basis has been superseded by the Family Law (Scotland) Act 1985, s 1 which provides, inter alia, that each spouse owes the other an obligation of aliment. Section 22 of the 1985 Act provides that expenses are no longer to be regarded as necessaries for which the other party to the marriage is liable. Accordingly current practice is to make such award of expenses as is reasonable in the circumstances. In *Craigie v Craigie*[6] the Inner House held that it was inappropriate to award expenses to a pursuer who was legally aided in a five year non-cohabitation action. At least in non-cohabitation cases conduct is irrelevant as regards liability for expenses. In other cases it may be that one party will be well able to meet the expenses of the divorce while the other may be in no position to do so. The party with assets may be ordered to pay some or all of the expenses but, particularly where the action is defended in whole or in part, the general rule that expenses follow success may be followed[7].

A party in receipt of legal aid who is found liable in expenses may apply to the court for modification of these expenses[8]. Where a legally-aided party enters into a joint minute agreeing inter alia expenses, and he wishes to apply for modification he should reserve his right to do so in express terms[9]. The

---

1 RC 168(9)(a).
2 Divorce (Scotland) Act 1976, s 1(5).
3 *McKidd v Manson* (1882) 9 R 270; *Dunnett v Dunnett* 1990 SCLR 135; *McCulloch v McCulloch* 1990 SCLR 155 1990 SLT (Sh Ct) 63; *Donnelly v Donnelly* 1990 SCLR 344.
4 *Milne v Milne* (1885) 13 R 304.
5 Eg *Sharp v Sharp* 1946 SLT 116.
6 1979 SLT (Notes) 60.
7 *Chalkley v Chalkley* 1984 SLT 281.
8 Legal Aid (Scotland) Act 1967, s 18(2) as amended by the Legal Aid Act 1988, Sch 4, para 7(b).
9 *Boughen v Scott* 1983 SLT (Sh Ct) 94; *Roy, Nicholson, Becker & Day v Clarke* 1984 SLT (Sh Ct) 16.

approach adopted by the court in regard to the modification of expenses in a consistorial case is set out in *Armstrong v Armstrong*[1].

Late formal withdrawal of defences may result in an award of expenses against the party withdrawing[2]. Appeals against awards of expenses alone are not likely to succeed unless it can be shown that the award was based on a wrong principle or was otherwise plainly wrong[3].

---

1 1970 SLT 247.
2 *Gow v Gow* 1987 GWD 24-887.
3 Eg *Cleghorn v Fairgrieve* 1982 SLT (Sh Ct) 17.

CHAPTER 8

INTERIM ORDERS

Interim orders may be obtained, broadly, at two stages: prior to service of the writ and after service of the writ. Some orders cannot be granted prior to service of the writ. Others, in the discretion of the court, may be granted at that stage but some are very unlikely to be granted, unless there are very exceptional circumstances.

Where it is desired to obtain an interim order in a sheriff court action the initial writ should contain a crave for such an order on an interim basis (eg 'and for interim interdict'), and an appropriate plea in law. In the Court of Session, while it is common for an interim order to be sought in the conclusions in similar terms, that is not thought to be necessary. The view is taken that the greater includes the less. Accordingly the order sought need make no mention of, for example, interim custody. There must be sufficient averments to enable the court to conclude that such an order is necessary and justified on the basis of these averments. While it may be possible to provide the court with supplementary information of events which have occurred since the writ was drafted, the court may be unwilling to pay much heed to information which could have been, but was not, included in the summons or initial writ unless the summons or writ is amended and re-served or the other party is present or represented. In the last-mentioned event it is likely that the court will adjourn the hearing of the motion if necessary to enable the representative of the other party to obtain instructions on the additional information.

OBTAINING INTERIM ORDERS PRIOR TO SERVICE OF THE WRIT

Warrants for intimation and the like are not interim orders and will, where applied for and where appropriate, be granted when the summons is signeted or when a warrant for citation is signed, as the case may be. As has been noted previously warrants for intimation may be applied for and granted or intimation may be ordered by the court *ex proprio motu* at any stage in the case.

Court of Session action

Once the summons has been signeted it should be lodged in the General Department along with a motion for the appropriate interim orders. The clerk of court will arrange for the matter to be put before a judge in court or in chambers. The pursuer must be present or represented on that occasion by counsel or solicitor or both[1]. Motions for interim custody and interim aliment, or for a variation thereof are made on a 7 day intimation except in a case of special urgency, when the normal 48 hour intimation applies[2]. In a Court of Session action an application under the Family Law Act 1986, s 35 for interdict or interim interdict prohibiting the removal of a child from the United Kingdom or any part of it or from the control of the person in whose control the child is must be made by motion[3]. But if a person other than a party to the marriage wishes authority to remove a child from the custody of a person claiming custody in the action of divorce the application must be by minute lodged in that action, of which notice would of course have to be given in the ususal way[4].

Sheriff court action

The initial writ should be lodged at the sheriff clerk's office along with the appropriate fee. The sheriff clerk should be informed that interim orders are sought prior to service. A time will be arranged when the application for the interim order(s) will be heard by a sheriff, usually in chambers. On that occasion the pursuer or his solicitor should appear.

The warrant for service will contain any interim orders made prior to service and may appoint parties to be heard on some or all of the interim orders sought on a day and at a time specified in the warrant. Any such orders which may have been granted will normally be expressed so as to expire at the time of that hearing. They should not be granted for a period greater than one week. Interim orders for custody and delivery of a child should not normally be granted without intimation to the party in whose care the child is[5]. If the pursuer wishes the interim order to continue beyond that time a motion must be made at the hearing for such continuation as well as for the granting of the other interim orders sought. Failure by the pursuer to appear or to be represented will result in the orders lapsing. Once they have lapsed the pursuer cannot complain of a breach of the order in respect of conduct after the lapse. If the warrant for service has not been successfully executed application should be made for a new warrant for service and, if appropriate, for new interim orders. The court is not likely to make repeated new orders where it has not proved possible to effect service on the defender. The court may take the view that there is no justification for continuing to grant interim orders with early dates for hearings if the defender has not acted in a manner contrary to any interim order while service is attempted but has not been successful, for example because his whereabouts are unknown or he is known to be residing abroad.

Procedure in the absence of the defender

It is inherently contrary to natural justice for a court to make orders without giving an opportunity to both parties to be heard. Thus there must be a sound justification for the making of an interim order on the basis of *ex parte* statements alone, as there may be when there is real urgency or else a very real risk

1 RC 79, 236.
2 Court of Session Practice Note, 13 November 1969.
3 RC 170C(1).
4 Children Act 1975, s 51(1); RC 170C(2).
5 *Nelson v Nelson* 1989 SLT (Sh Ct) 18.

that steps will be taken in the meantime to put the issue beyond the reach of the court. Thus the court will be more likely to grant interim orders which, for example, prohibit the removal of children from the jurisdiction of the court or the disposal of assets to the disadvantage of the pursuer[1]. The basis upon which it would do so would be that the order will preserve the status quo pending a further hearing of the issues. It will be less likely to grant orders prior to service where the pursuer appears to have a weak or possibly irrelevant or incompetent case or where either there is less urgency or the status quo would be altered or it would be unjust to deny the defender an opportunity to be heard.

Prior to service the court will normally be unwilling to make an interim order granting custody to the pursuer particularly if the defender currently has *de facto* custody of the child. Similarly an interim order for access to or for the delivery of a child is unlikely to be granted before service unless there is a very strong case for doing so. Courts are reluctant to make orders for custody which would have the effect of changing the parent who has day-to-day care of the child, on an interim basis. Exceptions are likely to occur when the child has been 'snatched' by the defender in which event the court may regard the return of the child as restoring the status quo.

If there is already an order for custody of that child in existence made by another court or if application has been made to another court for such an order this court may refuse to make such an order or may sist the application made to it[2]. It is mandatory to aver the existence of such orders and applications[3].

Supersession of earlier orders by later orders

Section 15 of the Family Law Act 1986 provides that where there comes into force either (a) a custody order, or an order varying a custody order, competently made by another court in any part of the United Kingdom, or (b) an order for the custody of that child made outside the United Kingdom and recognised in Scotland by virtue of section 26 of the 1986 Act an existing Scottish order ceases to have effect so far as it makes provision for any matter for which the same or different provision is made by the later order. Thus, for example, if a court in Scotland grants custody to the mother and, later, another competent court, whether in Scotland, elsewhere in the United Kingdom or in the circumstances mentioned above, a court outside the United Kingdom, grants custody of that child to either parent, the Scottish order thereupon ceases to have effect. If a person, as a result of the later order, loses custody of a child any existing order providing for the supervision of the child by a local authority under either the Matrimonial Proceedings (Children) Act 1958, s 12(1) or the Guardianship Act 1973, s 11(1)(b) ceases to have effect.

In the sheriff court where there is an existing decree for custody, aliment or access and a divorce action is raised, there is no need to lodge a minute in the original process. The new order should be sought in the usual way in the divorce action. When a court makes an order in the divorce process that order supersedes the earlier order which then ceases to apply[4].

1 Cf *Johnstone v Johnstone* 1967 SLT 248.
2 Family Law Act 1986, s 14.
3 RC 157(3); OCR 3(5).
4 OCR 129(4).

Because the court must be satisfied as to the welfare of the children on granting divorce, the court must have before it information which is up to date. An earlier decree, possibly granted long ago and in another court, is of limited value at the time of divorce and is most unlikely to be accepted as sufficient evidence by the court in which the divorce action is.

INTERDICTS

The court, when granting a warrant for service of the writ, will normally be willing to grant interim interdict if it is justified. The test which must be satisfied is that the grant is justified either on the balance of convenience or in order to preserve the status quo. That justification will be found, if at all, in the averments. Reliance should not be placed on *ex parte* statements which introduce new matter not the subject of averment.

A non-molestation interdict in the form approved in *Murdoch v Murdoch* 1973 SLT (Notes) 13 or similar may be granted prior to service if the averments justify it. But if an interim interdict for non-molestation is sought in some other form, close attention is likely to be paid to its terms by the court. For 'the terms of the interdict must be no wider than are necessary to curb the illegal actings complained of, and so precise and clear that the person interdicted is left in no doubt what he is forbidden to do'. The court must be satisfied that, 'unless interdict is granted, the pursuer is likely to be exposed, without other adequate protection, to conduct on the part of the defender which will put her at risk or in fear, alarm or distress; and where an interim order is made it must be sharply defined and related specifically to the particular risks which justify its grant' (*Murdoch* supra).

ORDERS FOR THE INTERIM POSSESSION OF PROPERTY

In any cause depending before the Court of Session the court may, on the motion of any party to the cause, make such order as to the interim possession of any property to which the cause relates, or regarding the subject matter of the cause, as the court thinks fit[1].

MATRIMONIAL HOMES ACT ORDERS

The Matrimonial Homes (Family Protection) (Scotland) Act 1981 contains express provision to the effect that many of the interim orders which may be made under that Act may not be made without affording the defender an opportunity of being heard by or represented before the court. These include applications for interim orders under section 3 (regulation by court of rights of occupancy of matrimonial home), section 4 (exclusion orders and orders ancillary thereto) and section 15 (attachment of power of arrest to matrimonial interdicts)[2].

---

1 Court of Session Act 1988, s 47(2).
2 Matrimonial Homes (Family Protection) (Scotland) Act 1981, ss 3(4), 4(6), 15(1)(b).

That requirement applies whether or not the non-applicant spouse has lodged defences or a notice of intention to defend[1]. The provisions of the 1981 Act innovate on the common law. It is not competent at common law to interdict another from removing his own property unless he has entered into an obligation not to do so. But in the Court of Session where the property is property to which the cause relates the court may make such order regarding interim possession as it thinks fit[2]. A similar conclusion was arrived at in the sheriff court on the basis that at common law a party could be restrained from removing moveable property which is the subject of litigation. The 1981 Act makes it possible to make the furniture and plenishings in a matrimonial home the subject of litigation[3].

In the Court of Session the following applications for orders under the 1981 Act are made by motion[4]: under section 3(4) (interim order for regulation of rights of occupancy), under section 4(6) (interim order suspending occupancy rights), under section 5 (variation and recall of orders regulating occupancy rights and exclusion orders), under section 15(1) (order attaching a power of arrest—if made after the application for a matrimonial interdict), under section 15(2) and (5) (variation and recall of matrimonial interdict and power of arrest) and the proviso to section 18(1) (extension of period). The motion must be intimated at least 7 days before it is enrolled unless the court orders a lesser period[5]. In a sheriff court action the warrant for service will normally include a date for a hearing within a week if the court is to be asked to make interim orders at an early stage. Application for such orders at a later stage of a pending action is by motion duly intimated.

Power of arrest

Unless it appears to the court to be unnecessary to do so, the court is required to attach a power of arrest to any matrimonial interdict ancillary to an exclusion order and an interim exclusion order. Such a power can be granted only after the defender has had an opportunity of being heard. The court is similarly required to attach such a power to any other matrimonial interdict where the defender has had such an opportunity[6]. Accordingly it is not competent for an application to be made for a power of arrest to be attached to an interim order granted prior to service of the writ. At the first hearing after service of the writ a motion may be made to the court to attach a power of arrest to any interdicts then granted. A power of arrest is ineffective until the interdict to which it is attached has been served on the defender[7].

HEARING OF MOTION FOR INTERIM ORDERS

Contested motions are heard in open court. It may well be of advantage to have available information in documentary form to assist the court. Otherwise

1 *Nelson v Nelson* 1988 SLT (Sh Ct) 26.
2 Court of Session Act 1988, s 47(2); *Black Arrow Group v Park* 1990 SCLR 99.
3 *Welsh v Welsh* 1987 SLT (Sh Ct) 30.
4 RC 188D(3) and (4).
5 RC 188D(9).
6 Matrimonial Homes (Family Protection) (Scotland) Act 1981, s 15(1).
7 Ibid, s 15(2).

the court will be dependent on *ex parte*, and often conflicting, statements. Such documentary evidence may usefully be in the form of affidavit evidence where an exclusion order is sought. Wages slips, bank statements, notice of the amount payable by way of mortgage and community charge and the like are of assistance when aliment is in issue. A doctor's report (eg of his findings of injuries to the pursuer) in the form of a written statement bearing to be by a duly qualified medical practitioner and signed by him once lodged in court is admissible in place of parole evidence[1]. Extract convictions for assault and breach of the peace if related to the marriage may assist in obtaining a non-molestation interdict or an exclusion order.

Affidavits

In the Court of Session affidavits are admissible in connection with any application under the Matrimonial Homes (Family Protection) (Scotland) Act 1981[2]. In the sheriff court they are admissible only when the application is opposed[3]. It is not appropriate to take the statements made on behalf of the pursuer *pro veritate*[4]. If both parties produce affidavits which are mutually conflicting the court may feel unable either on the basis of *ex parte* statements or on the basis of the affidavits produced to determine whether an interim exclusion order should be made. There are difficulties holding a proof at an early stage limited to such interim orders but in some courts an abbreviated procedure of making up a record of the pleadings and fixing a very early proof is followed. (Few proofs arranged thus have proceeded[5].)

Affidavits should follow the form of affidavits for an undefended divorce but should deal only with matters germane to the interim orders which are in issue. The practice notes printed as an appendix hereto give some guidance.

INTERIM CUSTODY

Both the Court of Session and the sheriff court have jurisdiction to make orders and interim orders for custody[6]. The sheriff court also has jurisdiction at common law to deal with applications for custody and access. Courts are less likely to make a custody order where the effect would be to alter the status quo than where the effect would be to confirm it. It is thought that children should not be moved from the care of one parent to the other on an interim basis unless there is good reason to believe that that will be in the best interests of the child, that the decision is unlikely to be changed and that there is some degree of urgency. Clearly that may be so if there has been abuse of the child by the party who has care of him, but it may be

---

1 RC 168(6); OCR 72(4).
2 RC 188D(15).
3 AS (Consistorial Causes) 1984 (SI 1984/255), para 3(15).
4 *Smith v Smith* 1983 SLT 275 at 278, per Lord Robertson; *Ward v Ward* 1983 SLT 472 at 475.
5 Cf *Byars v McDonald* 1990 GWD 28–1610
6 Sheriff Courts (Scotland) Act 1907, s 5(2C) provides that the sheriff court has jurisdiction in respect of orders relating to parental rights. Parental rights include custody and access: Law Reform (Parent and Child) (Scotland) Act 1986, s 3 and cf the Conjugal Rights (Scotland) (Amendment) Act 1861, s 9.

difficult for the court to know what weight to attach to an allegation of that nature which is denied. At that stage as a matter of practice the court will not have heard evidence. The court may be reluctant to reach a decision on the basis of conflicting *ex parte* statements[1]. While there is no reason why affidavits may not be put before the court in connection with a motion for interim custody this is not common. In such circumstances the court will be likely to order a report to be prepared by an independent reporter as a matter of urgency. The Law Reform (Parent and Child) (Scotland) Act 1986, s 3(2) provides that the court shall not make any order relating to parental rights unless it is satisfied that to do so will be in the interests of the child. It has been held that an order for interim access should be refused *in hoc statu* until the court had obtained a report which might provide sufficient material to meet the test set out in that subsection[2]. Although there were cases in which access was sought by the father of an illegitimate child the subsection does not differentiate between natural parents and others who may apply for such rights.

INTERIM ACCESS

The preceding considerations clearly also apply so far as applications for interim access are concerned[3]. Courts tend to assume that it is in the best interests of a child to keep in touch with both parents unless there is some good reason to suppose that there should be no access. Where it is intended to make an award of access subject to the supervision of a social work department the court will appoint intimation (by the party making the motion for access) to the chief executive of the local authority of the motion for access and an indication that the social work department may be required to supervise access. The motion will be adjourned to allow sufficient time for the local authority to make representations in court or in writing[4].

INTERIM ALIMENT

Aliment may be awarded on an interim basis before defences are lodged and before the action is sisted to enable a party to apply for legal aid[5], but the person claiming aliment must have made a prima facie case[6]. That would not be so if the pursuer depended for the divorce on the consent of her husband which was refused[7]. Where a party seeking interim aliment is carrying on a course of adultery difficult questions may arise as to whether it is appropriate to make an order in favour of the adulterous spouse who may be caring for the children of the marriage. Commission of adultery does not of itself result in loss of the right to interim aliment. Much will depend on whether the paramour is providing or could provide support[8]. In a desertion case it may be argued that the party seeking aliment is not willing to adhere and has

1 *Peploe v Peploe* 1964 SLT (Notes) 44.
2 *Montgomery v Lockwood* 1987 SCLR 525, followed in *McEachan v Young* 1988 SCLR 98.
3 Cf *Johnston v Carson* 1990 SCLR 460.
4 Court of Session Practice Note No 1 of 1988.
5 *Fyffe v Fyffe* 1954 SC 1.
6 *Barbour v Barbour* 1965 SC 158.
7 *Boyle v Boyle* 1977 SLT (Notes) 69.
8 *Juner v Juner* (1908) 15 SLT 732; *Barbour*, supra.

no reasonable grounds for non-adherence and so should not be awarded aliment. Though it may seem contrary to principle to make an award in such circumstances the court will not be well placed to assess the relative strength of the arguments and may make an interim order pending a decision in the case; but it would refuse to do so pending an appeal where it had been held that there was a genuine offer to adhere[1].

As much factual information should be put before the court as possible as to the income and expenditure of the parties and as regards the needs of the person for whom interim aliment is sought[2]. In assessing need the court will have regard to the standard of living which the parties enjoyed and any particularly onerous commitments. The amount of aliment must be determined having regard to the ability of both parents to maintain their children[3]. There is little point in making an award where both parties are in receipt of state benefits. The court may award aliment on the basis of an understanding that in addition to the aliment to be paid the payer will continue to make payments of, eg, the mortgage. An award will not be refused simply because the person seeking aliment has means of her own[4]. For the purposes of interim aliment the principles set out in sections 9 to 11 of the 1985 Act do not apply. Nor do the circumstances set out in section 4 of that Act[5]. Accordingly the court has a wide discretion which will not be easily challenged on appeal.

In a sheriff court action if it is intended to appeal against a decision on a motion for interim aliment or access[6] leave to appeal must be sought. There was a sharp divergence between sheriffs principal as to whether or not leave to appeal is necessary. But unanimity has now been reached that leave is required. The last sheriffdom to take a different view was Tayside, Central and Fife[7].

REPORTS

At a hearing of an application for interim orders the court may be asked to obtain a report from a reporter. Such reports are usually asked for in connection with the arrangements current and proposed for the children of the marriage. A reporter is not infrequently appointed in sheriff court actions before the period of notice has expired and the cause has tabled. The view is taken in some sheriff courts that the cause must table before any such report may be ordered. Until then it is not known that there will be a defended action. There may be difficulty recovering the fees and outlays of a reporter within a reasonable time from a party who may never enter the process. The reporter in a matter of custody or access may be a social worker employed by a local social work department. In that event the court will normally appoint the Director of Social Work for that area to investigate and report to the court on all the circumstances of the child and the proposed arrangements for the care and upbringing of the child[8]. The director then nominates a suitable

1 *Bonnar v Bonnar* 1911 SC 854; *Douglas v Douglas* 1932 SC 680.
2 *Fyffe*, supra; Family Law (Scotland) Act 1985, s 6.
3 *Scully v Scully* 1989 SCLR 757.
4 *Fyffe*, supra.
5 Family Law (Scotland) Act1985, s 27—definition of 'aliment' and 'action for aliment'.
6 *Black v Black* 1990 GWD 30–1777.
7 Cf *Rixson v Rixson* 1990 SLT (Sh Ct) 5 and cases there cited; *Dickson v Dickson* 1990 SCLR 542; *Hulme v Hulme* 1990 SCLR 181; *Richardson v Richardson* (23 October 1990, Alloa Sheriff Court, unreported).
8 Matrimonial Proceedings (Children) Act 1958, s 11.

social worker to prepare the report. Alternatively the court may appoint an independent reporter, often but not invariably a solicitor or advocate. Before the court is invited to appoint a reporter, it may be prudent to ascertain from the clerk of court how long a report from a particular source is likely to take.

If the pursuer and the defender live in different local authority areas there may be a disadvantage in obtaining a report through a Director of Social Work. What may happen is that the report will come in two parts—from two different social workers employed by different local authorities. Neither may have been in a position to compare the pursuer and the defender and see their accommodation. An independent reporter will be able to travel to see both. That may be expensive. Steps should be taken to agree who is to pay the fee and outlays which will be incurred.

Usually the party who moved for the report to be prepared will be liable in the first instance; if the motion was a joint one the expense will be equally shared; but if the court ordered the report *ex proprio motu* the pursuer will normally be liable in the first instance[1]. Where a local authority has been appointed to prepare a report similar conditions apply as regards the instruction of the report and as regards meeting the expenses of the local authority[2].

Solicitors whose clients are in receipt of legal aid should satisfy themselves that the legal aid fund will cover the cost. In recent experience this has not been a source of difficulty. On receipt of the report the clerk of court may refuse to release it to the parties until payment has been received or a satisfactory undertaking given that early payment will be made. In terms of the Matrimonial Proceedings (Children) Act 1958, s 11 the expense of a report by whomever it is prepared is to form part of the expenses of the action and ultimately will be payable by the party ordered to pay such expenses.

OBTAINING EVIDENCE OF WELFARE OF CHILDREN

If there is inadequate information available to the court as to the welfare of the child, the court may order any person whom it believes has relevant information to disclose it to the court. It is not a reason for non-compliance that to do so would incriminate that person or his spouse. But a statement made in compliance with such an order is not admissible against either of them in any proceedings for any offence other than perjury[3].

OTHER ORDERS WHICH MAY BE GRANTED AD INTERIM

Committal of child to care of local authority or an individual

In terms of the Matrimonial Proceedings (Children) Act 1958, s 10 the court has power as respects any child for whose custody it has power to make provision in connection with inter alia divorce to commit that child to the care of the local authority or any other individual. But this may be done only where it appears to the court that there are exceptional circumstances making it

1 Court of Session Practice Notes, 13 November 1969 and 9 July 1974.
2 Court of Session Practice Note, 30 October 1980.
3 Family Law Act 1986, s 33.

impractical or undesirable for the child to be entrusted to either of the parties of the marriage. Before the court makes such an order in relation to a local authority, the local authority must be given an opportunity of making representations.

Supervision order

In terms of the Matrimonial Proceedings (Children) Act 1958, s 12 the court has power as respects any child for whose custody it has power to make provision in connection with inter alia divorce to make an order placing the child under the supervision of a local authority. But this may be done only where it appears to the court that there are exceptional circumstances making it desirable that the child should be under the supervision of an independent individual. Where it is intended to make a supervision order whether in respect of custody or access it is suggested that prior to any such order being made by the court intimation should be made (by the party making the motion) to the local authority of the terms of the motion giving an indication that a supervision order may be made. Any such motion will be adjourned to allow sufficient time for the local authority to make representations in court or in writing[1].

---

[1] Cf Court of Session Practice Note No 1 of 1988.

CHAPTER 9

DEFENDED ACTION

ENTERING APPEARANCE

In a Court of Session action the defender's solicitor should enter appearance not later than three days after the date of calling[1]. In a sheriff court action a notice of intention to defend should be lodged before the expiry of the period of notice[2].

ARRESTMENT ON THE DEPENDENCE

Where a warrant for arrestment on the dependence has been executed in connection with a claim in an action of aliment or for financial provision on divorce the court may limit the arrestment[3].

INHIBITION

Inhibition may be recalled or restricted as regards the property affected by it[4].

EARLY HEARING ON INTERIM ORDERS

It is necessary for the defender to be present or represented at any early hearing of which he has notice if he wishes to contest the making or the continuation of interim orders. Failure to appear is likely to be regarded as amounting to acquiescence in the making of such interim orders as the pursuer seeks. In support of the defender's position it may well be advisable to have available for production to the court such documentary evidence as can be made available; if an exclusion order is sought, affidavits from those who from their own knowledge can refute the pursuer's evidence; if aliment is sought, evidence of income of the defender and of his regular outgoings. This may entail obtaining, for example, wages slips or the most recent profit and loss account of the defender's business, bank statements, or a statement of the mortgage payments due.

1 RC 81(1).
2 OCR 33.
3 Family Law (Scotland) Act 1985, s 19(1)(b).
4 *Pow v Pow* 1987 SLT 127; RC 74(h); Gretton *The Law of Inhibition and Adjudication* pp 13–14.

WHERE AGREEMENT CAN BE REACHED

In an action of divorce in the sheriff court where custody of a child is sought, if parties can agree what orders should be pronounced, the court may grant interpone authority to or grant decree in terms of a joint minute dealing with custody, access, aliment, periodical allowance, capital payment or transfer of property whether or not these have been craved in the summons, initial writ or minute[1]. In the Court of Session the parties may enter into a joint minute agreeing the parental rights of a child and the court may interpone authority to that joint minute[2]. Decree of divorce may be delayed pending implementation of the agreement and, if it is not implemented, decree in terms of the agreement may be pronounced along with decree of divorce[3].

WHERE AGREEMENT CANNOT BE REACHED

In the Court of Session if the defender wishes to seek an order for financial provision on divorce or to oppose such an application by the pursuer he or his curator *ad litem*, if any, must lodge defences[4].

WHERE ONLY ALIMENT, PERIODICAL ALLOWANCE, CAPITAL PAYMENT OR TRANSFER OF PROPERTY ARE DISPUTED

Sheriff court—rule 34 minutes

In the sheriff court where, in an action of divorce the defender intends only to dispute liability for or the amount of or to raise other matters relating to aliment, periodical allowance, capital payment or transfer of property, he may, in place of lodging a notice of intention to defend, lodge a minute setting out the relevant facts[5].

Alternatively or additionally where he wishes to apply to the court for any of the orders referred to in the foregoing paragraph the defender may, in place of lodging a notice of intention to defend, lodge a minute which must set out the order which he claims the sheriff should make and set out the relevant facts in support of it[6] The minute when lodged should be accompanied by any relevant documentary evidence in support of the defender's claim. Such a form of defence is known as a rule 34 minute.

Where a rule 34 minute has been lodged the sheriff clerk enrols the case for a hearing. He will give the defender or his agent the date. It is the responsibility of the defender to send a copy of the minute and intimate the date of hearing to the pursuer. The pursuer must then return the initial writ to the sheriff clerk at or before the hearing. No process is lodged in court unless the sheriff so directs. At the hearing the sheriff may resolve the matter or continue the cause for such further procedure as he considers appropriate.

1 OCR 34(6), 56(3).
2 RC 170B(5).
3 *Cuthbertson v Cuthbertson* 1987 GWD 30–1129.
4 RC 170D.
5 OCR 34(2).
6 OCR 34(3).

Accordingly parties should be prepared for the matter to be the subject of a decision by the sheriff at the hearing. They should not assume that the sheriff will be prepared to postpone the application. It will assist the early and economical resolution of these matters if productions to be relied on are lodged with the sheriff clerk well in advance of the hearing and their lodging intimated to the other side. OCR 78 (lodging productions for proofs) does not apply to hearings as such but, if at the hearing the sheriff orders proof to take place, it is submitted that rule 78 would apply. If the court decides to hear parties on a rule 34 minute it will not normally make an order for financial provision until it grants a divorce on the basis of affidavit evidence[1]. Until decree of divorce has been granted a decision on a rule 34 minute is not appealable[2].

THIRD PARTY ENTERING THE PROCESS

A third party to whom intimation has been made or who claims an interest[3], may enter the process by lodging defences, answers or a minute in the divorce process[4]. In a sheriff court action the minuter should ask that he be sisted as a party to the action and that he be allowed to lodge defences or answers as the case may be. The procedure thereafter is as the court directs[5]. Where a minute is lodged in terms of RC 170B(7) either party may lodge answers thereto within such period as the court may allow.

DEFENCES

In most ordinary actions if a party who is sued does not enter the process in an appropriate way the pursuer can move for decree in absence[6]. In a defended action other than an action of divorce or separation, if a party does not lodge a production or a step in process or does not implement an order of court within the time allowed, or does not appear at a diet, decree by default may be granted[7]. But in an action of divorce irretrievable breakdown must be established[8]. The court is not bound to grant decree of divorce even though irretrievable breakdown has been established if in its opinion to do so would result in grave financial hardship to the defender[9]. But failure to lodge defences or a notice of intention to defend or to take any notice of interim motions may result in the assumption being made that there is not a good defence[10].

Defences take the same form as those in any ordinary action, ie there will be articulate answers to each of the articles of condescendence. Where there are proceedings continuing which would affect the validity or subsistence of the marriage and the pursuer has failed to aver the existence of such proceedings

1 OCR 23(1)(c); *Monkman v Monkman* 1988 SLT (Sh Ct) 37.
2 *Monkman*, supra.
3 *Smith v Smith* 1964 SC 218, 1964 SLT 309.
4 RC 165, 170B(7); OCR 130(12).
5 OCR 130(13).
6 RC 89; OCR 21.
7 OCR 59(1).
8 Divorce (Scotland) Act 1976, s 1(1).
9 Divorce (Scotland) Act 1976, s 1(5); *Boyd v Boyd* 1978 SLT (Notes) 55; *Nolan v Nolan* 1979 SLT 293.
10 *Nelson v Nelson* 1988 SLT (Sh Ct) 26; *Gardezi v Gardezi* 1987 GWD 37-1327; *Stevens v Stevens* 1987 GWD 16-605.

the defender is obliged to do so, giving the same information as the pursuer is required to do[1]. Those sentences which are accepted as true should first be repeated in the same order in the answers with each sentence prefaced by the words 'Admitted that'. If a fact is within the knowledge of the defender, such as whether or not he has committed adultery, he must either admit or deny it. Those sentences which are neither admitted nor denied should be repeated similarly and be prefaced by the words: 'Not known and not admitted that. . .'. If he does not wish to admit adultery but does not deny it the correct averment is 'No admission is made'. There follows the time honoured phrase: '*quoad ultra* denied' or '*quoad ultra* not known and not admitted'. '*Quoad ultra*' means 'all the other averments are'. That is usually followed by the equally well-known phrase 'Explained and averred' which prefaces the defender's account. That should be a summary of what he intends to prove and not be a narration of the evidence by which that will be proved. Pleas in law should be added stating the propositions in law upon which the defence is based. If the defender fails to state a plea in law in respect of a particular aspect of the pursuer's case, it will be assumed that he is not contesting that aspect[2].

Where a defender seeks an order for financial provision in his own favour he should set out in his defences in a Court of Session action, in the form of one or more conclusions, the order(s) which he seeks. There should be supporting averments and pleas in law[3]. When defences are lodged in court a copy of them should be sent to the pursuer[4].

Adjustment

In a sheriff court action where defences have been lodged, adjustment is permitted during such period or periods as the court may permit. In the Court of Session in a consistorial cause adjustment is permitted for a period of not more than 6 weeks excluding vacations. That period may be extended if a motion is enrolled prior to its expiry but only on special cause shown. Thereafter the equivalent of a closed record is made up; three copies are lodged in process; one copy is sent to each of the other parties and a motion is enrolled to have the cause sent to the appropriate roll for proof or to the Procedure Roll[5].

An open record is made up only with leave of the court on special cause shown[6]. In the sheriff court an open record is made up only if the sheriff so directs[7].

COUNTERCLAIM OR CROSS ACTION

Where in a sheriff court action it is not appropriate to lodge a minute in terms of rule 34 of the Ordinary Cause Rules for the purpose of disputing aliment, periodical allowance, capital payment or transfer of property, the question may arise as to what issues may be raised by way of a counterclaim

1 RC 157(3)(c); OCR 3(7).
2 Maxwell *Court of Session Practice* p 189; OCR 43(2).
3 RC 170D(2).
4 RC 83(d); OCR 43(2).
5 Court of Session Practice Note, 4 January 1973.
6 Court of Session Practice Note, 4 January 1973.
7 OCR 47(1).

as an alternative to raising a cross action. In the Court of Session procedure by way of counterclaim does not apply to consistorial actions[1]. In an action of divorce the defender must oppose the making of such orders or seek such orders in defences[2]. In either court if both parties wish to seek divorce the proper procedure is to raise a separate action in the usual way. The actions may be conjoined and heard together. If actions of divorce are pending in two different courts if one of them is not sisted it should be remitted to the other court. The actions should be disposed of at the same time[3]. But there may be circumstances which justify hearing one action before the other[4]. It is not competent to seek decree of divorce in a counterclaim in the sheriff court[5]. In the sheriff court the defender may counterclaim for custody of, access to or maintenance of a child for whom such an order is or could have been sought by the pursuer[6]. Where the defender makes such a counterclaim he may seek an order for aliment, periodical allowance, capital sum or transfer of property. He does not also require to lodge a rule 34 minute. It is not competent for a defender to counterclaim for a capital payment where none of the orders mentioned in OCR 56(1) is sought by the pursuer[7]. But where variation of the financial provisions contained in a decree of divorce is sought in the sheriff court the court may entertain a counterclaim for variation of the order for access made in the same interlocutor[8].

SISTING OF THIRD PARTIES

A person to whom intimation has been given may apply to be heard in the action. In the Court of Session the third party may lodge a minute craving leave to be sisted as a party to the action and making such relevant averments in relation to the care, maintenance or education of the child as may be appropriate[9]. In the sheriff court application should be made within the period of notice by minute craving to be sisted as a party and for leave to lodge defences or answers as the case may be[10]. As to the action which a curator *ad litem* should take see RC 167(1)(c); OCR 133(3) and p 112 supra.

PARTICULAR LINES OF DEFENCE

Defences to an action of divorce

The effect of a successful defence on the merits of an action of divorce is that the parties remain married to one another. This trite comment is not always appreciated by a would-be defender whose anger has been roused by what he considers to be a pack of lies, ie the averments of the pursuer in

1 RC 84(j).
2 RC170D(2) and (5).
3 *Pringle v Pringle* 1967 SLT (Notes) 60.
4 *Robertson v Robertson* 1972 SLT (Notes) 64.
5 *Whyte v Whyte* 1989 SCLR 375; *Farley v Farley* 1990 SCLR 452 and see *McNab v Nelson* 1909 2 SLT 68.
6 OCR 51, 56(1).
7 *Hollywood v Hollywood* 1989 SCLR 521.
8 *Freel v Freel* 1987 SCLR 665.
9 RC 170B(7).
10 OCR 11A.

the summons or initial writ. While most defences are based on challenging these allegations or putting forward a different interpretation of the marital history, if the action is based on adultery there may be a defence that the adultery has been condoned or was connived at. Otherwise if a defence is to succeed it must challenge at least one essential fact without proof of which the pursuer cannot obtain the decree sought, for example, an allegation that the defender has committed adultery. Where the divorce is based on non-cohabitation for five years the court is not bound to grant decree of divorce if in its opinion grave financial hardship would result from doing so[1]. 'Grave' seems to mean more serious than 'serious'[2].

ADULTERY

It is not a defence that the adulterer believed that the other spouse was dead[3], nor that he believed that he had been divorced[4].

CONDONATION

Section 1(3) of the Divorce (Scotland) Act 1976 provides that irretrievable breakdown is not established if the adultery founded upon has been condoned 'by the pursuer's cohabitation with the defender in the knowledge or belief that the defender has committed the adultery'. But there is no condonation by reason only of the fact that after the commission of the adultery the pursuer, having the knowledge or belief mentioned above, continued or resumed cohabitation as husband and wife[5], provided that the pursuer has not cohabited with the defender at any time after the end of three months from the date on which cohabitation was continued or resumed[6]. Knowledge of one act of adultery which is condoned may amount to condonation of a course of adultery with the same person[7], but not necessarily if there has been earlier adultery with another person[8]. If there is conditional condonation that amounts to condonation even though the condition is not fulfilled[9].

LENOCINIUM (OR CONNIVANCE)

Section 1(3) of the Divorce (Scotland) Act 1976 makes similar provision in regard to the defence of lenocinium. To establish the defence the connivance at the adultery must involve some positive act such as participation or encouragement[10]. Inactivity will not amount to connivance[11]. There must be a causal connection between lenocinium and the adultery[12].

1   Divorce (Scotland) Act 1976, s 1(5).
2   Cf Family Law (Scotland) Act 1985, s 9(1)(e).
3   *Hunter v Hunter* (1900) 2 F 771.
4   *Sands v Sands* 1964 SLT 80.
5   *Paterson v Paterson* 1938 SC 251 at 270.
6   Divorce (Scotland) Act 1976, ss 2(2), 13(2).
7   *Steven v Steven* 1919 2 SLT 239.
8   *Ralston v Ralston* (1881) 8 R 371.
9   *Collins v Collins* (1884) 11 R (HL) 19.
10 *Riddell v Riddell* 1952 SC 475 at 481 et seq, per Lord President Cooper; *Thomson v Thomson* 1908 SC 179.
11 *McMahon v McMahon* 1928 SN 37, 158; for a fuller discussion see Clive *Husband and Wife* pp 473 et seq.
12 *Gallacher v Gallacher* 1934 SC 339.

Matrimonial Homes Act matters

Applications under section 3 of the Matrimonial Homes (Family Protection) (Scotland) Act 1981 for regulation of rights of occupancy can be opposed on the grounds *inter alia* that:

(1) they are not 'just and reasonable having regard to all the circumstances of the case'[1];

(2) the matrimonial home (and in some circumstances the furniture and plenishings) are used in connection with a trade, business or profession[2], and

(3) the effect of the order would be to exclude the defender from the matrimonial home[3].

COMPENSATION

The court may order the pursuer to pay compensation where either the defender has suffered a loss of occupancy rights or the quality of his occupation of the matrimonial home has been impaired in consequence of the act or default of the pursuer which was intended to result in such loss[4].

Applications under section 4 of the Matrimonial Homes Act for an exclusion order and related orders may be opposed on the grounds *inter alia* that:

(a) the test for the granting of an exclusion order set out in s 4(2) has not been met;

(b) the grant of an exclusion order would be unjustified or unreasonable in all the circumstances including those set out in s 3(3);

(c) the matrimonial home is or is part of an agricultural holding or is a tied house in which the defender or both of the parties are required to reside[5];

(d) the exclusion order should be suspended. The court may suspend an interim exclusion order which it is prepared to grant in order to allow the defender to find alternative accommodation[6]. In that event decree for summary ejection would not be granted if the court was satisfied that it was not necessary.

(e) the orders ancillary to an exclusion order for ejection and for interdict prohibiting the removal of furniture and plenishings are unnecessary[7].

POWER OF ARREST

The court may refuse to attach a power of arrest to a matrimonial interdict other than one which is ancillary to an exclusion order if it is persuaded that such a power is unnecessary[8].

1 Matrimonial Homes (Family Protection) (Scotland) Act 1981, s 3(3).
2 Ibid, s 3(3)(d).
3 Ibid, s 3(5).
4 Ibid, s 3(7).
5 Ibid, s 4(3).
6 *Mather v Mather* 1987 SLT 565.
7 Matrimonial Homes (Family Protection) (Scotland) Act 1981, s 4(4).
8 Ibid, s 15 (1)(b).

Orders for financial provision

In the course of discussion of such orders in chapter 4 defences are discussed incidentally. Reference should be made to that chapter. Application may be made under sections 7(2) and 16(1)(b) respectively of the Family Law (Scotland) Act 1985 for the variation or termination of an agreement to pay aliment on a material change of circumstances or for the setting aside or variation of an agreement as to financial provision which was not fair and reasonable at the time it was entered into. The procedure for such applications is contained in Rule of Court 170D(7) and Ordinary Cause Rule 132A[1]. Generally application is by minute lodged in the original process.

PROCEDURE IN A DEFENDED DIVORCE

Defended divorces proceed as ordinary actions in the sheriff court. An open record of the pleadings is not made up unless the sheriff so orders[2]. In the Court of Session no open record is made up except with leave of the court on special cause shown. In that court there is a six week period of adjustment which may be extended[3]. During the course of adjustment or even during the proof an action of divorce may be amended to found on a ground which would not have been competent at the date on which the action was raised[4]. If the divorce action is plainly incompetent, for example, because the requisite period of non-cohabitation has not elapsed the court will dismiss the action unless it is amended[5]. An action of separation may be amended so that it becomes an action of divorce but the same may not be permitted where the action commenced as one seeking custody and aliment[6]. If the defender alleges that the marriage was bigamous and void, a preliminary proof may be allowed on that matter[7]. A defender will not normally be ordered to lead in the proof even where the principal contentions are likely to centre on the defence to a claim for an order for financial provision[8]. That is principally because the pursuer has to establish irretrievable breakdown of the marriage. All or at least most of the other orders sought are likely to depend on the establishment of that fact.

Late appearance by the defender

The defender may be allowed to appear and be heard at the proof even though he has not lodged defences (or, in the sheriff court, a notice of intention to defend) but he cannot lead evidence without the consent of the pursuer or he may be allowed to lodge defences at any time prior to decree of divorce being pronounced. This procedure takes the place of reponing procedure[9]. Its justification is that it is inappropriate to change the status of a person without

1 And see OCR 129.
2 OCR 47(1).
3 RC 168A, which sets out the procedure to be followed.
4 *Duncan v Duncan* 1986 SLT 17; *Robertson v Robertson* 1989 SCLR 71.
5 *Matthews v Matthews* 1985 SLT (Sh Ct) 68.
6 *Edgar v Edgar*; *Porter v Porter* 1990 SCLR 96.
7 *Battu v Battu* 1979 SLT (Notes) 7.
8 *Williamson v Williamson* 1989 SLT 866.
9 RC 89; OCR 28.

giving him an opportunity of being heard[1]. But the discretion to refuse to allow defences to be lodged will be exercised against permitting that course where the only result would be a waste of time and money[2]. The defender may be allowed by the sheriff to appeal within fourteen days of the decree of divorce[3]. In the Court of Session the court may allow the defender to reclaim within the reclaiming days although he was not present or represented at the proof[4]. The reclaiming days means within twenty-one days of decree of divorce[5]. On a few occasions a defender has been allowed to appear and lodge defences on the quantum of an order for financial provision after decree of divorce has been granted but before extract[6] As to the effective date of the interlocutor granting divorce see *Smith v Smith* 1989 SCLR 308, 1989 SLT 668.

Other parties who may appear

In addition to a curator *ad litem* appointed to the defender any person to whom intimation has been made may apply to the court to be sisted as a party within the period of notice or induciae by way of a minute[7]. In the case of a sheriff court action the minute asks for leave to lodge defences or answers. The Lord Advocate may appear in an action of divorce and may lead such proof and maintain such pleas as he thinks fit. The court may direct that any such action be brought to the notice of the Lord Advocate[8].

If a defender alleges adultery with a named person there will be an order for intimation to that person. If a paramour appears and denies committing adultery the court should determine whether the paramour committed adultery or not[9].

Reconciliation

Where the parties resume cohabitation during the dependence of a divorce action the action will either be sisted or dismissed on the motion of the parties, but the court may continue the action where it appears that there is a reasonable prospect of a reconciliation[10].

Conciliation

In any action (and in the Court of Session that includes a petition for custody of or access to a child[11]), where the custody of or access to a child is in dispute the court may, at any stage in the action or proceedings where it considers it appropriate to do so, refer the parties to a specified family conciliation service. In an action in the Court of Session this may be done only if the parties to the dispute agree[12].

1 *Stirton v Stirton* 1969 SLT (Notes) 48.
2 *Watt v Watt* 1978 SLT (Notes) 55.
3 OCR 59A.
4 RC 169.
5 RC 264(a).
6 *MacFarlane v McFarlane* (1985) JLSS 126.
7 See, eg, RC 170B(7); OCR 11A(6).
8 Court of Session Act 1988, s 19; Sheriff Courts (Scotland) Act 1907, s 38B.
9 *Raeside v Raeside* 1913 SC 60; *Creasey v Creasey* 1931 SC 9.
10 Divorce (Scotland) Act 1976, s 2(1); Court of Session Practice Note 1977 No 3.
11 RC 260D(10).
12 RC 170B(15); OCR 132F.

RECOVERY OF DOCUMENTS

In *Gould v Gould* 1966 SLT 130 at 133 the court said in regard to the financial arrangements between a husband and wife on granting a divorce:

> 'The evidence which is required to justify an application will vary according to the circumstances of the particular case. In general, detailed evidence will not be required and only in the rarest cases will a specification, designed to ascertain the defender's means, be justified or necessary. Thus the court will normally be able to deal properly with an application for a periodical allowance on the basis of the pursuer's evidence as to the defender's wages or occupation and the parties general standard of living at the time when they last lived together and as to her own means at the date of the proof.'[1].

The court will not grant commission and diligence to recover documents in a divorce action unless there are special circumstances such as that the means of one or both of the parties are substantial and one party has not frankly disclosed essential details of assets known to him but not to the other party[2].

The procedure for the recovery of documents is provided for in RC 95 to 98 and in OCR 78, 80, 81 and 82. There are no special provisions in connection with the recovery of documents peculiar to a divorce action.

Specimen calls for the recovery of documents relevant to financial conclusions

The following calls were approved by the Inner House in *Douglas v Douglas* 1966 SLT (Notes) 43. What form will be appropriate in a particular case will depend on the circumstances of that case.

(1) All profit and loss accounts and balance sheets of (name of business) for the period from (specify date—no more than 3 years prior) to date.

(2) All books of the company aftermentioned so that excerpts may be taken therefrom at the sight of the Commissioner of all entries showing or tending to show the heritable property owned by the said (company).

(3) All title deeds, plans and other documents so that excerpts may be taken therefrom at the sight of the Commissioner of all entries showing or tending to show the heritable property owned by the defender between (date) and this date.

(4) All registration books of motor cars in the hands of the defender or anyone on his behalf showing or tending to show the motor vehicles owned by the defender at this date.

(5) All receipts and demand notices for income tax paid by or due by the defender since (date).

(6) All books of account, cash books, ledgers, fee books or other cash memoranda kept by or on behalf of the defender for the period from (date) to date so that excerpts may be taken therefrom at the sight of the Commissioner of all entries showing or tending to show the defender's income from his business as a (specify occupation) during said period.

---

1 See also *Douglas v Douglas* 1966 SLT (Notes) 43; *Savage v Savage* 1981 SLT (Notes) 17; for a contrary view see *Latter v Latter* 1990 SLT 805.
2 *Douglas*, supra.

(7) All lists of investments, all share, stock and debenture certificates and dividend counterfoils, national savings certificates, life insurance policies, bank pass books, building society bank books, bonds, deposit receipts, IOUs, and other similar documents in name of the defender or anyone on his behalf so that excerpts may be taken therefrom at the sight of the Commissioner of all entries showing or tending to show the amount of the defender's incorporeal moveable property.

(8) Failing principals, drafts, copies or duplicates of the above or any of them.

The court will be prepared to allow recovery of documents and records to show the valuation of a shareholding in a company but may refuse to allow such recovery for the purpose of valuing the assets of the company[1].

Consideration may be given to making calls for the records of the defender's employers so that excerpts may be taken to show the salary or wages paid to the defender; or the call could be for wage slips or salary payments. Forms P45 or P60, receipts or invoices for the payment of rent may be relevant, but income tax returns as such should not normally be sought[2].

Where the income of the defender is not known and not readily ascertainable, for example, because it is paid from an overseas source to an offshore tax haven, it may be worth making averments as to the style of life of the defender and then seeking to recover records showing the level of his expenditure.

---

1 *Demarco v Demarco* (1990) The Scotsman, 30 May, 6 CL 951.
2 Macphail *Sheriff Court Practice* 15–56.

CHAPTER 10

THE EVIDENCE REQUIRED

BURDEN OF PROOF

The burden of proof is on the pursuer. In divorce cases it is often necessary for the pursuer to prove a negative, for example, that there has been no cohabitation since a certain date. It is not necessary for a pursuer to prove that there will not be grave financial hardship if decree of divorce is granted[1]. Nor is there a burden upon the pursuer to establish that there is no bar to divorce being granted, for example, to negate condonation of adultery. If it appears to the court that there is a bar to divorce, for example, because of lenocinium (connivance) the court will take notice of the point even though it has not been pleaded and may require further evidence or may refuse decree[2]. But if such a bar is pleaded it will be for the party pleading it to establish it[3]. In a defended action the pursuer should lead at the proof. She has to establish irretrievable breakdown[4]. The defender should lead evidence in a divorce action. He should not content himself with arguing that the pursuer has not proved her case[5]. So far as the burden of proof in matters of custody and access is concerned there may be an onus on the party seeking the order. That is so in the sense that before decree of divorce can be pronounced the court must be satisfied that the arrangements for the children are satisfactory or are the best that can be devised in the circumstances or that it is impracticable for the parties appearing before the court to make any such arrangements[6] But so far as variation of an order is concerned the burden is on the party seeking variation[7].

STANDARD OF PROOF

The Divorce (Scotland) Act 1976, s 1(6) provides that in an action for divorce the standard of proof shall be on balance of probability. In other consistorial matters that is also the standard[8].

1 Cf Divorce (Scotland) Act 1976, s 1(5).
2 *A v B* (1858) 20 D 407 at 418; *Andrews v Andrews* 1961 SLT (Notes) 48.
3 *Andrews*, supra.
4 *Paterson v Paterson* 1938 SC 251.
5 *Bird v Bird* 1931 SC 731; *White v White* 1947 SLT (Notes) 51.
6 Matrimonial Proceedings (Children) Act 1958, s 8(1).
7 *Porchetta v Porchetta* 1986 SLT 105, criticised in *Reid v Reid* 1987 GWD 8–308.
8 *Sloss v Taylor* 1989 SCLR 407 at 411, disapproving *MacEachan v Young* 1988 SCLR 98 at 100 where a higher standard was suggested; *Fisher and Donaldson v Steven* 1988 SCLR 337.

SUFFICIENCY OF EVIDENCE

It was formerly necessary to lead the evidence of at least two witnesses in court to prove the ground of divorce unless an extract decree of separation on the same, or substantially the same, ground was relied on but in such cases the pursuer had to give evidence[1]. Adultery, sodomy and bestiality had to be proved beyond reasonable doubt[2]. No longer is that so.

The requirement[3] that in *inter alia* actions of divorce the evidence shall consist of or include evidence other than that of a party to the marriage does not apply to certain actions. These are those actions where:

(1) the action is undefended;
(2) the action is based on non-cohabitation with or without the defender's consent;
(3) no other proceedings are pending in any court which could have the effect of bringing the marriage to an end;
(4) there are no children under the age of sixteen;
(5) neither party applies for an order for financial provision on divorce; and
(6) neither party suffers from mental disorder within the meaning of section 1(2) of the Mental Health (Scotland) Act 1984[4].

The former law of corroboration was amended in respect of actions which may proceed by the simplified procedure, ie those to which the foregoing order applies[5] but has now been amended for all civil proceedings in ordinary courts of law as well as in certain other proceedings by the Civil Evidence (Scotland) Act 1988; cf ss 8, 9. Evidence relative to the welfare of children under sixteen for whose custody, maintenance and education the court has jurisdiction to make provision is by way of affidavits unless the court otherwise directs. At least one affidavit is to be emitted by a person other than either of the parties to the marriage[6].

The Civil Evidence (Scotland) Act 1988, s 1(1) provides:
'In any civil proceedings the court ..., if satisfied that any fact has been established by evidence in those proceedings, shall be entitled to find that fact proved by that evidence notwithstanding that the evidence is not corroborated.'
Furthermore s 2(1) of that Act provides that evidence shall not be excluded solely on the ground that it is hearsay. Hearsay is defined as including hearsay of whatever degree[7]. It is also provided that a statement made by a person otherwise than in the course of the proof shall be admissible as evidence of any matter contained in the statement of which direct oral evidence by that person would be admissible. The court, if satisfied that any fact has been established by evidence in those proceedings, shall be entitled to find that fact proved by the evidence notwithstanding that the evidence is hearsay.

It may be difficult to argue that there is insufficient evidence in law in a particular case but the court will be concerned with the weight to be attached to the evidence which has been led. It is safer not to rest a case on the evidence

---

1 Divorce (Scotland) Act 1976, s 3(1).
2 Cf, eg, *Burnett v Burnett* 1955 SC 183 at 186–7, per Lord President Clyde.
3 Civil Evidence (Scotland) Act 1988, s 8(3).
4 Evidence in Divorce Actions (Scotland) Order 1989, SI 1989/582.
5 Divorce Jurisdiction, Court Fees and Legal Aid (Scotland) Act 1983, s 2; Evidence in Undefended Divorce Actions (Scotland) Order 1983, SI 1983/949.
6 RC 168(5).
7 Civil Evidence (Scotland) Act 1988, s 9.

of one witness nor on hearsay when other or more direct evidence is available. In other fields of law where the requirement for corroboration has been removed it is advisable in many cases to lead corroborative evidence if it is available[1]. The court must be satisfied that the fact has been established.

Section 8 of the Civil Evidence (Scotland) Act 1988 provides that in certain types of action, including actions of divorce and separation, 'no decree or judgment in favour of the pursuer shall be pronounced until the grounds of action have been established by evidence'. In *inter alia* actions of divorce and separation 'the evidence ... shall consist of or include evidence other than that of a party to the marriage[2]. The Lord Advocate may by order provide that the last-mentioned requirement shall not apply to such classes of action as may be specified[2].

This means that a basis for divorce, such as adultery, cannot be proved either by the evidence of one party or by the evidence of both parties to the marriage. There must be evidence led from a person who is not a party to the marriage. The courts will expect the evidence of non-party witnesses to be of substance in relation to the establishment of the ground of divorce. The exemptions so prescribed are noted above.

Evidence of parties

The parties to a divorce action are competent[3], and are probably compellable in relation to the matters in issue in a divorce action. One party may cite the other as a witness.

ASPECTS OF THE EVIDENCE REQUIRED

The court must be satisfied that the marriage has broken down irretrievably. That is a matter of fact. Irretrievable breakdown can be established only by proof of at least one of the bases set out in the Divorce (Scotland) Act 1976, s 1(2). Each such basis is itself a matter of fact. The date at which irretrievable breakdown must be established is the date of the divorce proof. By then a marriage based on the defender's behaviour may also have broken down because the pursuer is associating with another man[4].

Many cases decided prior to the coming into effect of the Civil Evidence (Scotland) Act 1988 may no longer be of binding or even persuasive authority, but some will be followed, albeit for different reasons. For example, it was held that a judicial admission by the defender supported by the evidence of the pursuer was not sufficient to prove adultery[5]. That case turned on an interpretation of the Court of Session Act 1830, s 36 which has been repealed[6]. But it is submitted that section 8 of the 1988 Act would lead a contemporary

1 Cf Law Reform (Miscellaneous Provisions) (Scotland) Act 1968, s 9; *Morrison v J Kelly & Sons Ltd* 1970 SC 65; *McGowan v Lord Advocate* 1972 SC 68; *McArthur v Organon Laboratories Ltd* 1982 SLT 425.
2 Civil Evidence (Scotland) Act 1988, s 8(4).
3 Evidence (Scotland) Act 1853, s 3, as amended.
4 *Findlay v Findlay* 1988 GWD 24-1034.
5 *Macfarlane v Macfarlane* 1956 SC 472 at 480.
6 Civil Evidence (Scotland) Act 1988, s 10 and Schedule.

court to the same conclusion. It may be necessary to lead evidence of several witnesses in order to establish a pattern of behaviour[1].

At a proof where the divorce is defended on its merits oral evidence is led in the usual way. But where the merits of the divorce are not in issue proof of the divorce will be by way of affidavit evidence unless the court directs otherwise[2]. Affidavit evidence may be sufficient proof. Only in rare cases is there oral evidence. However a proof may proceed partly by way of affidavit evidence and partly by way of oral evidence. This could happen where, for example, there was no dispute as to the fact that the defender had committed adultery. Evidence from inquiry agents might be by affidavit. But other matters may be in dispute such as orders relating to children or finance. Oral evidence might be led in connection with those matters in which there was dispute and might supplement affidavit evidence on undisputed matters.

Affidavit evidence includes affirmation and statutory or other declarations. Provided that the affidavit is emitted before a notary public or other competent authority it may be taken as the equivalent of parole evidence[3]. In an undefended proof in the sheriff court the evidence is not recorded[4].

PRACTICE NOTES RELATING TO DIVORCE AFFIDAVITS

The practice note by the Sheriffs Principal relates to actions of divorce in the sheriff court. That practice note and notes by the Dean of the Faculty of Advocates and the President of the Law Society of Scotland to similar effect in relation to affidavits in Court of Session divorce actions are printed as an appendix hereto. The notes are in broadly similar terms. The paragraph numbers which follow refer to the former practice note. The practice notes specify the forms which affidavits should take, the duties of the person taking the affidavit and what the affidavits should contain. Paragraph 4 is headed 'No hearsay' and states that an affidavit should contain only matters of fact to which the witness can testify. That may appear to be inconsistent with the provisions of the Civil Evidence (Scotland) Act 1988. But it is submitted that the practice note does not require to be amended. Affidavits are required to be used as the means of proof where no notice of intention to defend has been lodged, may be used where an action proceeds as undefended and may be used in relation to the merits of the divorce action even if there is a defence on an ancillary matter[5]. Affidavit evidence is admissible in place of parole evidence but the court may refuse to grant decree based on such evidence[6].

As the practice note points out (at paragraph 12), with affidavits the court cannot ask any supplementary questions. It is therefore legitimate to require that minimum standards of evidence be reached. Affidavits, for example, from a pursuer's mother, even prior to the coming into effect of the 1988 Act, were occasionally little more than a narration of what her daughter had told

1 Eg *Walker v Walker* 1953 SC 297; *Tullis v Tullis* 1953 SC 312; *Michlek v Michlek* 1971 SLT (Notes) 50.
2 RC 168(4); OCR 23, 72.
3 RC 168(3); OCR 72(3).
4 OCR 73(4).
5 RC 168(1); OCR 23, 72.
6 RC 168(10); OCR 23(3).

her of her married life. That added little or nothing to the evidence of the pursuer.

The practice note also requires, in paragraph 10, that an affidavit or affidavits providing corroborating evidence about the welfare of the children should be provided. The matters to be dealt with in relation to their welfare are set out in that paragraph. Before the court can grant decree of divorce it must be satisfied as respects every child for whose custody it has power to make provision that arrangements have been made for the care and upbringing which are satisfactory or are the best that can be devised in the circumstances or that it is impracticable for the party or parties appearing before the court to make any such arrangements[1].

PROOF OF MARRIAGE

Before the court can grant a divorce it has to be satisfied that the parties are married. A recent extract certificate of the marriage should be lodged with the writ[2]. Extracts are admissible without further proof of the entries to which they relate[3]. The pursuer in evidence or in her affidavit will identify that as her marriage certificate. That is normally regarded, in the absence of challenge, as sufficient[4]. If the marriage certificate is in a foreign language a certified translation should be lodged. The certificate should bear to be by a person who is qualified to make such a translation and that person should not normally be a party to the marriage. Embassies and consulates of the country where the marriage took place are usually prepared to provide a translation or provide information as to where such a translation may be obtained. It is not necessary, unless the matter is put in issue, to establish that a foreign marriage would be recognised as valid in Scotland[5]. If no marriage certificate can be obtained, the marriage may be proved *prout de jure* by evidence from witnesses who were present at it or, in a case of marriage by habit and repute, by evidence relevant to that[6]. As was noted in chapter 7, where the defender's address is unknown, a letter should be lodged in process from the General Register Office, New Register House, Edinburgh stating that there is no trace of a divorce having been granted previously in respect of the marriage between the pursuer and the defender[7].

PROOF OF BIRTH OF CHILDREN

Similarly an extract certificate of the birth of each of the children under sixteen at the date when the writ is lodged in court should be lodged with the summons or writ[8]. Abbreviated birth certificates are not normally accepted except in an emergency and on the understanding that full certificates will be lodged.

1 Matrimonial Proceedings (Children) Act 1958, s 8(1).
2 In the sheriff court the relevant extract(s) must be lodged with the writ in order to obtain a warrant for citation: OCR 3(9).
3 Registration of Births, Deaths and Marriages Act 1965, s 41.
4 Walker and Walker on Evidence, para 155.
5 see Clive: *Husband and Wife* ch 22.
6 *Lacy v Lacy* (1869) 7 M 369; *Shaw v Henderson* 1982 SLT 211.
7 Court of Session Practice Note, 10 March 1966, 1984 SLT (Notes) 100.
8 In the sheriff court the relevant extract(s) must be lodged with the writ in order to obtain a warrant for citation: OCR 3(9).

In a Court of Session case while abbreviated certificates may be accepted for the purpose of signetting in such circumstances, full certificates should be lodged before the case calls. Extracts are admissible without further proof of the entries to which they relate[1]. But for the purpose of proving that a particular person gave birth to a child, eg in order to prove adultery, there will have to be additional evidence such as that the defender had been pregnant prior to the date of birth or had been seen with a young baby shortly after that date[2].

ADMISSIONS

It has always been competent to prove that the defender admitted the conduct complained of by leading evidence from witnesses to the admission[3]. Such admissions are commonly made in connection with the commission of adultery and, less frequently, of assaults and other unreasonable conduct. But an extract conviction may be lodged. Evidence could be led that the defender pled guilty to a charge, for example, of assaulting the pursuer. A judicial admission (eg in defences) may be founded on[4]. The Civil Evidence (Scotland) Act 1988 has not, it seems, made an admission by, for example, a paramour of adultery with the defender admissible against the defender unless that admission was made in the presence of the defender and he did not dissent from it[5]. In practice paramours are usually quite prepared to give evidence of adultery directly. Failure to defend the action does not provide support for the pursuer's case[6].

DIVORCE BASED ON EARLIER DECREE OF SEPARATION OR IN OTHER MATRIMONIAL PROCEEDINGS

Section 3(1) of the Divorce (Scotland) Act 1976 provides that in an action of divorce, other than one based on adultery, the court may treat an extract decree of separation based on the same, or substantially the same, facts as those averred in support of the divorce action as sufficient proof of the facts upon which the decree of separation was granted. That means that an extract decree and a certified copy of the initial writ or summons or closed record should be lodged in process. Evidence will still be required from the pursuer whether orally or by way of affidavit[7]. So far as adultery is concerned the Law Reform (Miscellaneous Provisions) (Scotland) Act 1968, s 11 provides that a finding that a person was guilty of adultery in any matrimonial proceedings is admissible for the purpose of proving in any civil proceedings that the defender committed the adultery to which the finding relates whether or not he defended the action and whether or not he is a party to the (later) civil proceedings[8].

1 Registration of Births, Deaths and Marriages Act 1965, s 41.
2 Cf *Risi or Keenan v Keenan* 1974 SLT (Notes) 10.
3 Cf, eg, *Campbell v Campbell* (1860) 23 D 99.
4 *Macfarlane v Macfarlane* 1956 SC 472.
5 See Civil Evidence (Scotland) Act 1988, s 2(1)(b); *Creasey v Creasey* 1931 SC 9.
6 *Barr v Barr* 1939 SC 696.
7 Divorce (Scotland) Act 1976, s 3(2); *Wilson v Wilson* 1939 SC 102; *Andrews v Andrews* 1971 SLT (Notes) 44.
8 See *Andrews*, supra.

PROOF OF EXTRACT CONVICTIONS

The Law Reform (Miscellaneous Provisions) (Scotland) Act 1968, s 10(1) provides that in any civil proceedings the fact that a person has been convicted of an offence by a court in the United Kingdom is admissible in evidence for the purpose of proving that he committed that offence whether he pled guilty or not. An extract conviction should be lodged in court. It should be obtained in a form which describes the particular conduct of which the defender was convicted. It will be necessary to lead evidence from some third party that the person named in the extract is the defender[1].

PROOF OF ADULTERY

Adultery has been defined as 'voluntary sexual intercourse between a married person and a person of the opposite sex, not being the marriage partner'.[2]. It is now common practice for divorces for adultery to be proved by the lodging of affidavits by the defender and the paramour in which they describe when and how their relationship commenced and its nature. Such affidavits not infrequently narrate (unnecessarily) that they have been informed that they do not need to make an affidavit but that they choose to do so. The misapprehension that such narrative is necessary proceeds on what was held to be an incorrect reading of the Evidence Further Amendment (Scotland) Act 1874, s 2 which provides that a witness may refuse to answer any question tending to show that he has been guilty of adultery. The evidence of a defender and of a paramour[3], is admissible as evidence that they committed adultery and may be sufficient to establish that fact whether proof is by affidavit or parole evidence[4].

Inquiry agents will require a relatively recent photograph of both the pursuer and the defender. In many cases they obtain admissions from the defender and the paramour and inspect their accommodation. It is essential that they identify the defender as the person whom they have seen in the company of a person not the pursuer in circumstances from which it may be inferred that an act or a course of adultery was being committed. The photographs should be docqetted by them and by the pursuer and referred to in their affidavits.

Where adultery is to be proved by witnesses who know the defender and either the pursuer or the paramour (or all three) it is not necessary to lodge photographs. However it will be necessary for such witnesses to state in their evidence the basis of their knowledge, eg by reason of relationship or friendship over a number of years. Opportunity to commit adultery is not likely, on its own, to be sufficient proof unless the circumstances are compromising and suspicious[5], but opportunity with evidence of familiarity may well be sufficient[6].

1 See *Andrews*, supra.
2 Clive *Husband and Wife* p 443.
3 *Don v Don* (1848) 10 D 1046; *Muir v Muir* (1873) 11 M 529.
4 *Sinclair v Sinclair* 1986 SLT (Sh Ct) 54, but see *Cooper v Cooper* 1987 SLT (Sh Ct) 37.
5 *Bennet Clark v Bennet Clark* 1909 SC 591; *McInnes v McInnes* 1954 SC 396; *Hall v Hall* 1958 SC 206.
6 Eg *Burnett v Burnett* 1955 SC 183; *White v White* 1990 GWD 12-612.

Love letters passing between the defender and the paramour[1], or a written admission by the defender in a diary[2], or to any other party, provided that they can be identified as such, will clearly be strong evidence.

Adultery may be proved on a non-access basis by evidence that the defender has had a child of whom the pursuer could not have been the father, for example, because he was working abroad at the time of conception[3]. A photostat of the birth certificate should be lodged in court and, if the defender has signed it her signature should be identified. Photostatic copies are treated as equivalent to principals. Application should be made to the Registrar General of Births, Marriages and Deaths in Scotland for such copies. In England application should be made to district registrars[4]. The birth certificate may also identify the father of the child. In addition to such evidence as the birth certificate may disclose there should be evidence consistent with the birth of a child to the defender on the date shown on the birth certificate. Such evidence may be to the effect that the defender has in fact had a child (eg she has been seen pushing a young baby in a pram) or was seen to have been pregnant shortly before the date of birth[5]. It is now possible to prove paternity of a child with great accuracy by testing the DNA in the blood of the child and the putative parents. Adultery may also be proved by evidence of the communication by one party to the other of a sexually transmitted disease.

Proof of bigamous marriage

While bigamy is a ground of nullity of marriage it is not of itself a basis for irretrievable breakdown of a marriage. Evidence of bigamy may be relevant to a divorce for adultery or unreasonable behaviour[6]. Where it is alleged that there has been bigamy, it is not enough to rely on production of the certificate relating to the allegedly bigamous marriage. Such a certificate is evidence of the entry in the register. It is not by itself sufficient evidence that the marriage took place. Accordingly evidence that that marriage took place is necessary[7]. That case involved consideration of the Court of Session Act 1830, s 36 which has been repealed[8]. The equivalent provision is now contained in section 8 of the Civil Evidence (Scotland) Act 1988.

PROOF OF UNREASONABLE BEHAVIOUR

There must be sufficient evidence that the behaviour of the defender has been such that the pursuer cannot reasonably be expected to cohabit with him[9]. General support for the particular evidence of the pursuer can be sufficient

1 Eg *Rattray v Rattray* (1897) 25 R 315; *MacColl v MacColl* 1946 SLT 312.
2 *Argyll v Argyll* 1963 SLT (Notes) 42.
3 *Currie v Currie* 1950 SC 10 at 14; *MacLennan v MacLennan* 1955 SC 105; *Passmore v Passmore* 1972 SLT (Notes) 18.
4 Court of Session Practice Note, 28 September 1956.
5 *Mackay v Mackay* 1946 SC 78.
6 At a divorce proof the writer once called as witnesses two subsequent 'husbands' to prove adultery by the wife. The wife who lived in Berlin seemed to have made a business of marrying servicemen then stationed there. It never became known whether she had also married that particular pursuer bigamously.
7 *Risi or Keenan v Keenan* 1974 SLT (Notes) 10.
8 Civil Evidence (Scotland) Act 1988, s 10(1) and Schedule.
9 Cf *Boyce v Boyce* 1986 SLT (Sh Ct) 26 - evidence held, possibly incorrectly, to be insufficient.

evidence[1]. What must be proved is set out above. Particular incidents need not be corroborated. The evidence will not be insufficient simply because the conduct is most unlikely to be repeated[2].

PROOF OF THE DEFENDER'S CONSENT TO DECREE UNDER SECTION 1(2)(d)

Evidence of one witness is sufficient to establish the signature on a consent form as being that of the person consenting. If the consent has been indicated in the prescribed manner that is sufficient evidence of such consent[3].

MEDICAL REPORTS

In undefended actions 'a written statement bearing to be that of a duly qualified medical practitioner which has been signed by him and lodged in process shall be admissible in place of parole evidence'[4]. In a defended action an attempt should be made to agree the terms of any such report.

REPORTS ON CUSTODY AND ACCESS

It is for the pursuer to provide evidence as to the welfare of the children. That cannot be done, unless in exceptional circumstances, simply by asking the court to order a report. It is for the court to decide whether a report should be obtained[5]. While it is not uncommon for the court to ask for a report to assist in the resolution of disputes about interim custody or access pending further progress in the action, it has been known in a contested case for the court, having heard evidence in a proof, to request a report from a reporter and, in the light of the findings of that report, to grant custody to one party on such terms as the court considered to be appropriate[6]. The court in that case did not hear evidence from the compiler of the report. However in a later, contested case where a report had been obtained and the compiler did not give evidence but the parties did, the report was not regarded as evidence[7]. It is suggested that the approach in the latter case is to be preferred[8]. Where a report has been obtained the parties may not cite the maker of the report as a witness unless the court either *ex proprio motu* or on a motion to that effect requires that person to appear as a witness[9]. That is in accordance with the Matrimonial Proceedings (Children) Act 1958, s 11(4). It is suggested that that practice should be followed in the sheriff court. The reporter is appointed as an independent officer of court. He or she should

1 *Yates v HMA* 1977 SLT (Notes) 42.
2 *Hastie v Hastie* 1985 SLT 146.
3 Divorce (Scotland) Act 1976, s 1(4) and cf RC 166(2) and OCR 72(4).
4 RC 168(6); OCR 72(4).
5 *Wallace v Wallace* 1963 SC 256.
6 *MacIntyre v MacIntyre* 1962 SLT (Notes) 70.
7 *Whitecross v Whitecross* 1977 SLT 225 at 228, per Lord Avonside.
8 *Oliver v Oliver* 1988 SCLR 285; *Kristiansen v Kristiansen* 1987 SCLR 462.
9 Court of Session Practice Note, 6 June 1968.

not be regarded as a witness to fact unless an incident has taken place which was witnessed by the reporter.

EVIDENCE OF WELFARE OF CHILDREN WHOSE WHEREABOUTS ARE UNKNOWN

If there is inadequate information available to the court as to the welfare of the child, the court may order any person whom it believes has relevant information to disclose it to the court. It is not a reason for non-compliance that to do so would incriminate that person or his spouse. But a statement made in compliance with such an order is not admissible against either of them in any proceedings for any offence other than perjury[1]. If adequate information is not available the court will be asked to grant divorce on the basis that it is impracticable to make arrangements for the care and upbringing of the children[2].

EVIDENCE OF THE WELFARE OF A CHILD IN THE CARE OF A LOCAL AUTHORITY

In such circumstances it is sufficient that there be an affidavit from a person qualified so to state that the child is in the care of a particular local authority. It is not necessary for that person to be aware of or speak to the arrangements for the child unless the welfare of the child is put in issue[3].

INTERVIEWING CHILDREN

The court may interview children in private, if it considers it appropriate to do so. That is not infrequently done if the parties consent or at least raise no objection[4]. The court would not interview a child if one of the parties objected. Judges differ as to whether to interview children, and if so in which cases, even if the parties agree that that should be done. A case should not be decided on the basis of interviews with the parties and the children alone[5]. Interviews with children may take place at any stage of a proof. The best stage may be at the conclusion of the evidence for the defender. A difficulty from the judge's point of view is that what a child says is said in private. The rest of the evidence will have been heard in public and subjected to cross-examination. If the child says something which has a material bearing on the other evidence in the case or raises points not dealt with in the evidence, what status and weight is the account given by the child to be accorded? How does a sheriff make findings in fact in regard to the child's evidence? Nonetheless, where matters are evenly balanced the child's wishes may be decisive[6].

1 Family Law Act 1986, s 33.
2 Matrimonial Proceedings (Children) Act 1958, s 8(1).
3 *Hunter v Hunter* 1979 SLT (Notes) 2.
4 Cf, eg, *Casey v Casey* 1989 SCLR 761.
5 *MacDonald v MacDonald* 1985 SLT 244.
6 Eg *Fowler v Fowler* 1981 SLT (Notes) 9.

AFFIDAVITS

Undefended action

In an undefended action affidavit evidence is admissible in place of parole evidence and may be sufficient evidence[1]. These rules provide that proof in all undefended actions of divorce shall be by way of affidavit evidence unless in that particular action the court directs otherwise. Affidavits dated prior to the raising of the action are competent[2].

Affidavits and written statements in defended actions

Affidavit evidence may be allowed in an action in which there is a contest on the merits of that action or in respect of non-contentious aspects of a case[3]. If the evidence would be admissible if it were oral evidence it may be admitted in the form of a written statement which may be in the form of an affidavit. Application must be made to the court by motion to receive the statement. The statement must be lodged with the motion along with (where the motion is not agreed to) an affidavit or affidavits setting out the name, designation and qualifications of the author of the statement, the circumstances in which it was written and the reasons for the application. The last-mentioned provisions may be complied with by including the necessary information in the original written statement or affidavit. But a motion to that effect is likely to be refused if the evidence is crucial to the case and is likely to be challenged at the proof[4].

Taking affidavits

The practice notes issued by the Dean of Faculty and President of the Law Society (11 April 1978) and by the sheriffs principal printed as an appendix hereto, which offer guidance as to the form, content and procedure which should be adopted when obtaining affidavit evidence, should be followed.

There is no objection to the solicitor acting for a party being the notary who swears the affidavit(s). A person entitled to swear an affidavit must be a notary public, justice of the peace, commissioner of oaths or other statutory authority within the meaning of the Statutory Declarations Act 1835. A separate affidavit should be sworn by each witness[5].

The affidavits should:

(1) Be in the form set out in the practice notes. An example is set out below.

(2) Make it clear whether the witness was sworn or affirmed.

(3) Contain evidence only of matters to which that witness can speak from his own knowledge and should indicate how that witness knows that fact, eg by seeing or hearing.

(4) Set out the evidence of the witness on the matters to which he can speak in the same order as these matters are set out in the writ. This makes it much easier to check the sufficiency of the evidence. This should be done in numbered paragraphs.

1 RC 168(2); OCR 23(1) and(2), 72(1) and (2).
2 *McInnes v McInnes* 1990 SCLR 327.
3 Civil Evidence (Scotland) Act 1988, s 2(1)(b), (3), (4); RC 108A; OCR 72A.
4 *Ebrahem v Ebrahem* 1989 SCLR 540.
5 *Sanderson v Sanderson* 1979 SLT (Notes) 36.

(5) Contain the evidence of the witness in terms which reflect what he or she would have said had the evidence been oral. There is an unwelcome tendency for affidavit evidence to look like word-processor excerpts from the writ.

(6) Refer expressly to all the documents or other productions, to which that witness speaks, by their number of process, if any, eg, the marriage and birth certificates, consent of the defender or photographs. Each such production must be docqueted as being the production referred to in the affidavit and must be signed by the witness and the notary.

(7) Where the pursuer does not seek a capital sum, periodical allowance or aliment for the children, explain why not. The absence of a claim for expenses need not be explained. Expenses should not be claimed in a five year non-cohabitation case, particularly when the pursuer is legally aided[1].

(8) Contain full, accurate and up to date information, particularly as regards the welfare of the children and the financial situation of the parties. How up to date the information on such matters is should be made clear in the evidence of the witness.

(9) Where there are children contain information, as a minimum as to the following:

(a) the qualifications of the witness, if not a parent, to speak about the child; the frequency of the occasions and the circumstances in which the witness sees the child;

(b) information about home conditions in which the child lives;

(c) observations upon the child's general appearance, interests and state of health and well-being;

(d) information, where relevant, about the school the child attends; whether and to what extent he has contact with other children and relatives;

(e) observations on the relationship between the child and the person in whose care he or she lives, on the child's attitude towards each of the parents and on the extent of contact with the parent or parents with whom the child is not living;

(f) details of arrangements made for the child while the parent having care of him is not available, eg because she is at work (other than during school hours);

(g) the means of the person seeking custody with reference to his or her ability to maintain the child in a suitable manner.

(10) Refer to any joint minute which may have been entered into by the parties.

(11) be signed by the witness and the notary on each page[2].

In adultery actions it is common for the affidavits of a defender and paramour to state that they have been warned that they need not incriminate themselves by making an affidavit. As has been remarked above such a statement is not necessary[3].

The notary should satisfy himself that the witness has the mental capacity to swear an affidavit. The witness should appreciate the importance of what is being done by him and, before signing the affidavit, should be given an opportunity to alter any typed draft affidavit which is put in front of him. For many people swearing an affidavit may be a somewhat intimidating event. They may not be willing to make corrections unless specifically given the opportunity to do so.

---

1 See chapter 7.
2 *Macalister v Macalister* 1978 SLT (Notes) 78.
3 *Sinclair v Sinclair* 1986 SLT (Sh Ct) 54 but cf *Cooper v Cooper* 1987 SLT (Sh Ct) 37.

Form of affidavit

COURT OF SESSION, SCOTLAND
(or)
SHERIFFDOM OF (eg TAYSIDE, CENTRAL AND FIFE AT PERTH)
AFFIDAVIT
of
(Full name)
in causa
(Here take in the parties as in the instance)

At , the day of 19 , in the presence of Compeared who being solemnly sworn *or* who being affirmed, Depones as follows:
1. (The full name, age and address of the deponent)
2. et seq.: set out the evidence of the deponent
All of which is truth as the Deponent shall answer to God or All of which is affirmed to be true.

(Signature of Deponent)
(Signature of Notary)
(Note: each page must be signed by both deponent and notary. Any alterations should be initialled by both.)

EVIDENCE OF THE FINANCIAL MATTERS

Where there are claims for orders for financial provision, and even where the action is undefended, there should be evidence, at least in the affidavits, dealing with the financial claims. The court is required to decide what order is justified by the principles set out in the Family Law (Scotland) Act 1985, ss 9–11 and reasonable having regard to the resources of the parties[1]. Where interim aliment is in issue the court may award any lesser sum than the sum claimed or may refuse to make such an award[2]. Accordingly such claims should not be regarded as being the same as undefended claims for payment of sums of money in which if there is no defence it is assumed that the pursuer will be entitled to what he claims. Many claims for orders for financial provision are resolved without oral evidence. Documentary evidence is lodged of the income, gross and net of the parties, the value of their capital assets, their major outgoings (eg mortgage, insurance). Where possible these documents should be agreed. The decision may then be made on the basis of *ex parte* statements. It may be necessary to obtain actuarial evidence where questions arise as to the value of interests in trusts, pension schemes and life assurance policies. The lack of such evidence may hamper a court in arriving at a fair decision[3]. Oral evidence is usually heard where it is alleged that there has not been full disclosure or where there are differences as to the value of major assets. It may be necessary in such cases to seek to recover documents. There are no specialities as to the procedure for such recovery in a divorce case[4]. But the court will allow such recovery only in exceptional cases[5].

If there are financial claims and one party does not give evidence or does not challenge in cross-examination the evidence for the other party inferences most favourable to that other party may be drawn[6]. The same approach may be adopted in criminal cases[7].

1 Family Law (Scotland) Act 1985, s 8(2).
2 Ibid, s 6(2).
3 *McDevitt v McDevitt* 1988 SCLR 206; *Phillip v Phillip* 1988 SCLR 427.
4 RC 95-98; OCR 78, 81 and 82.
5 Reference should be made to the concluding paragraphs of Chapter 9.
6 *O'Donnell v Murdoch Mackenzie & Co* 1967 SLT 229; *Berry v Berry* 1990 GWD 12-617.
7 *McIlhargey v Herron* 1972 SLT 185.

CHAPTER 11

ORDERS MADE AFTER DIVORCE, VARIATION AND RECALL OF ORDERS

ORDERS MADE AFTER DIVORCE

Making an order for payment of capital sum or transfer of property after divorce

An order for payment of a capital sum or transfer of property, if not made on granting decree of divorce, may be made within such period as the court on granting decree of divorce may specify. The court may stipulate that any such order will come into effect on a specified future date and be payable by instalments[1]. Thus it may be that there will be a further hearing in connection with the making of such orders notwithstanding that decree of divorce has been granted. This hearing may be fixed as a result of a motion in the divorce action by one of the parties. If the court, on granting decree of divorce, has not specified a period within which such an order may be made the court will be unable to make such an order at a later date.

Making an order for payment of periodical allowance after divorce

An order for a periodical allowance, if not made on granting decree of divorce, may be made within such period as the court on granting decree of divorce may specify. But if no such order has been made previously, if application is made after the date of the decree and if, since the date of decree, there has been a change of circumstances, an order for a periodical allowance may be made after decree of divorce[2]. It is to be noted that the change of circumstances does not have to be 'material' in this connection. An application at that stage for a periodical allowance raises some problems which the Family Law (Scotland) Act 1985 does not resolve. Taking sections 8 to 13 together it is clear that the principles to be applied in making an order for financial provision at the time of a divorce are also to be applied when application is made for a periodical allowance after divorce. In particular the court is enjoined by section 13(2) not to make an order for a periodical allowance unless it is satisfied that an order for a capital sum or for transfer of property would be inappropriate or insufficient. But the court may already have made an order for a capital sum or for the transfer of property or may, at the post-divorce stage, be prevented from doing so because it has no power to do so[3]. How a court is to reach such a decision in a post-divorce application for a periodical allowance where

1 Family Law (Scotland) Act 1985, s 12.
2 Ibid, s 13(1); *Bain v Bain* 1990 GWD 3–136.
3 Ibid, s12.

there has been a division of capital is not clear. There is unlikely to be a full record of the basis upon which the division was made and of the circumstances prevailing at that time.

Where a party wishes to apply for an order for a periodical allowance in circumstances in which one was neither applied for nor made at the time when decree of divorce was granted, in a Court of Session action, application is made by motion intimated on an induciae of fourteen days[1]. The court may then order that a minute and answers be lodged. But it seems that in the sheriff court a new action will have to be raised. This is because the rules of court do not make provision for such an application to be made by minute in the original divorce process in this particular connection[2].

ORDERS FOR FINANCIAL PROVISION FOLLOWING AN OVERSEAS DIVORCE OR ANNULMENT

Where there has been a divorce in an overseas country a court in Scotland may, in certain circumstances, entertain an application for an order for financial provision, provided that certain conditions are met[3]. Broadly speaking, an application may be competent when the circumstances, at the time that the overseas divorce was granted, were such that a divorce could have been granted in Scotland. Such an application may be made to the Court of Session[4], or to the sheriff court. But if the application is to the sheriff court there are additional jurisdictional requirements.

An overseas country means a country or territory outside the British Islands. An order for financial provision means not only an order which might have been granted under the Family Law (Scotland) Act 1985, s 8(1) had it been a Scottish divorce but also an order under the Matrimonial Homes (Family Protection) (Scotland) Act 1981, s 13, which makes provision for transfer of the tenancy of the matrimonial home.

For such an application to succeed the court to which application is made must first have jurisdiction. If jurisdiction would fall to be determined under Part I of the Civil Jurisdiction and Judgments Act 1982, the requirements of that Act must be met[5]. But if that is not the case there will be jurisdiction where the applicant was domiciled or habitually resident in Scotland on the date when the application was made and the other party to the marriage either:

(1) was domiciled or habitually resident in Scotland on that date; or

(2) was domiciled or habitually resident there when the parties last lived together as husband and wife; or

(3) when the application was made owned, was tenant of or had a beneficial interest in property in Scotland which had at some time been the matrimonial home.

Where the application is made in the sheriff court either one of the parties must be resident in the sheriffdom or the property referred to in (3) above must be wholly or partially in the sheriffdom.

1 RC 170D(3), 170B(10).
2 OCR 129(2)(c).
3 Matrimonial and Family Proceedings Act 1984, s 28(1).
4 RC 170M.
5 Matrimonial and Family Proceedings Act 1984, s 28(4).

Secondly all the following conditions must be satisfied:

(a) the divorce is one which would be recognised in Scotland;
(b) the other party initiated the divorce proceedings;
(c) the application was made within five years of the divorce taking effect;
(d) a court in Scotland would have had jurisdiction to entertain an action of divorce between the parties if such an action had been brought in Scotland immediately before the divorce took effect;
(e) the marriage had a substantial connection with Scotland, and
(f) the parties are alive at the date of the application[1].

If these conditions are satisfied the court will apply Scots law[2]. The court is required to exercise its powers so far as is reasonable and practicable to put the parties in the financial position in which they would have been if the action of divorce had been raised in Scotland and had been disposed of on the date when the foreign divorce took effect. Account must be taken of the parties' resources, present and foreseeable, and any order made by a foreign court for financial provision or the transfer of property.

Where the applicant has to rely on the basis of jurisdiction set out in (3) above in order to establish jurisdiction, the court may only make orders relating to the former matrimonial home or its furniture or plenishings, or that the other party pays a capital sum not exceeding that other party's interest in the matrimonial home[3].

In relation to other applications the court may make an interim order for the payment of periodical allowance if it appears from the averments that an order for financial provision will be made and that it is necessary to make such an order to avoid hardship to the applicant[4]

RESTRICTING THE REMOVAL OF A CHILD FROM THE JURISDICTION OF THE COURT

A court in Scotland may, at any time after the commencement of proceedings in connection with which the court would have power to make a custody order or in any proceedings in which it would be competent for the court to grant an interdict prohibiting the removal of a child from its jurisdiction, grant interdict or interim interdict prohibiting the removal of the child from the United Kingdom or any part of the United Kingdom or out of the control of any person in whose custody the child is[5]. Application in the Court of Session is by minute lodged in the cause to which the application relates[6]. The provision applies to sheriff courts as well as to the Court of Session. Accordingly a sheriff may grant interdict prohibiting the removal of a child from the United Kingdom or part of it. He is not restricted to prohibiting removal from his sheriffdom, still less from his sheriff court district.

1 Ibid, s 28(3).
2 Ibid, s 29(1).
3 Ibid, s 29(5).
4 Ibid, s 29(4).
5 Family Law Act 1986, s 35(3); see also chapter 5.
6 RC 170B(13).

ORDERS FOR DELIVERY OF A CHILD

A court having jurisdiction to make a custody order in relation to a child also has jurisdiction to make an order for the delivery of that child whether or not the order sought is in implement of a custody order[1].

VARIATION AND RECALL OF ORDERS AFTER DIVORCE

Setting aside or variation of agreements between spouses

Former spouses can enter into an agreement to vary the terms of court orders without the intervention of the court. That agreed variation may subsequently be set aside or varied by court order on a change of circumstances[2]. Where a husband and wife enter into a financial agreement to take effect on divorce the court, after divorce, may set aside any term of that agreement so far as it relates to periodical allowance and provided that the agreement makes provision for the court to do that. In a sheriff court action application will be by summary application[3]. The court may set aside an agreement or a term of it on granting decree of divorce or after divorce if the agreement was not fair and reasonable at the time it was entered into[4]. In a sheriff court action application will be by minute lodged in the divorce process[5].

Orders which may be varied or recalled

Application may be made to the court in the divorce process for variation or recall of orders including the following:[6]

    (1) variation or recall of an order for custody of or access to children under sixteen[7].

    (2) variation or recall of an order for periodical allowance.[8]
The application may be made by either party to the marriage or his or her executor. The court may also backdate such variation or recall to the date of the application or, on cause shown, to an earlier date; or convert the order into an order for payment of a capital sum or an order for the transfer of property. If there is a backdating of a variation or recall the court may order repayment of periodical allowance[9].

    (3) variation or recall of an order for aliment of a child[10].

1 Family Law Act 1986, s 17; for a more detailed discussion see chapter 5.
2 *Jenkinson v Jenkinson* 1981 SLT 65.
3 OCR 132A(3).
4 Family Law (Scotland) Act 1985, s 16.
5 OCR 132A(4); *Milne v Milne* 1987 SLT 45.
6 Cf RC 170B(8); OCR 129(2).
7 Test is: 'a material change of circumstances.'
8 Test is: 'a material change of circumstances': Family Law (Scotland) Act 1985, s 13(4).
9 For examples of applications by executors see *Sandison's Exrx v Sandison* 1984 SLT 111; *Finlayson v Finlayson's Exrx* 1986 SLT 19.
10 Test is: 'a material change of circumstances': Family Law (Scotland) Act 1985, s 5(1); cf RC 170P.

The powers of the court when dealing with such an application include power to order the payment of aliment for a definite or an indefinite period or until the happening of a specified event, to order payments of an occasional or special nature or for educational expenses, to backdate an award[1], and to order the repayment of sums paid under the decree[2]. The court also has power to award less than the sum claimed even if there is no dispute, eg when the defender has not entered any form of defence[3] In order to justify backdating to a date earlier than the date of the motion for variation there must be special cause shown, for such a power will be sparingly exercised[4]. Variation of an award of aliment may be granted after the definite period for which it was awarded has expired. A parent may seek such variation in the divorce process on behalf of a child over sixteen[5]. Recall of a sheriff court order is unnecessary where the order has been superseded by a Court of Session order[6].

(4) variation of the date or method of payment of a capital sum[7].
(5) variation of the date of transfer of property[8].
(6) variation or recall of an incidental order[9].
(7) by a trustee in bankruptcy or judicial factor if the payer was absolutely insolvent at the date of the order or was so rendered by the making of such order for recall of the order and for repayment or retransfer of any property handed over in implement of the order, or the value of such property[10].
(8) setting aside or variation of terms of agreements relating to periodical allowance where the agreement so provides[11].
(9) within a specified period after divorce has been granted for the setting aside or variation of an agreement as to financial provision or any term of it where the agreement was not fair and reasonable at the time it was entered into[12].
(10) variation or recall of orders made under the Matrimonial Homes (Family Protection) (Scotland) Act 1981, s 3 (occupancy rights) and s 4 (exclusion orders)[13].

Orders for periodical allowance or for payment of a capital sum or for the transfer of property may have been made after the date on which decree of divorce was granted in the circumstances mentioned above. An incidental order under section 14(2) and (3) of the Family Law (Scotland) Act 1985 may be made before divorce in certain circumstances or on or after granting decree of divorce. An order for custody in a divorce action may have been granted after decree of divorce[14]. Such orders may be varied and recalled by subsequent order in the same manner as such orders made on granting divorce.

Section 14(2) of the Family Law (Scotland) Act 1985 provides that an 'incidental order' means one or more of the following orders:

1 Family Law (Scotland) Act 1985, s 3(1); *Abrahams v Abrahams* 1989 SCLR 102, 1990 SLT (Sh Ct) 113.
2 Ibid, s 5(4).
3 Ibid, s 3(1).
4 *Foreman v Foreman* 1989 GWD 14–600.
5 *Nixon v Nixon* 1987 SLT 602.
6 *Cosgrove v Cosgrove* 1980 SLT (Sh Ct) 105.
7 Test is: 'a material change of circumstances': Family Law (Scotland) Act 1985, s 12(4).
8 Test is: 'a material change of circumstances': Ibid, s 12(4).
9 Test for variation or recall is: 'on cause shown': Ibid, s 14(4).
10 Bankruptcy (Scotland) Act 1985, s 35.
11 Family Law (Scotland) Act 1985, s 16, see supra; cf *Mills v Mills* 1990 SCLR 213.
12 Ibid, s 16, supra.
13 Matrimonial Homes (Family Protection) (Scotland) Act 1981, s 5(1).
14 Matrimonial Proceedings (Children) Act 1958, s 8(2).

(a) an order for the sale of property;
(b) an order for the valuation of property;
(c) an order determining any dispute between the parties to the marriage as to their respective property rights by means of a declarator thereof or otherwise;
(d) an order regulating the occupation of the matrimonial home or the use of furniture and plenishings therein or excluding either party to the marriage from such occupation;
(e) an order regulating liability, as between the parties, for outgoings in respect of the matrimonial home or furniture or plenishings therein;
(f) an order that security shall be given for any financial provision;
(g) an order that payments shall be made or property transferred to any curator bonis or trustee or other person for the benefit of the party to the marriage by whom or on whose behalf application has been made under section 8(1) of this Act for an incidental order;
(h) an order setting aside or varying any term in an antenuptial or post-nuptial marriage settlement;
(j) an order as to the date from which any interest on any amount awarded shall run;
(k) any ancillary order which is expedient to give effect to the principles set out in section 9 of this Act or to any order made under section 8(2) of this Act.

Variation and recall of orders for periodical allowance

Where there has been a material change of circumstances since the order was made either party or, where the payer has died, his executor may apply to the court to vary or recall the order. On such an application being made the court may do one or more of the following[1]:

(a) vary or recall the order;
(b) backdate such variation or recall to the date of the application or, on cause shown, to an earlier date. Where backdating is ordered the court may order that an appropriate amount of periodical allowance be repaid[2];
(c) convert the order into an order for payment of a capital sum or for a transfer of property.

It would not be difficult to show cause in relation to backdating where for example there had been concealment of a change of circumstances or where the change was such that it would be unrealistic to expect an application to be lodged immediately. The provision which permits conversion will be of particular value where the payer has died. It may be necessary where there are substantial amounts at stake to obtain an actuarial valuation of the interest of the payee although it may be difficult (or invidious) to quantify her prospects of remarriage.

As to whether there will be held to be a change of circumstances where there has been no attempt to oppose the order when it was applied for and made or where the order was made on the basis of incorrect information supplied to the court see: *Galloway v Galloway* 1973 SLT (Notes) 84; *Ritchie v Ritchie* 1987 SLT (Sh Ct) 7 and cases cited in *Ritchie*.

1 Family Law (Scotland) Act 1985, s 13(4).
2 Ibid, s 13(6).

Test for recall or variation

As has been noted above incidental orders in terms of section 14(4) of the Family Law (Scotland) Act 1985 may be varied or recalled 'on cause shown'. In relation to other orders of which variation or recall is sought the test is whether there has been a 'material change of circumstances'. If a party dies there will almost certainly be a change of circumstances[1]. While an executor may be a party to an application for variation or recall of an order for payment of a periodical allowance, there is no statutory provision in terms of which he is entitled to be a party to an application for variation or recall in relation to the payment of a capital sum or the transfer of property. But where there has been a joint minute settling the financial arrangements between the parties the jurisdiction of the court may have been ousted so far as a variation is concerned. If so a change of circumstances would be immaterial[2]. If the joint minute fails to set out the basis of agreement fully the court may conclude that there has been a change of circumstances when there has not been[3].

A change of circumstances may arise in many ways but to persuade the court to act that change must be 'material'. Increased cost of living may amount to such a change[4]. The court will ask itself not only whether the change is material but also whether the changed circumstances make the existing order inappropriate. If the net effect of the changes is neutral or approximately so the court will refuse recall or variation. It is not a change of circumstances that incomplete information was put before the court which made the original order[5]. Where the father has taken over from the mother as the person having custody of a child that change of circumstances may warrant the reduction of an award of periodical allowance payable by the father. It may also, despite his continuing liability to pay periodical allowance, warrant the making of an order requiring the mother to pay aliment for the child[6]. Where the payer has taken on extra responsibilities and the payee has made little effort to gain employment periodical allowance may be varied to nil[7].

Form of minute

If no order for access was made on granting divorce an application for access may be competent by way of a new action in the sheriff court as an alternative to lodging a minute in the divorce process[8]. But where the Rules require that a minute be lodged or the court so directs (cf, eg, RC 170D(3)) the minute should contain a conclusion or a crave which asks the court to recall or vary, or both (in the alternative), the interlocutor pronounced in the cause on (date) and that by (specify the new form of order sought). It is suggested that, in a variation application, a phrase should be added such as 'or by varying the same in such manner as to the court may consider proper'. The averments in the minute will vary with the circumstances. If an application were to

1 *Sandison's Exrx v Sandison* 1984 SLT 111; *Finlayson v Finlayson's Exrx* 1986 SLT 19.
2 *Milne v Milne* 1987 SLT 45.
3 *Sutherland v Sutherland* 1988 SCLR 346 and see *Sochart v Sochart* 1988 SLT 449, 799.
4 *Jenkinson v Jenkinson* 1981 SLT 65.
5 *Stewart v Stewart* 1987 SLT 246; *Ritchie v Ritchie* 1987 SCLR 90, 1987 SLT (Sh Ct) 7.
6 *Howarth v Howarth* 1990 SLT 289.
7 *Jenkins v Jenkins* 1990 GWD 8–425.
8 *Philp v Philp* 1988 SCLR 313; *Girvan v Girvan* 1988 SLT 866.

be made to vary an order for a periodical allowance the averments might include:

The date and terms of the order made of which recall or variation is sought—other relevant aspects of the arrangements made at the same time as or before the order was made, eg capital payments or transfers of property—the circumstances at the time the order was made so far as now known, eg income of each party—the circumstances now—that change of circumstances is material—reasons why the order is now sought—reasons why the new order is one which should be granted in that form—why variation should be backdated to the date of the application or converted into an order for a capital sum or order for transfer of property or why the order should be recalled—that the order sought is reasonable.

There should be a suitable plea or pleas in law. The form which these take will depend on the nature of the order sought. Since in relation to orders for payment of a capital sum, transfer of property or for a periodical allowance the test is whether there has been a 'material change of circumstances'[1], the plea in law might be: 'There having been a material change of circumstances since the said order was granted as condescendenced upon variation (or recall) thereof should be granted as concluded for/as craved.' As has been remarked, in terms of the Family Law (Scotland) Act 1985, s 14(4) incidental orders may be varied or recalled 'on cause shown.' So a plea in law might be: 'Cause having been shown to warrant variation (or recall) of said order as condescendenced upon, variation (or recall) thereof should be granted as concluded for/as craved.'

Variation or recall of custody order

Where a child is subject to supervision of a local authority the local authority may bring to the notice of the court any material development affecting custody or access if in its opinion a change in the arrangements is desirable in the interests of the child[2].

In the course of an action of divorce in the sheriff court a party may, without lodging a minute in terms of OCR 129(1), crave an order relating to custody, aliment of or access to the children of the marriage or aliment for that party, even though an order to the same or a different effect has been made in a previous sheriff court process. When a new order is made in the divorce process the previous order ceases to apply[3]. Any application for variation or recall of any such order should be made by minute lodged in the original process in which decree was pronounced or the order was granted[4].

In the Court of Session where a party seeks an order for custody of a child where either no order was pronounced on granting divorce or a variation is sought of an order pronounced on granting divorce, application must be made by minute lodged in the divorce process. Where variation of aliment or access is sought the application is made by motion lodged in the original process[5]. The court may order a minute and answers to be lodged if the application is opposed.

1 Family Law (Scotland) Act 1985, ss 12(4), 13(4).
2 *Black v Black* 1988 SLT (Sh Ct) 24.
3 OCR 129(4).
4 OCR 129(1).
5 RC 170B(10).

Jurisdiction to vary or recall a custody order

A court in Scotland does not have jurisdiction to entertain an application for a variation of a custody order made under section 9(1) of the Matrimonial Proceedings (Children) Act 1958 (ie in the course of an action of inter alia divorce in which the action has been dismissed after proof on the merits has been allowed or decree of absolvitor has been granted) if on the date of the application there are matrimonial proceedings continuing in another court in the United Kingdom[1]. That would not be so if the other court has declined jurisdiction or has sisted the proceedings before it[2]. In terms of section 42 of the 1958 Act matrimonial proceedings in Scotland are treated as continuing until the child is sixteen.

If a court in Scotland has made a custody order it may, notwithstanding that it would no longer have jurisdiction to make the original order, make an order varying or recalling the original order with respect to a child referred to in the original order. But if the original order has been superseded by another order[3], that court may not do so[4]. Nor may the court vary or recall such an order if there are proceedings continuing in another court in the United Kingdom for divorce, nullity or separation.

Procedure for variation and recall of orders relating to custody, access and financial provision

COURT OF SESSION

In the Court of Session the procedure varies depending on the nature of the order of which variation or recall is sought. In the decree granting divorce the court will have granted leave to any person claiming an interest to apply for variation or revocation of any order under Part II of the Matrimonial Proceedings (Children) Act 1958 until the child is sixteen[5]. In the case of applications in relation to periodical allowance (including interim variation) or the variation of the date or the method of payment of a capital sum or the date of transfer of property, a motion, setting out the reasons for it, should be enrolled in the divorce process and intimated to the other party or to his solicitor on an induciae of 14 days by recorded delivery[6]. That procedure also applies to applications to vary or recall decrees of aliment but the motion is lodged in the process of the action for aliment[7]. But applications to vary or terminate an agreement on aliment must be by summons[8]. In the case of an application for variation or recall under section 14(4) of an incidental order made in terms of sections 8(2) and 14(1) of the Family Law (Scotland) Act 1985, for the setting aside or variation of an agreement as to financial provision under section 16 of that Act or relating to avoidance transactions under section 18 of that Act after decree of divorce, a minute should be lodged in the divorce process[9].

1 Family Law Act 1986, s 13(4).
2 Cf Ibid, s 13(5).
3 See Family Law Act 1986, s 15(1).
4 Ibid, s 15(2).
5 RC 170B(8).
6 RC 170D(3) and (8), 170B(10). Recorded delivery is not necessary where variation or recall of an order for access.
7 RC 170P. Where application for financial provision is made after an overseas divorce RC 170M applies.
8 RC 170R. Interim variation may be granted.
9 RC 170D(7).

Where variation or recall of an order for aliment is sought a copy of the letter of intimation and the relative Post Office receipt must be lodged in process along with written evidence of that party's earnings or written evidence that he or she is unemployed. Where the motion is opposed the court may order that the application be by minute and may direct the lodging of answers. Any minute so lodged must contain conclusions, averments and pleas in law[1]. Interim variation may be granted of an order for periodical allowance[2].

SHERIFF COURT

Where recall or variation of decrees for aliment, for custody of and access to children, of orders for financial provision or of incidental orders made in terms of section 14 of the Family Law (Scotland) Act 1985 are sought, application may be made to the court by minute lodged in the divorce process in which decree was pronounced or the original order was granted[3]. OCR 129 does not cover all the possible circumstances in which variation may be sought: eg in terms of the Bankruptcy (Scotland) Act 1985, s 35. It is suggested that the procedure specified in OCR 129 be followed unless it is clearly inappropriate to do so. If application is made for variation of an order for aliment notice should be given that backdating of the variation is sought[4]. If the applicant wishes to apply for a periodical allowance after decree of divorce and no order for such allowance had been made previously or to apply for orders other than those listed above, such as orders in terms of the Family Law (Scotland) Act 1985, ss 16 and 18, it will be necessary to make a separate application to the court by initial writ. Applications to vary orders under sections 3 and 4 of the Matrimonial Homes (Family Protection) (Scotland) Act 1981 are made by minute lodged in the original process. The minute is served on the opposite party and is intimated to the landlord if the property is tenanted and to any third party who permits the entitled spouse to occupy the property[5].

Procedure where minute lodged

The minute is served on the other party. Thereafter the procedure is at the discretion of the court but answers will usually be ordered[6]. There is no closed record. A proof may be ordered but in practice, in many cases, the facts are agreed and a hearing takes place either on the basis of a joint minute agreeing the facts or on the basis of ex parte statements supported by documents lodged in court.

Before making a variation of or recalling a custody order the court may, but need not, hear evidence[7].

1 RC 170B(10).
2 RC 170D(3).
3 OCR 129.
4 *Olds v Olds* 1990 SCLR 347.
5 AS (Applications under the Matrimonial Homes (Family Protection) (Scotland) Act 1981) 1982, SI 1982/1432.
6 OCR 129(3).
7 *Beverley v Beverley* 1977 SLT (Sh Ct) 3.

VARIATION OF PRE-1985 ACT ORDERS FOR FINANCIAL PROVISION

The Family Law (Scotland) Act 1985 came into force on 1 September 1986[1], except for section 25 which came into force on 30 November 1988[2].

The Divorce (Scotland) Act 1976, s 5(1) provided that application could be made to the court for an order for a periodical allowance. In terms of s 5(2) the court, on granting decree of divorce, 'shall make ... such order, if any, as it thinks fit, having regard to the respective means of the parties to the marriage and to all the circumstances of the case, including any settlement or other arrangements made for financial provision for any child of the marriage'. Section 5(3) provides that where no application for a periodical allowance was made or was made but was withdrawn or refused the court may make an order for a periodical allowance in favour of either party after the divorce has been granted if, since the divorce was granted, there has been a change of circumstances[3]. The word 'material' is not used in relation to such change.

Section 5(4) of the Divorce (Scotland) Act provides that the court may vary or recall an order for a periodical allowance at the instance of a party or his executor on a change of circumstances[3]. The Family Law (Scotland) Act 1985, while repealing that section, preserved it in relation to actions commenced prior to the commencement of the Family Law (Scotland) Act 1985. Section 28(3) of the 1985 Act provides that in the continued operation of section 5 of the 1976 Act the powers of the court to make an order for a periodical allowance under section 5(2) or vary such an order under section 5(4) shall include power to make such an order for a definite or an indefinite period or until the happening of a specified event. The reference to section 5(2) is to be noted. In an application under section 5(3) for a periodical allowance after divorce (eg for the first time) it is not competent for a court to make the order for a limited period[4]. If an order for payment of a periodical allowance has been made with a time limit, that time limit may be varied. The court should be asked to order that the allowance be paid until a specified date[5]. In *Ross* (supra) no order was made because the wife applicant was largely responsible for her financial situation. The coming into operation of the 1985 Act was not itself a change of circumstances[6]. The court may refuse recall or variation of an order even though the payee is cohabiting[7].

Differences arose after the 1985 Act came into operation as to whether the principles set out in sections 9 to 11 of that Act applied to applications to vary a pre-1985 Act order. The question was resolved in the negative[8]. The criteria to be applied are those set out in section 5 of the 1976 Act. It was pointed out by the court in *Wilson* that the principles referred to in sections 9 to 11 may properly be regarded as part of the circumstances of the case. The court may find that there are or were cross-actions of divorce, one under the 1976 provisions and one under the 1985 Act provisions. Somewhat different

---

1 Family Law (Scotland) Act 1985 (Commencement No 1) Order 1986, SI 1986/1237.
2 Family Law (Scotland) Act 1985 (Commencement No 2) Order 1986, SI 1988/1887.
3 Cf *Mills v Mills* 1990 SCLR 213.
4 *Ross v Ross* 1988 SCLR 267; *Grindlay v Grindlay* 1987 SLT 264.
5 *Macpherson v Macpherson* 1989 SCLR 132, 1989 SLT 231.
6 *Grindlay*, supra; *Caven v Caven* 1987 SLT 761.
7 *Kavanagh v Kavanagh* 1989 SLT 134; for a contrary example see *Brunton v Brunton* 1986 SLT 49. As to the relevance of the income of the payer's cohabitee see *Munro v Munro* 1986 SLT 72.
8 *Wilson v Wilson* 1987 SCLR 595, 1987 SLT 721; *Smith v Smith* 1988 SCLR 520, 1988 SLT 840.

considerations may arise in each of these actions if variation or recall of orders made in them is sought[1]. The same considerations apply to variation as applied to the original order[2]. If a limitation on the duration of a periodical allowance is to be sought in the course of an application to vary, it is at least desirable to give the other party notice of that[3]. However, such notice is not essential[4]. In *Smith* (supra) periodical allowance was restricted to a period which expired three years after the youngest child attained sixteen.

In applying the criteria mentioned above the court may take account of the duration of the marriage, the ages of the parties and the period for which periodical allowance has already been paid. The fact that one party is in receipt of social security benefit and is likely to remain so should be taken into account. But it is not for the court to save the husband from the need to maintain his spouse thereby devolving that responsibility onto the community[5]. The court may be invited to fix a termination date[6].

As was pointed out in *Sutherland v Sutherland*[7] there are two basic approaches when a variation is sought. One is to use the previous award as a baseline and, if there has been a change of circumstances, to work from there. The alternative is to regard the fact that there has been a change of circumstances as a key which opens the door to an assessment *de novo*. It is submitted that the former, which was adopted by the Inner House in *Macpherson v Macpherson*[8] is to be preferred to the latter which was adopted by the sheriff in *Sutherland*. There are practical difficulties if the latter approach prevails, not the least of which would be the need to retain records of what information was put before the court on the earlier occasion.

The court does not have power to 'terminate the payment of periodical allowance'. An application to that effect is incompetent[8]. The motion should be to vary the order so that it is for a definite or indefinite period or until the happening of a specified event, as the case may be, or to have the amount referred to in the order varied, for example to nil. Any such motion in a Court of Session case must comply with RC 170B and 170D, ie reasons must be given in the motion[9]. But the court may order that a minute and answers be lodged[10]. In the sheriff court application is by minute lodged in the divorce process[11].

There is no power to backdate a variation of a periodical allowance granted in connection with a pre-1985 Act divorce[12]. But a variation may be granted where the period for payment of the periodical allowance has expired. That variation may be of the amount of the periodical allowance but may also involve the removal of the terminal date of the order. The onus will be on the party

1 *MacLeod v MacLeod* 1990 GWD 14-768.
2 *Clark v Clark* 1983 SLT 371.
3 As was done in, eg, *McRae v McRae* 1988 SCLR 257 where a period of one year was fixed though the order sought was for a period of no more than two years or such other period as the court might determine.
4 *Robertson v Robertson* 1989 SCLR 71.
5 *Smith v Smith*, supra; but see *Olds v Olds* 1990 SCLR 347.
6 *Gow v Gow* 1987 SCLR 610: a period of four years fixed.
7 1988 SCLR 346.
8 1989 SCLR 132, 1989 SLT 231.
9 *Wilson v Wilson* 1987 SCLR 595, 1987 SLT 721.
10 *McCallum v McCallum* 1989 GWD 21-890.
11 OCR 129.
12 *Abrahams v Abrahams* 1989 SCLR 102, 1989 SLT (Sh Ct) 113 and cf *Wilson* supra and *Smith* 1988 SCLR 520, 1988 SLT 840 and *Hannah v Hannah* 1988 SLT 82.

seeking such a variation to show a change of circumstances and to show that an extension was warranted, an onus which at that stage it may not be easy to discharge[1].

RECALL OR VARIATION OF COURT OF SESSION DECREES BY THE SHERIFF COURT

Certain Court of Session decrees (which are not interim orders) may be recalled or varied by the sheriff court[2]. These are:

(1) awards of aliment;
(2) orders for periodical allowance;
(3) orders made by virtue of the Conjugal Rights (Scotland) (Amendment) Act 1861, s 9 (as substituted by the Law Reform (Parent and Child) (Scotland) Act 1986, Sch 1, para 2);
(4) orders under the Matrimonial Proceedings (Children) Act 1958, Part II;
(5) orders under the Guardianship Act 1973, Part II;
(6) any order varying such an order.

Applications for recall of such orders are commenced by initial writ lodged in the appropriate sheriff court[3]. That is the sheriff court having jurisdiction to deal with the application. As to jurisdiction generally see the Domicile and Matrimonial Proceedings Act 1973, s 10 and Sch 2. The basis upon which a particular sheriff has jurisdiction in respect of a variation of aliment or periodical allowance or an order varying such an order depends not on the Law Reform (Miscellaneous Provisions) (Scotland) Act 1966 nor on the 1973 Act. The sheriff must have jurisdiction over the party upon whom the application must be served. That jurisdiction may arise by reason of residence, place of business or prorogation[4]. Where the application relates to one of the other orders listed above or an order varying such an order the basis of jurisdiction is either habitual residence, presence of the child within the sheriffdom or the emergency provisions set out respectively in the Family Law Act 1986, ss 9, 10 or 12.

The initial writ is lodged along with a certified copy of the interlocutor whose variation is sought. A copy of the initial writ must first be sent by recorded delivery to the Court of Session where it will be lodged in the Court of Session process in which the order was made. A certificate of intimation must be attached to the initial writ. The procedure is governed by AS (Variation and Recall of Orders in Consistorial Causes) 1984, SI 1984/667. Where a notice of intention to defend has been lodged the pursuer must lodge in the sheriff court process within fourteen days after tabling the originals or copies of: the pleadings, interlocutor sheets, opinions of the court and the inventory of productions from the Court of Session process along with any documents on which he seeks to found. The sheriff may, on cause shown, prorogate the time for lodging the certified copy interlocutor of the Court of Session[5]. The

1 *Macpherson* 1989 SCLR 132, 1989 SLT 231. The application in that case was lodged prior to the terminal date.
2 Law Reform (Miscellaneous Provisions) (Scotland) Act 1966, s 8(1) as amended.
3 Law Reform (Miscellaneous Provisions) (Scotland) Act 1966, s 8(5).
4 Sheriff Courts (Scotland) Act 1907, s 6(a), (b) and (j).
5 SI 1984/667, para 3(3).

applicant or his solicitor may sign a minute requesting that the application be remitted to the Court of Session. That minute must be lodged in the sheriff court at or before tabling. The court is required then to remit the application to the Court of Session[1].

If it is undefended the application will call in court when the pursuer or his solicitor will be heard. Where the application is defended proof may be dispensed with. Parties may be heard whether or not defences have been lodged[2]. After decree has been granted the sheriff clerk returns any Court of Session documents to that court along with the sheriff court process.

---

1 Law Reform (Miscellaneous Provisions) (Scotland) Act 1966, s 8(3); SI 1984/667, para 8.
2 SI 1984/667, para 6.

CHAPTER 12

ENFORCEMENT

BREACH OF INTERDICT

Breach of interdict is a contempt of court which arises because a party has refused to comply with an order of the court. Where a breach is alleged application is made to the court which granted the interdict to have the offending party appear before that court. Warrant may be granted to officers of court to apprehend the offending party if he refuses to appear. Breach of interdict proceedings are most commonly used where a non-molestation interdict or an order to return or not to remove children has been breached. It is not every order of court with which a party has failed to comply which may be the subject on breach of interdict proceedings. It is competent to raise an action for civil imprisonment for wilful failure to pay aliment[1]. But it is not competent to use the procedure for contempt of court for the purpose of securing compliance with an order to pay aliment[2]. It is suggested that where there are alternative means of enforcement available to a party, such as the use of diligence, the court will not countenance attempts to achieve compliance with court orders by means of proceedings for contempt of court.

Procedure for breach of interdict

The Court of Session Act 1988, s 47(1), after providing that in any case containing a crave or conclusion for interdict the Division of the Inner House or Lord Ordinary may on the motion of any party grant interim interdict, provides that it shall be competent for the Division or the Lord Ordinary before whom any cause (in which interim interdict has been granted) is pending to deal with any breach of interim interdict without the presentation of a petition and complaint.

The appropriate procedure in an action pending in the Court of Session, and, it is submitted in an action pending in the sheriff court, is to lodge a minute as was done in *Gribben v Gribben*[3]. If no action is pending, as when the divorce action has concluded and the interdict granted is not on an interim basis, a new action will have to be raised by way of an initial writ, in the sheriff court and by way of petition and complaint in the Court of Session.

The petition and complaint, initial writ or minute sets out the alleged breaches of interdict. It requires to have the concurrence of the Lord Advocate. The

1 Debtors (Scotland) Act 1880, s 4; Civil Imprisonment (Scotland) Act 1882, s 4.
2 *Hay v Lefelier-Lebos* 1989 SCLR 501, 1989 SLT (Sh Ct) 55.
3 1976 SLT 266.

instance should narrate after the name and designation of the pursuer that it is raised with the consent and concurrence of the Lord Advocate. This concurrence will normally be endorsed on the petition and complaint, initial writ or minute, by the Lord Advocate or his representative who, in a sheriff court case, will be the procurator fiscal. The reason for this requirement is that the Crown may be contemplating or may have instituted criminal proceedings as a result of the incident or incidents complained of (*Gribben*, supra). The practice approved in *Gribben*[1] is for the minute and motion of the complainer to be intimated to the Lord Advocate.

Form of application for breach of interdict

Order

To ordain the defender to appear personally before the court on (date) at ... am or at such other time as the court may appoint to answer the charge that he is in breach of the interdict granted by (eg the sheriff of Tayside Central and Fife at Stirling) on (date) whereby the defender was interdicted from (specify terms of interdict) and is guilty of contempt of court; and failing his appearance to grant warrant to officers of court to apprehend the defender and bring him before the court to answer as aforesaid; on breach of interdict being admitted or proved, to find that the defender has been in breach of the said interdict and is guilty of contempt of court; to impose such punishment as to the court shall seem just; and to find the defender liable in expenses.

Averments

Interdict granted on (date)—terms of interdict—service of interdict on defender—defender well aware of its terms—defender in breach of interdict in the following respects: (specify)—the defender is in contempt of court.

Plea in law

The defender being in breach of interdict as condescended upon should be found guilty of contempt of court and punished accordingly.

If the breach is not admitted answers or defences may be lodged and a period for adjustment may be allowed. If necessary a proof will take place. The standard of proof is beyond reasonable doubt[2]. The penalty which the court imposes will vary with the circumstances of the case. The options available to the court are to admonish the party in breach or to impose a fine or imprisonment. If imprisonment is imposed it must be for a fixed term although the contemnor may be discharged at an earlier date by order of the court[3]. The maximum penalties which may be imposed in the sheriff court for contempt of court, which is what a breach of interdict is, are three months' imprisonment, or a fine on level 4 on the standard scale, or both. But in the Court of Session the maximum penalties are two years' imprisonment or a fine or both. There is no upper limit on the fine which may be imposed by the Court of Session.[4]. The court should not normally 'defer sentence'. The procedure is a summary

---

1   1976 SLT 266 at 269.
2   *Gribben*, supra; *Nelson v Nelson* 1988 SCLR 663.
3   Contempt of Court Act 1981, s 15(1).
4   Contempt of Court Act 1981, s 15(2)(a).

one and should be disposed of promptly. A sentence for contempt of court is appealable[1].

Powers of arrest

Where in terms of the Matrimonial Homes (Family Protection) (Scotland) Act 1981, s 15 a power of arrest has been attached to a matrimonial interdict and has been served on the non-applicant spouse, a police officer may arrest without warrant a spouse reasonably suspected by him to be in breach of interdict. Thereafter the Procurator Fiscal may decide to instigate criminal proceedings. If he decides not to do so, proceedings may be taken by the applicant spouse for breach of interdict in the usual way. But if the arrest was made in the exercise of the power of arrest attached to the interdict, if the non-applicant spouse was not liberated by the police and the Procurator Fiscal decides not to instigate criminal proceedings, the non-applicant spouse will be brought before a sheriff. The Procurator Fiscal will present a petition setting out the matters referred to in the Contempt of Court Act 1981, s 17(5)(a). If it appears that there has prima facie been a breach of interdict, that proceedings for breach of interdict will be taken and that there is a substantial risk of violence by the non-applicant spouse against the applicant spouse or any child of the family, the sheriff may order the non-applicant spouse to be detained for a further period of not more than two days[2].

CIVIL IMPRISONMENT

Civil imprisonment may be imposed in connection with wilful failure to pay within the days of charge any sum or sums of aliment together with the expenses of process for which decree has been pronounced by a competent court[3]. It is essential that non-payment be 'wilful'[4]. But it will be presumed to be so unless that is rebutted[5]. Unpaid periodical allowance is not 'aliment' for the purposes of the Civil Imprisonment (Scotland) Act 1882[6]. The maximum period of imprisonment is 6 weeks. The period of imprisonment does not extinguish the debt to any extent[7]. In the sheriff court summary application is made for a warrant to imprison. There are printed forms for this purpose, containing blank interlocutors. The application cannot follow directly on the decree awarding aliment[8]. There are no written pleadings. A minute containing a charge for payment 'under the pain of poinding and imprisonment, so far as competent' is in proper form. The minute is not incompetent simply because at the date of the charge the child has attained sixteen[9]. The sheriff should not continue the case to see if the defender's circumstances improve[10]. The

1 *Cordiner, Petitoner* 1973 JC 16 at 18–19.
2 Contempt of Court Act 1981, s 17(5)(b).
3 Civil Imprisonment (Scotland) Act 1882, s 4 and see Debtors (Scotland) Act 1880.
4 *Cassells v Cassells* 1955 SLT (Sh Ct) 41.
5 *McWilliams v McWilliams* 1963 SC 259.
6 *White v White* 1984 SLT (Sh Ct) 30.
7 Civil Imprisonment (Scotland) Act 1882, s 4.
8 *Whiteford v Gibson* (1899) 7 SLT 233; *Glenday v Johnson* (1905) 8 F 24.
9 *Hardie v Hardie* 1984 SLT (Sh Ct) 49.
10 *Cain v McColm* (1892) 19 R 813 though see *Brunt v Brunt* 1954 SLT (Sh Ct) 74.

sheriff cannot order the arrest of the debtor[1]. There is no appeal unless the order made is incompetent[2]. New applications may be made at intervals of six months[3]. The procedure is at the creditor's expense[4].

ENFORCEMENT OF MAINTENANCE ORDERS

Enforcing agreements for maintenance

Where there is an agreement in which the parties set out agreed financial arrangements following on the breakdown of their marriage and that agreement has been registered in the Books of Council and Session for preservation and for execution, diligence may be done to enforce the terms of the agreement[5]. The procedure to be followed is regulated by AS (Proceedings in the Sheriff Court under the Debtors (Scotland) Act 1987) 1988, SI 1988/2013 made under and in terms of the Debtors (Scotland) Act 1987, s 102.

Aspects of diligence

The ordinary rules of diligence apply to the enforcement of orders for financial provision[6]. So far as periodical payments are concerned the provisions for current maintenance arrestments (as to which see below) are of particular importance where the payer is employed. There are provisions in the 1987 Act dealing with competing diligences including competition between current maintenance arrestments *inter se* and between a current maintenance arrestment and other diligences[7].

But there may be cases where there is no moveable property owned by the defender within the jurisdiction against which diligence can be done. In that event where the parties are *pro indiviso* proprietors of heritable property, eg the matrimonial home in which the pursuer lives, and the defender refuses to pay a capital sum in terms of a decree of court, it has been held that the court can order that the heritable property be sold to the pursuer at an open market price to be fixed by a reporter. Payment of the price is satisfied *pro tanto* by the pursuer granting a discharge of the debt to the defender[8].

Current maintenance arrestments

The Debtors (Scotland) Act 1987 ss 51–56 set out the procedure for the arrestment of earnings to enforce an award of maintenance. This is known as a current maintenance arrestment. This procedure may be used to enforce awards of maintenance whether they were made in Scotland or were made in another part of the United Kingdom or abroad. For the full list of the orders to which this procedure applies, see the Debtors (Scotland) Act 1987, s 106. In the case of orders made outside Scotland there is a requirement in the case of most

1 *Cook v Wallace & Wilson* (1889) 16 R 565.
2 *Strain v Strain* (1886) 13 R 1029; *Gavin v Gavin* 1989 GWD 19–785.
3 Civil Imprisonment (Scotland) Act 1882, s 4.
4 *Wilson v Wilson* (1936) 52 Sh Ct Rep 200.
5 Writs Execution (Scotland) Act 1877, s 3 (substituted by the Debtors (Scotland) Act 1987, s 87(4)).
6 See generally the Debtors (Scotland) Act 1987.
7 Eg Debtors (Scotland) Act 1987, ss 59, 62.
8 *Scrimgeour v Scrimgeour* 1988 SLT 590.

of them that, prior to enforcement, they be registered in Scotland or be confirmed by a court in Scotland.

Such an arrestment requires an employer, so long as the arrestment is in effect, to deduct a sum from the debtor's net earnings every payday and as soon as reasonably practicable to pay it to the creditor. It comes into effect on the date on which a current maintenance arrestment schedule is served on the employer. The form of that schedule is prescribed by Act of Sederunt[1]. It ceases to have effect if the debtor leaves the employment of the employer or if the arrestment has been recalled, abandoned or has ceased to have effect for any reason.

A single current maintenance arrestment may cover more than one maintenance order[2]. There are formulae set out in the 1987 Act by which the amount to be deducted from net earnings is to be calculated.

Unless the maintenance order has been registered and at the time of registration a certificate of arrears was produced to the court in Scotland which registered the order, it is necessary, before a current maintenance arrestment can be served, that the creditor must have intimated to the debtor (in the manner prescribed in the Act of Sederunt) the making, registration or confirmation, as the case may be, of the order; that at least four weeks have elapsed since such intimation; and that a total value of at least three instalments of maintenance must remain unpaid[3].

Generally the sheriff having jurisdiction over the place where the current maintenance arrestment was executed or if that is unknown, an established place of business of the employer[4], has power inter alia to recall a current maintenance arrestment or to declare it invalid or to have ceased to have effect[5].

Enforcement in one part of the United Kingdom of orders made in another part for payment of a capital sum, periodical allowance and aliment

The basic scheme is that where a maintenance order made in one jurisdiction in the United Kingdom has been registered in another the decree may be enforced as if it had been made by the court in which it is registered and that court had jurisdiction to make it[6]. Accordingly an order made in England and registered in Scotland may be enforced as if it had been made in Scotland. Thus a decree registered in Scotland may be extracted. On extract a warrant for diligence will be granted and it may be enforced in the usual way. There are comparable arrangements for the enforcement of decrees granted in Scotland following upon registration in other jurisdictions within the United Kingdom.

Part II of the Maintenance Orders Act 1950, as amended, provides the procedure for enforcing such orders and many other types of order in terms of which a person is required to pay money or transfer property. This is done by defining a maintenance order widely[7], so that it includes, for example,

1 AS (Proceedings in the Sheriff Court under the Debtors (Scotland) Act 1987) 1988, SI 1988/2013, r 42, form 34.
2 Debtors (Scotland) Act 1987, s 52.
3 Ibid, s 54(1).
4 Ibid, s 73.
5 Ibid, s 55.
6 Maintenance Orders Act 1950, s 18(1).
7 Maintenance Orders Act 1950, s 16 (1)(b).

orders for financial provision under the Family Law (Scotland) Act 1985, s 8 as well as orders under the Divorce (Scotland) Act 1976, s 5, its predecessors and the Matrimonial and Family Proceedings Act 1984, s 29. Section 8 of the Family Law (Scotland) Act 1985 includes orders for payment of a capital sum or of a periodical allowance and orders for the transfer of property.

PROCEDURE

An application to register a Scottish decree in England, Wales or Northern Ireland is made to the clerk of the court which granted the decree. In the case of sheriff court decrees that will be the appropriate sheriff clerk but if the decree was granted in the Court of Session the application is made to the Deputy Principal Clerk of Session.

THE RULES

The procedure for enforcement of maintenance orders is set out in the Maintenance Orders Acts Rules 1980. There are separate Rules for orders made or registered in the Court of Session and in the sheriff court. These Rules are set out in SI 1980/1727 (Court of Session) and SI 1980/1732 (sheriff court). The Rules deal both with the registration in other parts of the United Kingdom of decrees granted in Scotland and with the registration and enforcement in Scotland of orders made in courts in other parts of the United Kingdom.

Registers of maintenance orders are kept by the Deputy Principal Clerk and by sheriff clerks and are open to inspection by persons entitled to or liable to make payments under such orders or their solicitors or, in certain circumstance, others having an interest[1].

If a person who is under an obligation to make payments under a maintenance order which has been registered in a court of summary jurisdiction in England fails to inform the clerk of court of a change of address he may be convicted of an offence[2]. There is no comparable provision for Scotland.

Outgoing orders

Where it is desired to register an order made in Scotland in another part of the United Kingdom an application is made by sending to either the Deputy Principal Clerk of Session in the case of an order made by the Court of Session or to the sheriff clerk of the court by which the order was made:

(1) a letter of application;
(2) an affidavit by the applicant;
(3) a copy of that affidavit;
(4) a certified copy of the decree.

So far as the certified copy 'decree' is concerned in a sheriff court case it may be necessary to send a certified copy of the writ and of the relevant interlocutor. The affidavit must include the name and address of the person

1 SI 1980/1727, r 4; SI 1980/1732, r 4.
2 Maintenance Orders Act 1950, s 18(2A).

liable to make payments under the decree; the arrears, if any, due and the date to which they are calculated; the reason for the application and a statement that the decree is not already registered under the Maintenance Orders Act 1950.

If the decree appears to be enforceable in another part of the United Kingdom there will be sent to the appropriate officer of that court by the Deputy Principal Clerk or by the sheriff clerk the affidavit of the applicant, a certified copy of the decree and a letter stating that the application has been granted and requesting that the decree be registered, and (in the case of a Court of Session decree) that registration be notified[1]. Where a decree has been registered in the High Court in England or Northern Ireland, application may be made to the Court of Session for re-registration of it in a magistrates' court[2]. Application may be made to a sheriff to have a decree which has been registered in a magistrates' court re-registered in the High Court in England[3]. In either of these events a similar procedure is followed.

So long as the decree of a Scottish court is registered elsewhere it cannot be enforced in Scotland[4]. Nor can it be registered in more than one court elsewhere in the United Kingdom at a time[5].

CANCELLATION OF REGISTRATION

Cancellation may be appropriate where the payer has returned to the jurisdiction of the court which made the order, say, Scotland although the order is registered in, say, Northern Ireland. It may also be appropriate where the order is registered in one jurisdiction, say, Northern Ireland, and the payer has moved to another jurisdiction, say, England. In the former case Scottish procedure will be used to enforce it. In the latter Northern Irish procedures for enforcement would be likely to prove ineffective, simply because the payer would no longer be subject to the jurisdiction of the Northern Irish court.

Cancellation does not affect the validity of the original decree. It may thereafter be enforced in the courts of the jurisdiction where it was made. Cancellation may be sought by either the payer or the payee. If the payee seeks cancellation it must be granted unless proceedings for variation of the order are pending in that court[6].

VARIATION AND DISCHARGE OF THE ORDER

If the Court of Session varies or discharges a decree which is registered elsewhere in the United Kingdom the party on whose application the order for variation or discharge was made is required to inform the Deputy Principal Clerk. He in turn will inform the court which has registered the decree[7]. If the sheriff court varies a decree which has been registered elsewhere the sheriff clerk

1 Court of Session: Rule 7; Sheriff Court: Rule 8.
2 Court of Session: Rule 9.
3 Sheriff Court: Rule 10.
4 Maintenance Orders Act 1950, s 19(2).
5 Ibid, s 18(6).
6 Maintenance Orders Act 1950, s 24.
7 Court of Session: Rule 13.

informs the court which has registered the decree[1]. But the court in Scotland cannot vary the rate of payments. That may be done only by the court in which the order is registered[2]. The court in which the order is registered cannot extend the period during which maintenance is payable[3].

Incoming orders

REGISTRATION

An order of the High Court in England or Northern Ireland can be registered only in the Court of Session. An order made by any other court in those countries must be registered in the sheriff court[4]. The Deputy Principal Clerk or the sheriff clerk as the case may be register incoming orders and make a note of the arrears, if any. The certificate, declaration or affidavit as to the amount of any arrears lodged with an application for registration in Scotland of a maintenance order is sufficient evidence of those arrears[5]. Once registered an extract may be obtained with a warrant for diligence in the usual way[6].

VARIATION OF RATE OF PAYMENTS

An application may be made by either the payer or the payee to the sheriff for a variation under section 22(1) of the Maintenance Orders Act 1950 of the rate of payments under a maintenance order made by a court in England or Northern Ireland and registered in the sheriff court[7]. This provision allows the sheriff court to vary the rate of payments due under a High Court order which has been re-registered as well as those due under an order of a court of summary jurisdiction. Variation may be granted on a change of circumstances[8]. Application in the sheriff court must be made by initial writ. The court which made the registered order will retain power to alter the order in other respects[9]. There are provisions for evidence to be adduced before the court in which the order is registered where the payer wishes to have the terms of the order altered (other than as regards the rate of payments) The evidence so adduced is transmitted to the original court which then decides whether or not to alter the order[10].

In the Court of Session there is no power to vary or discharge an order registered in that court[11]. That power is retained by the court which made the order. Where the payer wishes to have the rate of payments altered he applies to the court in which the decree is registered to adduce evidence in that connection. The evidence so adduced is transmitted to the original court which then decides whether or not to alter the order[12].

1 Sheriff Court: Rule 12.
2 Maintenance Orders Act 1950, s 22; *Thompson v Thompson* (1953) 69 Sh Ct Rep 193; *Allum v Allum* 1965 SLT (Sh Ct) 26.
3 *Allum,* supra.
4 Maintenance Orders Act 1950, s 17(1)(c); RC 15(1).
5 Ibid, s 20(2).
6 Court of Session: Rule 15; Sheriff Court: Rule 14.
7 Sheriff Court: Rule 15; *Thompson,* supra; *Allum,* supra.
8 *Cowan v Cowan* 1952 SLT (Sh Ct) 8.
9 Maintenance Orders Act 1950, s 22(4).
10 Ibid, s 22(5).
11 Ibid, s 21.
12 Ibid, s 21(2).

CANCELLATION OF REGISTRATION OF AN ORDER

Application for cancellation may be made by or on behalf of the person entitled to payments under the order. On an application being made in the prescribed manner to the court in which the order is registered that court will cancel the registration of the order unless proceedings for variation are pending in that court[1]. The person liable to make payments under the order may also apply for cancellation of the registration of an order on the ground that he has ceased to reside in the part of the United Kingdom in which the order is registered. But he must apply to the court which originally made the order[2]. That court sends a notice to the court in which the order is registered. The latter court then cancels the registration.

In a Court of Session application it is necessary to send to the Deputy Principal Clerk of Session a letter applying for cancellation along with an affidavit by the applicant. That affidavit must include the date of registration of the order, the reason for the application and a statement of the arrears, if any, due under the order[3].

In the sheriff court an application must be lodged with the sheriff clerk along with a copy of the order sought to be cancelled. The application must be signed by or on behalf of the applicant and must state the date of registration of the order[4].

Decrees may not be registered in more than one court at a time[5]. Nor can a decree registered in Scotland be enforced in another part of the United Kingdom[6]. Its registration should be cancelled before any such enforcement is attempted.

ENFORCEMENT OVERSEAS OF MAINTENANCE ORDERS MADE IN SCOTLAND

The principal statutory provisions for the enforcement of decrees granted by a Scottish court outside the United Kingdom or for the enforcement within the United Kingdom of orders for maintenance made by a court outside the United Kingdom are the Maintenance Orders (Reciprocal Enforcement) Act 1972 along with the Maintenance Orders (Reciprocal Enforcement) Act 1972 Rules 1974, SI 1974/939, and the Civil Jurisdiction and Judgments Act 1982.

Enforcement under the Civil Jurisdiction and Judgments Act 1982

The following countries have reciprocal rights to recognition and enforcement of maintenance orders under the Civil Jurisdiction and Judgments Act 1982, s 5: Belgium, Denmark, Federal Republic of Germany, France, Greece, Italy, Luxembourg, Netherlands, Republic of Ireland.

Section 5 of the 1982 Act provides for the registration of maintenance orders in the sheriff court having jurisdiction in accordance with the second paragraph of Article 32 of the 1968 Brussels Convention on Judgments set out in Schedule

1   Ibid, s 24(1).
2   Ibid, ss 24(2), 17.
3   SI 1980/1727, r 17.
4   SI 1980/1732, r 18.
5   Maintenance Orders Act 1950, s 17(7).
6   Ibid, s 18(6).

1 of the 1982 Act. That jurisdiction is determined by reference to the place of domicile of the party against whom enforcement is sought, but if he is not domiciled in the state in which enforcement is sought, jurisdiction is to be determined by reference to the place of enforcement. The order is transmitted to the court by the Secretary of State. There are corresponding arrangements for the enforcement of Scottish decrees in the courts of the countries listed above. Once registered in Scotland the order may be enforced in Scotland in the same manner as a comparable decree of a Scottish court.

Enforcement under the the Maintenance Orders (Reciprocal Enforcement) Act 1972

The provisions of the Maintenance Orders (Reciprocal Enforcement) Act 1972 are relatively complicated and should be referred to. What follows is an outline of these provisions so far as they may be relevant to the enforcement of orders for maintenance granted in the course of an action for divorce. This is not a comprehensive account of these provisions.

There are separate arrangements for 'reciprocating countries' (Part I of the Act) and for 'convention countries' (Part II of the Act). Provision is made in Part III of the Act for the making of bilateral arrangements. The countries with which there are such arrangements are listed below. Some of these arrangements are modifications of the provisions contained in Part I of the Act. Others are modifications of the provisions contained in Part II of the Act.

The reciprocating countries are, broadly, those jurisdictions which fall, or at one time fell, within the Commonwealth, though not all such jurisdictions are included. The convention countries are those which have acceded to the United Nations Convention on the Recovery Abroad of Maintenance 1956. They include many countries in Western and some in Eastern Europe as well as in other parts of the world. Bilateral arrangements under Part III are made with countries who are outside the 1956 Convention. Orders have been made in respect of the Republic of Ireland, most of the states of the United States and a number of countries which have acceded to the Hague Convention on the Recognition and Enforcement of Decisions relating to Maintenence Obligations (1973). Bilateral arrangements come into operation when an Order in Council is made after satisfactory arrangements have been agreed between the United Kingdom government and the government of the other country concerned. The arrangements with the states of the United States and the Republic of Ireland are a modification of the arrangements which apply to convention countries and which are set out in Part II of the Act.

Part I—reciprocating countries

The reciprocating countries are:
Anguilla[1], Australia (Australian Capital Territory, New South Wales, Northern Territory, Queensland, South Australia, Tasmania, Victoria[2], Western

---

1 SI 1983/1125.
2 SI 1974/556.

Australia[1], Barbados, Bermuda[2], Canada[3], Falkland Islands & Dependencies[4], Fiji[5], Ghana[6], Gibraltar[7], Hong Kong[8], India[9], Isle of Man[10], Kenya, Malta[11], Nauru[12], New Zealand[13], Norfolk Island[14], Papua New Guinea, St Helena[15], Singapore[16], Rebublic of South Africa[17], United Republic of Tanzania (except Zanzibar), Turks and Caicos Islands[18], Zimbabwe[19].

Hague Convention Countries to which modified provisions of Part I apply: Czechoslovakia[20], Federal Republic of Germany[21], Finland[22], France[23], Italy[24], Luxembourg[25], Netherlands (Kingdom in Europe and Netherlands Antilles)[26], Norway, Portugal, Sweden, Switzerland[27], Turkey[28].

Arrangements with reciprocating countries

Maintenance orders made in the United Kingdom may be transmitted to the reciprocating country for enforcement there. Alternatively a provisional order may be made in a court in the jurisdiction in which the pursuer resides, on her application. The provisional order is then transmitted to the reciprocating country in which the defender resides. The defender is given an opportunity to put forward his case there. The court in the reciprocating country decides whether to confirm the provisional order. The law applicable is that of the jurisdiction in which the application is first made. The defences which may be stated are those which would be available in that jurisdiction. The Maintenance Orders (Reciprocal Enforcement) Act 1972 makes reciprocal provision for orders coming to Scotland from an overseas court. That is a matter beyond the scope of this book.

1 SI 1979/115.
2 Both SI 1975/2187.
3 Alberta: SI 1979/115; British Columbia and Manitoba: both SI 1974/556; New Brunswick and North West Territories: both SI 1975/2187; Nova Scotia and Ontario: both SI 1974 /556; Saskatchewan: SI 1979/115.
4 SI 1983/1125.
5 SI 1979/115.
6 SI 1975/2187.
7 SI 1974/556.
8 SI 1979 /115.
9 SI 1975 /2187.
10 SI 1983/1125.
11 Both SI 1975/2187.
12 SI 1983/1125.
13 SI 1974/556.
14 SI 1979/115.
15 Both SI 1983/1125.
16 SI 1979/115.
17 SI 1975/2187.
18 Both SI 1979/115.
19 SI 1983/1125.
20 SI 1979/1317.
21 SI 1987/1282.
22 SI 1983/885.
23 SI 1979 /1317.
24 SI 1981/1674.
25 SI 1981/1545.
26 SI 1981/837.
27 All SI 1979/1317.
28 SI 1983/1523.

MAINTENANCE ORDERS WHICH MAY BE ENFORCED

A maintenance order for this purpose is an order which provides for the periodical payment of sums of money towards the maintenance of any person whom the person ordered to pay was liable to maintain in accordance with the law of the place where the order was made. An order made in Scotland on or after the granting of decree of divorce for payment of a periodical allowance is expressly included as is the variation of a maintenance order[1].

ENFORCEMENT OF MAINTENANCE ORDERS

Direct enforcement

If the person liable to pay in terms of an order made in Scotland resides or has assets in a reciprocating country, the person entitled to payment may apply for the order to be sent to that country for enforcement[2]. The application is made either to the Deputy Principal Clerk of Session in the case of a Court of Session application or to the sheriff clerk[3]. The application should be made by letter[4] The letter should be accompanied by:

(1) a certified copy of the relevant order;
(2) a statement signed by the applicant or his solicitor of any arrears outstanding in respect of the order;
(3) a statement similarly signed giving such information as to the whereabouts of the payer as the applicant possesses;
(4) a statement similarly signed giving such information as the applicant possesses for facilitating the identification of the payer;
(5) where available, a photograph of the payer.

An extract decree duly certified by the court should be sufficient to satisfy the requirement in (1) above.

The Deputy Principal Clerk or the sheriff clerk, as the case may be, sends to the Secretary of State for Scotland a certified copy of the maintenance order, a certificate certifying that the order is enforceable in the United Kingdom, a certificate of arrears and the other information provided in the application as to the whereabouts and identification of the payer together with the photograph. These are then transmitted by the Secretary of State to the appropriate authority in the reciprocating country if, but only if, he is satisfied that there is sufficient information as to the whereabouts of the payer to justify that[5].

Provisional order

If he has jurisdiction in terms of rule 2(5) of Schedule 8 to the Civil Jurisdiction and Judgments Act 1982 a sheriff has power to make a provisional order where the defender resides in a reciprocating country[6]. Rule 2(5) states that in relation to maintenance the court having jurisdiction is the court of the place where the maintenance creditor is domiciled or habitually resident, or where the

1 Maintenance Orders (Reciprocal Enforcement) Act 1972, s 21(1).
2 Maintenance Orders (Reciprocal Enforcement) Act 1972, s 2(1).
3 Maintenance Orders (Reciprocal Enforcement) Act 1972 Rules 1974, rule 3(1).
4 Ibid, para 4(1) (C of S); para 10(1) (Sh Ct).
5 Maintenance Orders (Reciprocal Enforcement) Act 1972, s 2.
6 Ibid, s 4.

matter is ancillary to an action concerning the status of a person (such as an action of divorce) the court which has jurisdiction to entertain such an action.

The application, which in the sheriff court would be commenced by initial writ[1], should include the information and photograph referred to in (3), (4) and (5) above. The sheriff has to be satisfied that to the best of the knowledge and belief of the pursuer, the defender resides in a reciprocating country. There does not need to be citation of the defender[2] But the court may not make an order unless the grounds of action are substantiated by sufficient evidence[3]. If a provisional order is made the sheriff clerk sends to the Secretary of State a certified copy of the maintenance order, a document, duly authenticated, setting out or summarising the evidence given, a certificate certifying the grounds on which the making of the order might have been opposed by the payer and a statement giving information as to the whereabouts of the payer, his identification and a photograph if available[4].

The evidence led in support of an application for a provisional order should normally be taken down by a shorthand writer so that a transcript can be sent to the confirming court[5]. The applicant or his solicitor is required to provide the sheriff with a transcript of the evidence where the evidence has been taken down by a shorthand writer[6]. The Secretary of State must be satisfied that there is sufficient information as to the whereabouts of the payer.

Section 5 of the 1972 Act makes provision for revocation and variation of a provisional order made in Scotland and confirmed in a reciprocating country. The court to which the order is transmitted is required to apply the law of the place where the order was made. It may confirm the provisional order with or without such alteration as the court thinks reasonable[7].

A Scottish order registered in a reciprocating country may be varied or revoked by the Scottish court and by the court of the country in which the order is registered. This would be done by the reciprocating country making a provisional order which would be sent to Scotland for confirmation[8].

Part II—Convention countries

The Convention countries for the purposes of Part II of the Act are:
Algeria, Austria, Barbados, Belgium, Brazil, Central African Republic, Chile, Czechoslovakia, Denmark, Equador, Finland, France (including: the overseas Departments of Guiana, Martinique and Reunion, Comoro Archipelago, French Polynesia, French Territory of the Afars and Issas, New Caledonia and Dependencies, St Pierre and Miquelon), Federal Republic of Germany (including West Berlin), Greece, Guatemala, Haiti, Holy See, Hungary, Israel, Italy, Luxembourg, Monaco, Morocco, Netherlands (Kingdom in Europe and Netherlands Antilles), Niger, Norway, Pakistan, Philippines, Poland, Spain, Sri Lanka, Surinam, Tunisia, Turkey, Upper Volta, Yugoslavia. The Order

1 Maintenance Orders (Reciprocal Enforcement) Act 1972 Rules 1974, r 18(a).
2 Maintenance Orders (Reciprocal Enforcement) Act 1972, s 4(4)(a).
3 Ibid, s 4(4)(b).
4 Ibid, s 3(5).
5 *Killen v Killen* 1981 SLT (Sh Ct) 77 at 81.
6 Maintenance Orders (Reciprocal Enforcement) Act 1972 Rules 1974, r 17(2).
7 Maintenance Orders (Reciprocal Enforcement) Act 1972, s 7(2); for an example of such an alteration see *Killen*, supra.
8 Maintenance Orders (Reciprocal Enforcement) Act 1972, s 5(5).

in Council relating to all these countries except Surinam and Switzerland is contained in the Recovery Abroad of Maintenance (Convention Countries) Order 1975, SI 1975/423; for Surinam see SI 1982/1530; for Switzerland see SI 1978/279.

PROCEDURE

There is no procedure for a provisional order such as there is where a reciprocating country is involved. A claim for maintenance, or for the variation of a maintenance order is made in a convention country, ie by the pursuer in her own jurisdiction. Maintenance for this purpose includes aliment and any sums payable, following divorce, by one former spouse for the support of the other, eg periodical allowance.[1]. The sheriff court has jurisdiction to deal with applications by a person in a convention country by virtue of the Sheriff Courts (Scotland) Act 1907, s 5(2A) and the 1972 Act, s 31(1).

To recover maintenance from the payer in another convention country in the case of a Scottish order an application is made to the Secretary of State for Scotland, through the sheriff clerk of the court in Scotland to whose jurisdiction the pursuer is subject. Application may also be made by this means where a person in Scotland seeks to vary a provision made in a convention country for payment of maintenance to the applicant[2]. The application contains a request that the claim be transmitted to the convention country to whose jurisdiction the defender is subject[3]. The sheriff clerk is required to assist the applicant to complete the application. The application must comply with the requirements of the law of the convention country. The sheriff clerk will transmit it to the Secretary of State who, if he considers it to be in order, will transmit it to the appropriate officer in the convention country. Sheriff clerks have notes for guidance as to the requirements of the convention countries. Accordingly before any such application is made it is desirable to consult the appropriate sheriff clerk as to the form of the application, the evidence necessary and the productions required. Reference should be made to AS (Reciprocal Enforcement of Maintenance Orders) (Hague Convention Countries) 1980, SI 1980/291.

Part III—bilateral arrangements

Bilateral arrangements exist between the United Kingdom and countries in which the Hague Convention of 1973 on the Recognition and Enforcement of Decisions Relating to Maintenance Obligations is in force. Such arrangements have been entered into with the United States in respect of most jurisdictions in that country, and Eire. The Order in Council may apply the provisions of the Act with or without modification.

As has been noted above in relation to reciprocating countries bilateral arrangements have been made with a number of countries and jurisdictions which are modifications of Part I of the Maintenance Orders (Reciprocal Enforcement) Act 1972. The arrangements with the states of the United States and the Republic of Ireland are in essence modifications of the arrangements set out in Part II of the Act. In relation to the states of the United States

1 Maintenance Orders (Reciprocal Enforcement) Act 1972, s 39.
2 Ibid, s 26(2).
3 Ibid, s 26.

there are certain additional requirements as to registration with which the sheriff clerk must comply.

The states of the United States with which arrangements have been made are:

Alaska[1], Arizona, Arkansas, California, Colorado, Connecticut[2], Delaware[3], Florida[4], Georgia, Hawaii[5], Idaho, Illinois, Indiana[6], Iowa[7], Kansas, Kentucky, Louisiana, Maine[8], Maryland, Massachussetts[9], Michigan, Minnesota[10], Missouri[11], Montana, Nebraska, Nevada, New Hampshire[12], New Jersey[13], New Mexico, New York, North Carolina, North Dakota, Ohio, Oklahoma, Oregon, Pennsylvania[14], Rhode Island, South Dakota, Tennessee [15], Texas[16], Utah [17], Vermont, Virginia, Washington, Wisconsin and Wyoming[18].

For the procedures applicable to a particular jurisdiction reference must be made to the statutory instrument concerned. Assistance in this connection may be obtained from the Scottish Courts Administration.

REPUBLIC OF IRELAND

Modified provisions of Part II also apply to the Republic of Ireland under a bilateral agreement. The relevant order which was made under Part III of the 1972 Act is the Reciprocal Enforcement of Maintenance Orders (Republic of Ireland) Order 1974[19]; see the Reciprocal Enforcement of Maintenance Orders (Republic of Ireland) Order 1974 Rules 1975[20]. It was intended that this arrangement would lapse on the coming into force in the Irish Republic of the Brussels Convention on Jurisdiction and Enforcement of Judgments in Civil and Commercial Matters on 1 June 1988. That, however, has not so far happened.

The arrangements, in outline, are that, in certain circumstances, the sheriff is given jurisdiction by the Order over defenders who owe a duty to pay maintenance and who are resident in the Republic of Ireland. These circumstances require that the defender has been given an opportunity to defend the claim for maintenance in accordance with the agreed arrangements. If so, a Scottish court may transmit a decree to the Irish Republic for enforcement. There are corresponding arrangements for the enforcement in Scotland of Irish decrees. These arrangements apply to both the Court of Session and the sheriff court.

1   SI 1984/1824.
2   All SI 1979/1314.
3   SI 1981/606.
4   SI 1979/1314.
5   Both SI 1984 /1824.
6   All SI 1979/1314.
7   SI 1984/1824.
8   All SI 1979/1314.
9   Both SI 1981/606.
10 Both SI 1979/1314.
11 SI 1981/606.
12 All SI 1979/1314.
13 SI 1984/1824.
14 All SI 1979/1314.
15 All SI 1981/606.
16 SI 1979/1314.
17 SI 1981/606.
18 All SI 1979/1314.
19 SI 1974/2140; see particularly Sch 2.
20 SI 1975 /475.

Procedure

In terms of the 1975 Rules, in any action for the payment, variation or revocation of aliment or other periodical payment for the maintenance of a person whom the payer is liable to maintain, which is competent in the sheriff court, the sheriff has jurisdiction in respect of a person residing in the Republic of Ireland if[1]

(1) The pursuer resides within the jurisdiction of that sheriff.
(2) The sheriff is satisfied that, to the best of the information or belief of the pursuer, the defender resides in the Republic of Ireland.
(3) The sheriff does not otherwise have jurisdiction in the action.

A copy of the initial writ and a copy of the warrant for citation must be sent to the responsible authority in Ireland and have been served on the defender in accordance with Irish practice in sufficient time for the defender to arrange for his defence. The grounds of action must be substantiated by sufficient evidence.

Any variation or revocation of an outgoing decree from Scotland must made by the court in Scotland.

A pursuer who has custody of a child for whom aliment is sought is deemed to have custody of the child by order of the court for the purpose of obtaining decree for aliment.

Where an application is made to the court for transmission of an order for enforcement in the Republic of Ireland the application is by letter addressed to the Deputy Principal Clerk of Session in respect of Court of Session decrees and to the sheriff clerk in respect of sheriff decrees. The letter should be accompanied by the documents referred to in the 1975 Rules (supra) paras 4 or 7 as the case may be. The Deputy Principal Clerk or the sheriff clerk, in the case of an application to him, must be satisfied that the defender resides in the Republic of Ireland. If so he will transmit the decree for enforcement.

So far as transmission is concerned the procedure is similar to that for transmission of a decree for enforcement under Part I of the 1972 Act in regard to a reciprocating country (see above). Transmission is through the Secretary of State for Scotland. But there must also be provided a signed document establishing that notice of the order made by the Scottish court was sent to the payer, a certificate, if applicable, that the pursuer received legal aid and, if the payer did not appear, a certified copy of the execution of service on the payer.

ENFORCING ORDERS FOR CUSTODY

Registration of custody orders elsewhere in the United Kingdom

Custody orders made in Scotland by the Court of Session or the sheriff court will be recognised by and may be registered in an appropriate court in England, Wales or Northern Ireland and vice versa[2]. The procedure for variation, registration and cancellation of court orders is set out in RC 260R to 260W and in AS (Rules for Registration of Custody Orders of the Sheriff Court) 1988, SI 1988/613. As regards sheriff court orders application is made

---

1 SI 1975/475, supra, Sch 2, para 4(1).
2 Family Law Act 1986, ss 25, 27.

to the sheriff clerk of the court which made the order. The application must be accompanied by:

(1) a copy of the letter of application;
(2) an affidavit by the applicant (sworn in the usual way);
(3) a copy of that affidavit;
(4) a certified copy of the interlocutor granting custody[1];
(5) a certified copy of any interlocutor containing a variation of that order which is in force;
(6) any other relevant document, in duplicate.

The affidavit should set out:

(a) the name and address of the applicant and his right under the custody order;
(b) the name and date of birth of the child in respect of whom the custody order was made, the present whereabouts or suspected whereabouts of the child and the name of any person with whom he is alleged to be;
(c) the name and address of any other person who has an interest in the custody order[2];
(d) whether the custody order is to be registered in England and Wales or in Northern Ireland or both and the court in which it is to be registered;
(e) whether the custody order is in force;
(f) whether the custody order is already registered and, if so, where it is registered;
(g) details of any order known to the applicant which affects the child and is in force in the jurisdiction in which the custody order is to be registered;

If the custody order which it is sought to register is not still in force, it will not be capable of registration. If that is the case the applicant will be notified in writing.

Similar procedure is followed where registration of the order is sought in the Court of Session.

The court in which the custody order is registered has the same powers to enforce it as if it had made the order itself. Where an application has been made for the enforcement of a registered order the court may give interim directions to secure the welfare of the child and to prevent changes in the circumstances relevant to the determination of the application[3]. The defender should be given a chance to oppose an order for delivery of the child[4]. Such an application may be sisted if proceedings have been taken or if it is intended to take such proceedings as a result of which the registered order may cease to have effect or may have a different effect. These proceedings may be in the United Kingdom or elsewhere[5]. After a custody order has been registered in Scotland steps may be taken to obtain interdict and delivery of the child[6].

A registered custody order may be revoked, recalled or varied[7]. Where an interlocutor awarding custody is revoked, recalled or cancelled, the sheriff

---

1 The clerk of the court in which the interlocutor was pronounced will certify the interlocutor.
2 That could include a local authority, eg where a supervision order has been made in terms of the Matrimonial Proceedings (Children) Act 1958, s 12 or a grandparent who has been granted access.
3 Family Law Act 1986, s 29.
4 *Woodcock v Woodcock* 1990 SCLR 535.
5 Family Law Act 1986, s 30.
6 *Woodcock v Woodcock*, supra.
7 Family Law Act 1986, s 28.

clerk sends a certified copy of that order to the court where the custody order is registered. Similar procedure applies in the Court of Session[1].

Tracing the whereabouts of a child

The court has power in connection with proceedings for or relating to a custody order, if the court does not have adequate information as to where the child is, to order any person, whom it has reason to believe may have any relevant information, to disclose that information to the court. It is not a reason for non-compliance with such an order that to do so would incriminate that person or his spouse. But a statement made in compliance with such an order is not admissible against either of them in any proceedings for any offence other than perjury[2]. In the Court of Session when the court orders disclosure it may order the person concerned to appear before the court or to lodge an affidavit[3]. It is suggested that in similar circumstances the sheriff court would adopt a similar course.

Enforcing delivery of children

The court may grant warrant to officers of court to search for and take possession of the child for the purpose of delivering him to the person entitled to custody. An order for delivery of a child is a decree *ad factum praestandum* and may be enforced by diligence[4]. The court may order delivery of a child to a parent so that the child may be returned to the jurisdiction in which he is a ward of court[5]. There is no duty on the police or Procurators Fiscal to assist messengers-at-arms and sheriff officers in the search for children whose delivery has been ordered by the court[6].

UNAUTHORISED REMOVAL OF CHILDREN

Removal of a child from one United Kingdom jurisdiction to another or from the United Kingdom

In terms of section 35(3) and (4) of the Family Law Act 1986 a court may make an order granting interdict or interim interdict prohibiting the removal of a child from the United Kingdom or any part thereof or out of the control of the person in whose custody the child is. The effect of such an order is that it has effect in each part of the United Kingdom other than the part in which it was made as if it had been made by the appropriate court in that part. Where the order prohibits the removal of the child to that other part it has effect as if the order included a prohibition of the further removal of the child except to the part where he should be[7]. These provisions apply

1 RC 260U.
2 Family Law Act 1986, s 33; *Abusaif v Abusaif* 1984 SLT 90.
3 RC 260EB.
4 *Brown v Brown* 1948 SC 5 at 11.
5 *Thomson Petr* 1980 SLT (Notes) 29.
6 *Caldwell v Caldwell* 1983 SLT 610.
7 Family Law Act 1986, s 36.

to both the Court of Session and to the sheriff court. Where such an order is in force the court which made the order may order the surrender of a United Kingdom passport relating to the child[1] The Rules of Court provide that application for such an interdict be made by minute in the cause in which the application is to be made[2]. But where there has been breach of such interdict new proceedings for breach of interdict would require to be taken in the appropriate court in the part of the United Kingdom where the child is. It is suggested that High Court proceedings are likely to be taken in respect of a High Court order. A child does not lose his place of habitual residence when, in contravention of such a prohibition, he leaves the part of the country in which he resided[3].

Child abduction

TAKING A CHILD OUT OF THE UNITED KINGDOM

It is a criminal offence punishable by imprisonment of up to two years or a fine or both for a person connected with a child to take that child out of the United Kingdom without the appropriate consent if custody of that child has been awarded to any person by a court in the United Kingdom or the child is a ward of court in England, Wales or Northern Ireland and if there is in force an order prohibiting the removal of that child from the United Kingdom or from any part of it[4]. If a prohibition order has been made by a court in one part of the United Kingdom, that court should revoke that prohibition if it is appropriate to do so and not the court in the part of the United Kingdom where the child happens to be[5]. A person is connected with the child inter alia if he is a parent or guardian of that child or if there is an award of custody of that child in his favour whether the award was of sole or joint custody.

Consent in this context means the consent of each parent or guardian of the child or any person who has been awarded custody of the child, whether jointly or not, or the leave of the court. Statutory defences are provided in the Child Abduction Act 1984, s 6(4) and (5).

A police constable may arrest without warrant any person whom he reasonably suspects of committing or having committed such an offence[6]. It is suggested that where abduction has taken place the party aggrieved should obtain a certified copy of the order of court awarding custody or prohibiting the removal of the child so that, when information becomes available as to the whereabouts of the child, evidence can be produced to the police. Such an order or document or a copy thereof, duly authenticated, is sufficient evidence of any matter to which it relates[7] The child named in the order is presumed to be the child in respect of whom the proceedings have been taken unless the contrary is proved[8].

1 Ibid, s 37.
2 RC 170B(13) and 260EC; OCR 132E.
3 Family Law Act 1986, s 41.
4 Child Abduction Act 1984, s 6.
5 *Deans v Deans* 1988 SCLR 192.
6 Child Abduction Act 1984, s 7.
7 Ibid, s 9.
8 Ibid, s 10.

THE CHILD ABDUCTION AND CUSTODY ACT 1985

The Child Abduction and Custody Act 1985 implements two conventions. Part I gives effect to the Convention on the Civil Aspects of International Child Abduction signed at The Hague on 25 October 1980. Part II gives effect to the European Convention on Recognition and Enforcement of Decisions concerning Custody of Children and on the Restoration of Custody of Children signed at Luxembourg on 20 May 1980.

Part I—Child abduction—The Hague Convention

The other countries which are currently contracting states are Australia, Austria, Belize, Canada, The French Republic, Hungary, Luxembourg, Norway, Portugal, Spain, Sweden, Switzerland and the United States[1].

The convention is set out in Schedule 1 to the Child Abduction and Custody Act 1985. Briefly it provides that the removal or the retention of a child under sixteen is considered wrongful if it is in breach of rights of custody attributed to an individual or an institution or other body according to the law of the place where the child was habitually resident and such rights were being or would have been exercised but for the removal. For example, if an Australian court awards custody of a child resident in Australia to the father and the mother removes that child to the United Kingdom without the father's consent there would be a breach of custody rights under Article 3 of the 1980 Hague Convention[2]. If a child leaves a state where he is habitually resident with the consent of both parents he will lose his habitual residence there and it will not revive[3].

The scheme of the convention is that any person, institution or other body claiming that a child has been removed or retained in breach of custody rights (defined in art 5) may apply either to the central authority of the child's habitual residence or to the central authority of any other contracting state for assistance in securing the return of the child (art 8). The central authority for the United Kingdom is the Lord Chancellor but in Scotland it is the Secretary of State for Scotland. The application should contain the information set out in article 8 of the Convention. In terms of article 7 the central authority is obliged to take all appropriate measures to initiate or facilitate the institution of judicial or administrative proceedings with a view to obtaining the return of the child and, in a proper case, to secure the effective exercise of rights of access.

The Court of Session has jurisdiction to entertain applications under the Convention. The sheriff court does not have jurisdiction[4]. Schedule 1 of the Child Abduction and Custody Act 1985 does not take effect retrospectively[5]. There are likely to be three types of application to the court under the Convention whether in this country or in another contracting state. These are for the return of a child wrongfully removed or retained[6], for declarator to establish that such an event has occurred, and to secure satisfactory arrangements for access.

1 See The Child Abduction and Custody (Parties to Conventions) (Amendment) (No 3) Order 1989, SI 1989/1332.
2 *Re C (a minor)* (1988) The Times, 19 December.
3 *Dickson v Dickson* 1990 GWD 23–1265 (Inner House).
4 Family Law Act 1986, s 4.
5 *Re B (minors)* (1987) The Times, 29 October, 1987 CLY 2467.
6 See *MacMillan v MacMillan* 1989 SCLR 243, 1989 SLT 350.

APPLICATION FOR RETURN OF CHILD

An application for the return of a child is by petition presented to the Outer House[1]. That Rule of Court sets out the averments which must be made. With the petition there must be produced a certified or authenticated copy of any relevant decision or agreement and a certificate or affidavit from a central authority or other competent authority of the contracting state of the habitual residence of the child concerning the relevant law of that state.

The court may give interim directions for the purpose of securing the welfare of the child or to prevent a change of circumstances[2]. The court is enjoined to act expeditiously and at least within 6 weeks (art 11). If the child has been wrongfully removed or retained for less than a year the judicial or administrative authority of the state where the child is must order the return of the child forthwith. Where the period exceeds one year the return of the child will be ordered unless the child is settled in its new environment (art 12)[3]. Provision is made for return to be refused in certain circumstances including where there is a grave risk that the return of the child would expose him to physical or psychological harm or otherwise place him in an intolerable situation (art 13). In deciding whether that is so the court may consider what is likely to happen on the child's return[4]. But a parent cannot rely on the risk of psychological harm if that risk has been caused by his own conduct[5]. There may have to be a balancing exercise weighing the consequences of the order to return the child[6]. A decision should be taken by the court at the time when the matter is before it and should not be delayed[7] The court is required to take account of information relating to the child's social background but is not obliged to delay a decision in order to obtain such information[8]. The court of the state to which the child has been removed can normally consider the custody of the child only after it has been determined that the child is not to be returned[9].

APPLICATION FOR DECLARATOR

An application for declarator that the removal or retention of a child was unlawful is made by petition presented to the Outer House. Any person appearing to the court to have an interest in the matter may seek declarator that the removal of any child from, or his retention outside, the United Kingdom was wrongful within the meaning of article 3 of the Convention[10]. That Rule sets out the averments which should be made.

ACCESS

Application may be made by the same means to secure the effective exercise of access[11]. Application for the return of a child is by petition presented to

1 RC 260J(1).
2 Child Abduction and Custody Act 1985, s 5.
3 *Kilgour v Kilgour* 1987 GWD 4–107.
4 *Re A (a minor) (Abduction)* (1988) 18 Fam Law 54.
5 *C v C* [1989] 2 All ER 465 (minor: abduction: rights of custody abroad).
6 *Re A*, supra.
7 *MacMillan v MacMillan* 1989 SCLR 243, 1989 SLT 350; *Re E (A minor)* 1989 FLR 35 (Abduction).
8 *Viola v Viola* 1987 SCLR 529. Nor is it obliged to hear evidence: *Dickson v Dickson* 1990 GWD 23–1265.
9 Hague Convention, art 16.
10 Family Law Act 1986, s 8; Hague Convention, art 15; RC 260J(3).
11 Hague Convention, art 21.

the Outer House[1]. That Rule of Court sets out the averments which must be made. With the petition there must be produced a certified copy of any relevant decision or agreement.

Part II—Recognition and Enforcement of Decisions concerning Custody of Children—Restoration of Custody of Children

The Contracting States currently are:

Austria, Belgium, Cyprus, France, Luxembourg, Norway, Portugal, Spain, Sweden, Switzerland[2].

The Convention is set out in Schedule 2 to the Child Abduction and Custody Act 1985. The Convention is concerned primarily with two matters: the international recognition of decisions relating to custody of children under sixteen and the enforcement of custody decisions. With regard to recognition the Convention is concerned with decisions including those relating to the care of the child, deciding the place of the child's residence and the right of access to him[3]. With regard to enforcement the Convention is concerned with improper removal of children across international frontiers. That includes failure to return a child and a removal which is subsequently declared to be unlawful.

SCHEME OF THE CONVENTION

The scheme of the Convention is that a decision in one contracting state will be recognised and will normally be registered[4] in another contracting state where it may then be enforced as if it had been a decision of a court in the country where it is registered[5]. The Court of Session may refuse registration on any of the grounds set out in articles 9 and 10 of the Convention[6]. Application for registration of a decision is made to the central authority along with the documents specified in Article 13. That authority is required to take all steps which it considers appropriate, if necessary by instituting proceedings: to discover the whereabouts of the child, to avoid prejudice to the interests of the child, to secure registration and enforcement of the decision, to secure delivery of the child to the applicant where enforcement is granted and to inform the requesting authority of what has occurred[7]. The court has power to make interim directions to secure the welfare of the child or to prevent a change of circumstances[8].

The grounds specified upon which recognition or registration may be refused[9] include, broadly: that the decree was granted in absence and either the defender

1 RC 260J(2).
2 The Child Abduction and Custody (Parties to Conventions) (Amendment) (No 2) Order 1989, SI 1989/980.
3 Hague Convention, art 1.
4 Child Abduction and Custody Act 1985, s 16.
5 Ibid, s 18.
6 Ibid, s 15.
7 Hague Convention, art 5.
8 Child Abduction and Custody Act 1985, s 19.
9 Hague Convention, arts 9 and 10.

did not have a proper opportunity to defend it or there was not jurisdiction, that there is not sufficient connection between the child and the state which made the order, that there exists an incompatible decision relating to custody or that there has been a change of circumstances[1]. Registration and enforcement may also be refused where there has been a delay in applying for an order[2]. Application may be made to the Court of Session for declarator that on any of the grounds referred to in Articles 9 or 10 the decision is not to be recognised in any part of the United Kingdom[3]. The substance of a foreign decision on custody may not be reviewed.[4] But a decision as to access may be altered.[5] The Convention applies to an order relating to custody made after the unlawful removal of a child.[6] Section 23(2) of the Child Abduction and Custody Act empowers courts in Scotland to declare the removal of a child to have been unlawful. For the procedure for such applications see RC260K(4); OCR 132B. The effect of proceedings being taken under this Part of the Act on pending proceedings in Scotland in relation to the same child are set out in section 20. Registered decisions may be varied or revoked[7].

Part II of the 1985 Act provides that the same persons as those mentioned in Part I are to be the central authority in the United Kingdom, ie the Lord Chancellor or, in Scotland, the Secretary of State for Scotland[8]. Once a decision is registered in one part of the United Kingdom it is recognised throughout the United Kingdom[9].

PROCEDURE

Applications under section 15 (to declare a decree not to be recognised), section 16 (for registration), section 18 (for enforcement), or both of the last two, are made by petition presented to the Outer House. Applications for variation or revocation of a registered decision are by note in the registration process. Applications to have the removal of a child declared unlawful are made by minute in a process commenced by summons or by note in a process commenced by petition[10]. The averments to be made and the procedure to be followed are set out in the subsequent provisions of that Rule of Court.

Compelling disclosure of the whereabouts of a child

In the course of proceedings under either Part I or Part II of the Child Abduction and Custody Act 1985 where there is inadequate information available as to where the child is, the court may order any person, whom it has reason to believe may have relevant information, to disclose that information to the

1 *Campins-Coll Petr* 1989 SLT 33.
2 *F v F (minors)* [1988] 3 WLR 959 (Custody: Foreign Order).
3 Child Abduction and Custody Act 1985, s 15(2)(a).
4 Hague Convention, art 9.
5 Ibid, art 11(2).
6 Ibid, art 12.
7 Child Abduction and Custody Act 1985, s 17(4); RC 260K(3).
8 Child Abduction and Custody Act 1985, s 14.
9 Ibid, s 15(2).
10 RC 260K.

court. This applies to applications for the return of the child (the Hague Convention) and to applications for the recognition, registration and enforcement of decisions in respect of a child (the Luxembourg Convention)[1]. This section empowers the court to require witnesses to attend to give evidence as to the whereabouts of a child but does not permit the court to order an abductor to give evidence when the child has been found[2].

---

1 Child Abduction and Custody Act 1985, s 24A.
2 *Re D* (A Minor) (Child Abduction) (1988) 18 Fam Law 336, 1989 1 FLR 97.

APPENDIX 1

Practice Notes by the Sheriffs Principal — Affidavits in Undefended Actions of Divorce other than Simplified Divorce.

1. An affidavit is no substitute for a reliable and adequate precognition though a precognition may eventually be the basis for an affidavit.

2. The affidavit should be typed on substantial paper, should be backed up longways, and should be stitched or stapled. It must commence with the words 'At   , the   day of   19   , in the presence of   Compeared   who being solemnly sworn, Depones and follows   ,' The full name, age, address and occupation must be given, and it must thereafter proceed in the first person and should take the form of numbered paragraphs. The witness should be made to appreciate the importance of the affidavit. The witness must be placed on oath, or must affirm, and each page will require to be signed by both the witness and the notary. It is not essential that it should be sealed by the notary. The document should be of shape and size convenient to be lodged as part of the process. The affidavit should end with the words 'All of which is truth as the Deponent "shall answer to God." or "All of which is affirmed to be true," as appropriate.'

3. Affidavits of parties and witnesses should follow step by step the averments in the initial writ. The drafter of an affidavit should provide himself, before drawing it, with a copy of the initial writ, a copy of the appropriate precognition, and the relative productions. The affidavit to be taken from a witness should follow the averments in the initial writ to the extent that these are within the knowledge of that particular witness. It is not a requirement that the wording of an affidavit should follow exactly the wording of the initial writ.

4. *No hearsay.* The drafter must take care that an affidavit contains only matters of fact to which the party or the witness in question can testify, and that it is correct at the date at which it is sworn.

5. On the matter of the qualifications of the person before whom the affidavit is taken, the rules provide that the affidavit is admissible if it is duly emitted before a notary public or other competent authority. This means a notary public, justice of the peace, commissioner of oaths or other statutory authority within the meaning of the Statutory Declarations Act 1835. In the examples given hereafter, it is assumed that the affidavit is in fact taken before a solicitor who is a notary public, and therefore the references to the party before whom the affidavit is sworn are 'the notary'. The solicitor acting in the action may well be called on also to act in a notarial capacity when the affidavit is subsequently sworn. This is permissible. In acting in a notarial capacity he must, however, as a competent authority, observe all the normal rules in this connection, and must satisfy himself as to the capacity of the witness to make the statement, and ensure that the witness understands that it constitutes his or her evidence in the case.

6. On the matter of productions, those required, when an affidavit is being taken, may already have been lodged in process, but there may be some productions (such as photographs) which are produced by the witness to the notary when the affidavit is sworn, and which may not by that time have been lodged in process.

7. Productions already lodged in process must be borrowed up, and put to the party or the witness who makes them part of his or her evidence in the appropriate part of the affidavit. Each production will require to be referred to in the affidavit by its number of process and must be docqueted and signed by the party or witness and the notary. If a production has not yet been lodged when the affidavit is being taken, it will require to be identified by the witness in his evidence in the affidavit, and will then be docqueted with regard to the affidavit and signed by the party or witness and the notary. It will then be lodged as a production. Obviously, certain productions will be docqueted with regard to more than one affidavit.

8. In adultery cases, photographs of both the pursuer and the defender will require to be produced, put to the appropriate party or witnesses in the affidavit, and signed and docqueted with reference thereto in the manner already described. In certain circumstances, a photograph may have to be identified and docqueted by more than one person, as in the case of the photograph of a party requiring to be spoken to by the pursuer and two inquiry agents.

9. All affidavits lodged must be of as recent a date as is possible in the circumstances. This factor is particularly important in (1) cases involving children, (2) those in which financial craves are involved, or (3) in any other circumstances where the evidence of a party or witness is liable to change through the passage of time. The notary will require to ensure, therefore, than an affidavit represents the deponent's evidence on such matters at the time the affidavit is sworn.

10. In cases involving custody of or access to children, an affidavit or affidavits providing corroborating evidence about the welfare of the children should be provided. The evidence of that witness must present the court with a full picture of the position regarding the child or children. It is, however, clear that such independent evidence in no way relieves the pursuer from testifying fully the position regarding the children in his or her own affidavit, so far as within his or her knowledge. Whatever else the affidavits of the pursuer and the independent witness contain, their evidence should certainly include the following:

    (a) the qualification of the witness, if not a parent, to speak about the child; how often, for example, and in what circumstances, does the witness normally see the child.

    (b) a description of the home conditions in which the child lives;

    (c) observations upon the child's general appearance, interests, state of health and well-being;

    (d) information, where relevant, about the school the child attends; whether and to what extent he has contact with other children and relatives;

    (e) observations on the relationship between the child and the person in whose care he or she lives, on the child's attitude towards each of the parents and on the extent of contact with the parent or parents with whom the child is not living.

(f)　details of child care arrangements at all times including arrangements during working hours (outwith school hours).

(g)　the means and status of the person craving custody with a view to enabling him or her to maintain and bring up the child in a suitable manner.

11.　The attention of solicitors is drawn to the provisions of the Matrimonial Proceedings (Children) Act 1958. The court will not (unless the provisions of section 8(2) are shown to apply) grant decree of divorce until the court is satisfied as respects every child for whose custody, maintenance and education the court has jurisdiction to make provision in that action (a) that arrangements have been made for the care and upbringing of the child and that those arrangements are satisfactory or are the best which can be devised in the circumstances; or (b) that it is impracticable for the party or parties appearing before the court to make any such arrangements.

12.　Where financial conclusions are involved, it is even more important that the evidence is full, accurate and up to date. In parole proofs the evidence of the pursuer and the witnesses on these matters can be supplemented at the proof by questions from the Bench or from the solicitor for the pursuer. This will not be possible where evidence is taken by affidavit, and the affidavits must be so framed as to exclude the necessity for supplementary questions. Failure to do so may result in the sheriff requiring the attendance of the solicitor in court. If, after an affidavit has been taken, and the solicitor concerned has parted with it, a material change of circumstances occurs, it is essential that the court be immediately informed, and where necessary, that a further affidavit be sworn.

13.　Where the pursuer in an action is speaking in the affidavit of the financial position of the defender, it is essential that the affidavit should state the date, as precisely as possible, at which the information was valid. Otherwise it may be assumed by the court that the pursuer is speaking to the defender's position at the date of the affidavit. The court must be provided with as up-to-date information as possible about the defender's ability to pay the sums the pursuer is seeking, and these sums should be such as that evidence justifies. The pursuer must, of course, speak also to his or her own financial position, at the date of the affidavit. Where the pursuer cannot obtain recent information as to the defender's means, it is suggested that, if the pursuer's advisers approve, assessment should be left to the sheriff, and in such cases it may be that the solicitors representing the pursuer would be willing to incorporate in the terms of the minute for decree, after the words 'in terms of the crave of the initial writ' the words 'or such other sum (or sums) as the Court may think proper'.

14.　The minute for decree must be signed by a solicitor who has examined the affidavits and other documents and takes responsibility therefor, whether or not he is the person who drew the summons or affidavits.

15.　In consent cases, the defender's written consent form will also have to be borrowed up, put the pursuer in his or her affidavit, and docqueted and identified in the same way as other productions.

16.　Affidavit procedure will not prevent the parties to the action agreeing the financial or other ancillary craves by joint minute. For so long as these ancillary craves are opposed, the affidavit procedure can not be used for them, but it can be used for the merits of the action. If a joint minute is signed before an affidavit or supplementary affidavit is emitted by the pursuer, that affidavit must refer to the arrangements in the joint minute. Decree of divorce will not be granted before any issues relating to financial provisions consequent upon the divorce which require to be decided by the court, have been so decided.

17. Where the pursuer has craved a capital allowance, a periodical allowance, aliment for the child or children, or expenses, and in the minute for decree does not seek decree for one or any of these, it is essential that the reasons for this are fully narrated in the affidavit. Where these reasons are capable of corroboration by witnesses, they should be dealt with in the witnesses' affidavits.

18. Solicitors are reminded that the normal rules of evidence about corroboration still apply except where—
- (a) the action is brought in reliance on the facts set out in section 1(2)(d) (2 years non-cohabitation and the defender's consent to decree) or in section 1(2)(e) (5 years non-cohabitation) of the Divorce (Scotland) Act 1976;
- (b) no other proceedings are pending in any court which could have the effect of bringing the marriage to an end.
- (c) there are no children of the marriage under the age of 16 years.
- (d) neither party applies for an order for financial provision on divorce, and
- (e) neither party suffers from mental disorder within the meaning of Section 6 of the Mental Health (Scotland) Act 1960[1].

---

1 See now the Mental Health (Scotland) Act 1984, s 1.

APPENDIX 2

Notes by the Dean of the Faculty of Advocates and the President of the Law Society for the Guidance of Members of the Faculty and of the Society in regard to Affidavit Evidence in Undefended Divorce Actions

1. It has been suggested to us by the Lord President that we might give guidance to the profession regarding the procedure to be followed in connection with the Act of Sederunt which comes into operation on 25th April 1978. In the hope that it might be helpful, we now do so on entirely general lines. Decisions in regard to particular situations will fall to be made by the legal advisers of the party concerned, and these notes do not claim to be in any way exhaustive.

2. Precognitions of parties and witnesses should be as ample and as relevant as it is possible to make them, bearing in mind that, except for the very small proportions of cases defended on the merits of the case, they will eventually become the basis of affidavits. The procedure at the initiating stage of the action will follow the same pattern as at present. Precognitions will be taken from the pursuer and witnesses and will be provided to counsel, who will draft the summons in the ordinary way. The one exception is that, where matters relating the children are involved, a precognition should be taken from the witnesses referred to in rule 2 (5) of the Act of Sederunt.

3. Once it has been ascertained that the action is not to be defended, it will be imperative that all the productions are uplifted from the process and passed to the solicitor concerned with the taking of the affidavits.

4. We do not feel it possible to provide a style of affidavit, but suggest that the affidavits of parties and witnesses should follow step by step the averments in the summons. The drafter of an affidavit should provide himself, before drawing it, with a copy of the summons, a copy of the appropriate precognition, and the relevant productions. The affidavit to be taken from a witness should follow the averments in the summons to the extent that these are within the knowledge of that particular witness. The drafter must take care that an affidavit contains only matters of fact to which the party or the witness in question can testify, and that it is correct at the date at which it is sworn.

5. On the matter of the qualifications of the person before whom the affidavit is taken, the Rules provide that the affidavit is admissible if it is duly emitted before a notary public or other competent authority. This means a notary public, Justice of the Peace, Commissioner of oaths or other statutory authority within the meaning of the Statutory Declarations Act 1835. In the examples given hereafter, we shall assume that the affidavit is in fact taken before a solicitor who is a notary public, and therefore we refer to the party before whom the affidavit is sworn as 'the notary'. The solicitor acting in the action may well be called on also to act in a notarial capacity, when the affidavit is subsequently sworn. We consider that he is in no way disqualified from doing so merely because of his interest in the action. In acting in a notarial capacity he must, however, as a competent authority, observe all the normal rules in this connection, and must satisfy himself as to the capacity of the witness to make the statement, and ensure that the witness understands that it constitutes his or her evidence in the case.

6. The pursuer or the witness must appreciate the importance of the affidavit. The affidavit should be typed on substantial paper, should be backed up longways, and should be stitched or stapled. It must commence with the words 'At   , the   day of   19   , in the presence of   , Compeared   who being solemnly sworn, Depones as follows   .' The full name, age, address and occupation must be given, and it must thereafter proceed in the first person and should take the form of numbered paragraphs. The witness must be placed on oath, or must affirm, and each page will require to be signed by both the witness and the notary. We do not think it is essential that it should be sealed by the notary, but it is of importance that the document should be of a shape and size convenient to be lodged as part of the process. The affidavit should end with the words 'All of which is truth as the Deponent shall answer to God,' or 'All of which is affirmed to be true', as appropriate.

7. On the matter of productions, those required, when an affidavit is being taken, may already have been lodged in process, but there may be some productions (such as photographs) which are produced by the witness to the notary when the affidavit is sworn, and which may not by that time have been lodged in process.

8. As earlier indicated, productions already lodged in process must be borrowed up, and put to the party or the witness in the appropriate part of the affidavit. Each production will require to be referred to in the affidavit by its number of process and must be docqueted and signed by the party or witness and the notary. If a production has not yet been lodged when the affidavit is being taken, it will require to be identified by the witness in his evidence in the affidavit, and will then be docqueted with regard to the affidavit and signed by the party or witness and the notary. It will then be lodged as a production. Obviously, certain productions will then be docqueted with regard to more than one affidavit.

9. In adultery cases, under the old procedure, a photograph of the defender was usually required, but a photograph of the pursuer was often unnecessary because the pursuer required to appear in court. Under the new procedure, in such cases, photographs of both the pursuer and the defender will require to be produced, put to the appropriate party or witnesses in the affidavit, and signed and docqueted with reference thereto in the manner already described. In certain circumstances, a photograph may have to be identified and docqueted by more than one person, as in the case of the photograph of a party requiring to be spoken to by the pursuer and two inquiry agents.

10. All affidavits lodged must be of as recent a date as is possible in the circumstances. The aim should be to submit these to counsel immediately after they are taken, because once counsel has signed the minute, they will be brought before a judge very quickly. This factor is particularly important in (1) cases involving children, (2) those in which financial conclusions are involved, or (3) in any other circumstances where the evidence of a party or witness is liable to change through the passage of time. The notary will require to ensure, therefore, that an affidavit represents the deponent's evidence on such matters at the time the affidavit is sworn.

11. In cases involving custody and welfare of children, the terms of rule 2 (5) relating to an independent witness should be borne in mind. The evidence of that witness must present the court with a full picture of the position regarding the child or children. It is, however, clear that such independent evidence in no way relieves the pursuer from testifying fully the position regarding the children in his or her own affidavit, so far as within his or her knowledge. Whatever else the affidavits of the pursuer and the independent witness contain, their evidence should certainly include the following:

    (a) the qualifications of the witness, if not a parent, to speak about the child; how often, for example, and in what circumstances, does the witness normally see the child;

    (b) a description of the home conditions in which the child lives;

    (c) observations upon the child's general appearance, interests, state of health and well-being;

    (d) information, where relevant, about the school the child attends; whether and to what extent he has contact with other children and relatives;

    (e) observations on the relationship between the child and the person in whose care he or she lives, on the child's attitude towards each of the parents and on the extent of contact with the parent or parents with whom the child is not living.

12. Where financial conclusions are involved, it is even more important that the evidence is full, accurate and up to date. In the past, the evidence of the pursuer and the witnesses on these matters has often required to be supplemented at the proof by questions from the Bench or from counsel. This will no longer be possible, and the affidavits must be so framed as to exclude the necessity for supplementary questions. Failure to do so might result in the case being sent to the by order roll. If, after an affidavit has been taken, and the solicitor concerned has parted with it, a material change of circumstances occurs, it is essential that counsel be immediately informed, and, where necessary, that a further affidavit be sworn.

13. Where the pursuer in an action is speaking in the affidavit of the financial position of the defender, it is essential that the affidavit should state the date, as precisely as possible, at which that information was valid. Otherwise it may be assumed by the court that the pursuer is speaking to the defender's position at the date of the affidavit. The court must be provided with as up-to-date information as possible about the defender's ability to pay the sums the pursuer is seeking, and these sums should be such as that evidence justifies. The pursuer must, of course, speak also to his or her own financial position, at the date of the affidavit. Where the pursuer cannot obtain recent information as to the defender's means, we would suggest that, if the pursuer's advisers approve, assessment should be left to the judge, and in such cases it may be that counsel and solicitors would be willing to incorporate in the terms of the minute, after the words 'in terms of the conclusions of the Summons' the words 'or such other sum (or sums) as the Court may think proper'.

14. Where the pursuer does not seek a capital allowance, or a periodical allowance, or ailment for the child or children, it is essential that the reasons for this are fully narrated in the affidavit. Where these reasons are capable of corroboration by witnesses, they should be dealt with in the witnesses' affidavits. Similarly, where a wife pursuer does not seek an award of expenses against the defender, she must give reasons for this in her affidavit, especially where she has a legal aid certificate.

15. We take the view that the minute must be signed by the counsel who has examined the affidavit evidence and no one else. This should be the case, whether or not the counsel who examined the affidavit evidence also drew the summons.

16. In consent cases, the defender's written consent form will also have to be borrowed up, put to the pursuer in his or her affidavit, and docqueted and identified in the same way as other productions.

17. In our view, the new procedure will not prevent the parties to the action agreeing the financial or other ancillary conclusions by joint minute. For so long as these ancillary conclusions are opposed, the affidavit procedure cannot be used for matters covered thereby, but it can be used for the merits of the action. If and when the ancillary conclusions are successfully negotiated, a joint minute may then be lodged and the case brought under the rules by Rule 2 (c). If a joint minute is signed before an affidavit or supplementary affidavit is emitted by the pursuer, that affidavit should refer to the arrangements in the joint minute.

18. As far as those members of the profession who are called upon to advise defenders are concerned, the new procedure does not alter the rules that defences in this type of action may be lodged at any time before the granting of decree, or that the decree may be reclaimed against within twenty-one days. Advisers are, however, reminded that the whole procedure from start to finish may well take a much shorter time than at present, and defenders who wish to contest any of the conclusions in whole or in part should be advised to enter the process without delay, and if appropriate, steps should be taken to sist the proceedings to enable the defender to apply for legal aid.

19. These notes have the general approval of the Lord President.

INDEX

Abduction
Child Abduction and Custody Act 1985 . . ., 186–90
Hague Convention, 186–8
taking child out of UK, 185
Access
averment, 88
interim, 124
order relating to, 53–54, 88
plea in law, 89
recall of order relating to, 161–2
report on, 147–8
simplified procedure not appropriate, 18
variation of order relating to, 161–2
Action
defended. See DEFENDED ACTION
raising. See RAISING ACTION
sist of, 109
undefended. See UNDEFENDED ACTION
Address
defender, of, 80
pursuer, of, 80
unknown, 80
Adherence
obligation to adhere, presumptions relating to, 7–8
Administration of Justice (Scotland) Act 1972, s 1
application for order under, 98
Admission
evidence relating to, 144
Adultery
averment, 81
defended action, 133
number of decrees based on, 1987 . . ., 145–6
simplified procedure not appropriate, 16

Affidavit
defended action, 149
form of, 151
interim order, hearing of motion for, 123
lodging of, 115
practice notes relating to, 142–3
taking, 149–50
undefended action, 149
Agreement
aliment, on,
 financial provision, setting aside or varying, 28
 husband and wife, 27
 parent and child, 28
spouses, between, setting aside or variation of, 156
Aliment
award,
 circumstances to be taken into account in making, 9
 test for making, 9
child, for. See CHILD
conduct, relevance of, 9–10
disputed, 129–30
generally, 24–5
interim,
 generally, 124–5
 pursuer, for,
  averment, 86
  order, 86
  plea in law, 86
jurisdiction relating to, 70–1
person to whom obligation owed, 8
prior agreement on,
 financial provision, setting aside or varying agreement on, 28
 husband and wife, 27
 parent and child, 28
quantum of, 26

Aliment—*contd*
simplified procedure not appropriate, 19
See also FINANCIAL PROVISION

Allowance
housekeeping, presumptions relating to, 7
periodical. *See* PERIODICAL ALLOWANCE

Amendment
ground of divorce, of, 115

Ancillary order
access, 53–4
aliment. *See* ALIMENT
child's whereabouts, disclosure of, 56
custody, relating to. *See* CUSTODY
delivery of child, relating to, 57–8, 156
divorce action raised prior to 1 September 1986 . . ., 22
interdict. *See* INTERDICT
interim order. *See* INTERIM ORDER
Matrimonial Homes (Family Protection) (Scotland) Act 1981, under. *See* MATRIMONIAL HOME
parental rights, 49
removal of child,
jurisdiction of court, from, restriction of, 56–7, 155
obtaining authority of court,

Annulment
order for financial provision following, 154–5

Appeal
simplified procedure, 97

Appearance
entering, 128
late, by defender, 135–6

Arrest, powers of
interdict, form of application for breach of, 169
matrimonial home, 122, 134
order relating to, 63–4, 122
simplified procedure, 21

Assets. *See* CAPITAL ASSETS

Averment
adultery, 81
aliment for child, 88
assets,
alienation, prevention of, 85
recovery of, 85
behaviour, 81–2
capital sum, 83–4
cohabitation, resumption of, 82

Averment—*contd*
delivery of child, 89
desertion, 82
exclusion order, relating to, 91
interdict, form of application for breach of, 168
matrimonial home, rights of occupancy of, 91–2
molestation, 90
periodical allowance, 84
preventing removal of child, 89
property, transfer of, 84–5
relative, example of, 80–1
resources, order to give details of, 87
separation,
five year, 82–3
two year, 82–3

Avoidance transactions
order relating to, 66–7
simplified procedure not appropriate, 21

Award
aliment, of,
circumstances to be taken into account in making, 9
test for making, 9

Before divorce. *See* SITUATION BEFORE DIVORCE

Behaviour
averment, 81–2
unreasonable. *See* UNREASONABLE BEHAVIOUR
See also CONDUCT

Bereavement
breakdown of marriage, comparison with, 1

Bigamous marriage
proof of, 146

Breakdown of marriage
bereavement, comparison with, 1
client's position on, 1–5

Capital assets
alienation, prevention of,
averment, 85
order, 85
plea in law, 85–6
periodical allowance, division to have priority over, 42
recovery of,
averment, 85

Capital assets—*contd*
recovery of,—*contd*
　　order, 85
　　plea in law, 85–6
simplified procedure not appropriate, 19–20
Capital payment
disputed, 129–30
Capital sum
averment, 83–4
order for payment of, made after divorce, 153
plea in law, 84
variation of, 31
Check list
access, 18
adultery, 16
aliment, 19
arrest, powers of, 21
avoidance transactions, 21
basis of divorce, 15
capital assets, 19–20
children,
　　access, 18
　　current marriage and, 14
　　custody, 18
custody, 18
defender, consent of, 17
desertion, 17
earlier marriage/relationship, 14–15
general, 17–18
interdict, 21
jurisdiction, 15
marriage,
　　brief history of, 15
　　current, and children of it, 14
　　earlier, 14–15
matrimonial home, 20–1
non-cohabitation,
　　five year, 17
　　two year, 17
periodical allowance, 19
unreasonable behaviour, 16–17
Child
abduction, 185, 186–90
access. *See* ACCESS
aliment for,
　　averment, 88
　　generally, 25–6
　　order, 87–8
　　parent and child, 28
　　plea in law, 88

Child—*contd*
best interests of, 50–1
birth, proof of, 143–4
custody. *See* CUSTODY
delivery of,
　　averment, 89
　　enforcing, 184
　　order for, 57–8, 89, 156
　　plea in law, 90
divorce, lack of experience of, 4
economic burden of caring for, 38–9
interdict relating to, 90
interviewing, 148
local authority, committal to care of, 126–7
meaning, 50
molestation
　　averment, 90
　　order, 90
　　plea in law, 90
parent and, prior agreement on aliment, 28
removal of,
　　abduction, 185, 186–190
　　jurisdiction of court, from, restriction of, 56–7, 155
　　obtaining authority of court, 57
　　prevention of,
　　　averment, 89
　　　order, 89
　　　plea in law, 89
　　unauthorised, 184–5
simplified procedure, cases where not appropriate, 14, 18
welfare of, evidence of, 126, 148
whereabouts of,
　　disclosure of, 56, 189–90
　　tracing, 184
Citation. *See* RAISING ACTION
Civil imprisonment
enforcement by, 169–70
Client
breakdown of marriage, position on, 1–5
Cohabitation
cessation of, 34
resumption of, averment, 82
See also NON-COHABITATION
Commencing ordinary action. *See* RAISING ACTION

Conciliation
defended action, 136
local conciliation service, assistance from, 3
reconciliation, court's requirement to encourage, 1
Conclusion
divorce, 81
example, 80–1
Condescendence
Court of Session, example of, 74–6
initial writ, example of, 78–9
Condonation
defended action, 133
Conduct
aliment, relevance to, 9–10
party, of, relevance of, 45–6
See also BEHAVIOUR
Connivance
defended action, 133
Consent of defender. *See* DEFENDER
Contributions
meaning, 37
Convention countries
ordinary action, commencement of, 103–4
Counterclaim
defended action, 131–2
Court
choice of,
simplified procedure, 13–14
writ, considerations relating to, 68
fees, exemption from, 96
jurisdiction of, restricting removal of child from, 56–7, 155
obtaining authority to remove child, 57
sheriff court. *See* SHERIFF COURT
Court of Session
citation in, 99–100, 102–3
decree, recall or variation by sheriff court, 165–6
jurisdiction, 69
Practice Note 1977 No. 3, 1
recall of orders, 161–2
remit from sheriff court, 108
remit to sheriff court, 108
summons, example of, 73–6
total decrees granted, 1987 and 1988 . . ., 1
transmission of process to, 108–9

Court of Session—*contd*
variation of orders, 161–2
writ, obtaining interim order prior to service of, 118–19
Crave
divorce, 81
example, 80–1
Cross action
defended action, 131–2
Curator *ad litem*
appointment of, 112–13
Custody
averment, 87
best interests of child, 50–1
Hague Convention, 188–9
interim, 50, 123–4
joint, 52–3
jurisdiction relating to, 70–1
one party, to, 51–2
order,
enforcement of, 182–4
example, 87
jurisdiction in relation to, 54–5
recall of,
generally, 160
jurisdiction to recall, 161
procedure, 161
variation,
generally, 160
jurisdiction to vary, 161
procedure, 161–2
parents, splitting children between, 52
plea in law, 87
report on, 147–8
simplified procedure not appropriate, 18

Decree
adultery, based on, 1987 figures, 1
consent to, 106–7
Court of Session, recall or variation by sheriff court, 165–6
defender's consent to, proof of, 147
desertion, based on, 1987 figures, 1
minute for, 115–16
non-cohabitation, based on, 1987 figures, 1
separation, of, decree based on, 144
Defence. *See* DEFENDED ACTION
Defended action
affidavit in, 149
agreement can be reached, where, 129

Defended action—*contd*
agreement cannot be reached, where, 129
aliment, dispute related to, 129–30
arrestment on dependence, 128
capital payment, dispute related to, 129–30
counterclaim, 131–2
cross action, 131–2
defence,
   adjustment, 131
   divorce, action of,
      adultery, 133
      condonation, 133
      connivance, 133
      generally, 132–3
      lenocinium, 133
   financial provision, order for, 135
   generally, 130–1
   matrimonial home, action relating to,
      arrest, power of, 134
      compensation, 134
      generally, 134
   particular lines of, 132–5
documents, recovery of, 137–8
entering appearance, 128
inhibition, 128
interim order, early hearing on, 128
periodical allowance, dispute related to, 129–30
procedure,
   conciliation, 136
   defender, late appearance by, 135–6
   generally, 135
   other parties who may appear, 136
   reconciliation, 136
process, third party entering, 130
sisting of third party, 132
third party,
   entering process, 130
   sisting of, 132
transfer of property, dispute related to, 129–30
written statement in, 149
Defender
absence of, procedure on interim order, 119–20
address, 80
consent of,
   averment for, 82
   simplified procedure, 17

Defender—*contd*
late appearance by, 135–6
name, 80
proof of consent to decree, 147
service on, 105
Delivery of child. *See* CHILD
Dependence
warrant for arrestment on, 92–3, 128
Desertion
averment, 82
number of decrees based on, 1987 . . ., 1
simplified procedure not appropriate, 17
Disclosure
whereabouts of child, of, 56, 189–90
Divorce
basis of, simplified procedure not appropriate, 15
coping with, 1–5
situation before,
   generally, 6–7
   presumptions. *See* PRESUMPTIONS
Documents
recovery of,
   before action raised, 98
   defended action, 137–8
service, which must accompany, 105–6
Domicile
jurisdiction, essential basis of, 70
Duration
periodical allowance, order for, 43–4

Economic advantage and disadvantage
contributions, meaning, 37
economic advantage, meaning, 37
economic disadvantage, meaning, 37
financial provision, principles to be applied when making order for, 37–8
Ejection
order relating to, 63
Enforcement
Child Abduction and Custody Act 1985 . . . 186–90
civil imprisonment, 169–70
custody order, of, 182–4
interdict, breach of. *See* INTERDICT
maintenance order, of. *See* MAINTENANCE
unauthorised removal of child, 184–5

Evidence
access, report on, 147–8
admission, 144
affidavit. *See* AFFIDAVIT
aspects of evidence required, 141–2
custody, report on, 147–8
financial matters, of, 152
interviewing child, 148
local authority, welfare of child in care of, 148
medical report, 147
other matrimonial proceedings, 145
parties, of, 141
proof of. *See* PROOF
report,
  access, on, 147–8
  custody, on, 147–8
separation, divorce based on earlier decree of, 144
sufficiency of, 140–1
welfare of child, of, 126, 148
See also PROOF

Exclusion order
averment, 91
ejection, 63
example, 90–1
interim, 60–1
nature of, 59–60
orders which must or may be granted along with, 61–2
plea in law, 91

Expenses
action, of, 116–17
matrimonial home, relating to, 92

Extract conviction
proof of, 145

Fees
exemption from, 96

Financial hardship
divorce, as result of, 40–1

Financial matters
evidence of, 152

Financial provision
conduct of party, relevance of, 45–6
dependent spouse, for, 39–40
interest on order for, 44
maintenance payment, taxation of, 46–8
order for,
  alienation of assets, prevention of, 85–6

Financial provision—*contd*
order for,—*contd*
  annulment, following, 154–5
  capital sum,
    averment, 83–4
    example, 83
    payment of, 31
    plea in law, 84
    variation of, 31
  cohabitation, cessation of, 34
  defended action, 135
  general, 28–9
  incidental, 29–31
  interest on, 44
  interim aliment for pursuer, 86
  matrimonial property,
    date at which valued, 33–4
    division of net value of, 35–7
    meaning, 32–3
    net value of, 34–5
    relevant date, 33–4
  overseas divorce, following, 154–5
  periodical allowance,
    averment, 84
    division of capital assets to have priority over, 42
    example, 83
    plea in law, 84
  pre-1985 Act, variation of, 163–5
  principles to be applied when making,
    child, economic burden of caring for, 38–9
    dependent spouse, financial support for, 39–40
    economic advantage and disadvantage, 37–8
    financial hardship, 40–1
    matrimonial property, division of net value of, 35–7
  property, transfer of, 31, 84–5
  quantum of financial provision, 41–2
  recall of, 161–2
  resources, details of, 86–7
  variation of, 161–2
  which may be made, 29
  writ, 83
periodical allowance. *See* PERIODICAL ALLOWANCE
quantum of, 41–2
setting aside agreement on, 28
varying agreement on, 28

Five year case
raising action, 95
simplified procedure, cases where not applicable, 17
Furniture
Matrimonial Homes (Family Protection) (Scotland) Act 1981, order under, 62-3

Gifts
spouses, between, presumptions relating to, 11
wedding presents, 10
Goods
household, presumptions relating to, 7

Habitual residence
jurisdiction, essential basis of, 70
Hague Convention
child abduction, 186-8
custody of child, 188-9
Hardship. *See* FINANCIAL HARDSHIP
History
marriage, of, 15
Home. *See* MATRIMONIAL HOME
Household goods
presumptions relating to, 7
Housekeeping allowance
presumptions relating to, 7
Husband and wife
aliment, prior agreement on, 27
wife, number of actions at instance of, 1988..., 1
See also SPOUSES

Identity
unknown, 80
Immigrant spouse
presumptions relating to, 11
Imprisonment
civil, enforcement by, 169-70
Incidental order
nature of, 29-31
Individual
committal of child to care of, 126-7
Induciae
citation, for, 100
extending, 101
shortening, 101
Inhibition
defended action, 128
Initial writ. *See* WRIT

Interdict
avoidance transaction, order relating to, 66-7
breach of,
  arrest, powers of, 169
  form of application for, 168
  generally, 167
  procedure, 167-8
child, relating to, 90
interim, 121
jurisdiction, 65
nature of, 64-5
simplified procedure not appropriate, 21
tenancy, transfer of, 66
terms of, 65
undertaking in lieu of, 65-6
Interest
financial provision, order for, 44
Interim order
access, 124
aliment. *See* ALIMENT
arrest, power of, 122
committal of child, 126-7
custody, 123-4
early hearing on, 128
generally, 22-4, 118
hearing of motion for,
  affidavit, 123
  early, 128
  generally, 122-3
interdict, 121
local authority, committal of child to care of, 126-7
matrimonial home, relating to, 121-2
property, interim possession of, 121
reports, 125-6
service of writ, obtained prior to,
  Court of Session action, 118-19
  defender, procedure in absence of, 119-20
  generally, 118
  later order, supersession of earlier order by, 120-1
  sheriff court action, 119
sist, effect of, 111
supervision, 127
welfare of child, obtaining evidence of, 126
Interview
child, of, 148

Intimation
ordinary action, commencement of, 104–6
warrant for, 92–3
writ, of, 107

Jurisdiction
aliment, 70–1
court, of, restricting removal of child from, 56–7, 155
Court of Session, 69
custody, 70–1
custody order,
  relating to, 54–5
  variation or recall of, 161
domicile, 70
generally, 68
habitual residence, 70
interdict, relating to, 65
prorogation of, 71
sheriff court, 69–70
simplified procedure not appropriate, 15

Legal aid
initial writ, style of, 73
raising action, 96

Legal capacity
presumptions relating to, 8

Lenocinium
defended action, 133

Litigation
bitterly contested, expense of, 2

Local authority
committal of child to care of, 126–7
evidence of welfare of child in care of, 148

Lodgment
affidavit, of, 115

Lord Advocate
involvement of, 113

Maintenance
order, enforcement of,
  agreement for maintenance, 170
  aliment, 171–2
  capital sum, payment of, 171–2
  current arrestments, 170–1
  diligence, aspects of, 170
  incoming order, 174–5
  outgoing order, 172–4

Maintenance—*contd*
order, enforcement of,—*contd*
  overseas,
    Civil Jurisdiction and Judgments Act 1982, under, 175–6
    generally, 175
    Maintenance Orders (Reciprocal Enforcement) Act 1972, under,
      bilateral arrangements, 180–2
      convention countries, 179–80
      generally, 176
      reciprocating countries, 176–9
  periodical allowance, 171–2
payment, taxation of, 46–8

Marriage
bigamous, proof of, 146
breakdown of. *See* BREAKDOWN OF MARRIAGE
brief history of, 15
earlier, simplified procedure not appropriate in case of, 14–15
polygamous, presumptions relating to, 11
proof of, 143
simplified procedure, cases where not appropriate, 14

Matrimonial home
arrest, powers of, 63–4, 122, 134
defended action,
  arrest, power of, 134
  compensation, 134
  generally, 134
dependance, warrant for arrestment on, 92–3
ejection, 63
exclusion order,
  averment, 91
  ejection, 63
  example, 90–1
  interim, 60–1
  nature of, 59–60
  orders which must or may be granted along with, 61–2, 91
  plea in law, 91
expenses, 92
furniture, 62–3
interim orders, 121–2
intimation, warrant for, 92–3
Matrimonial Homes (Family Protection) (Scotland) Act 1981, orders under, 58–64

Matrimonial home—*contd*
occupancy, regulating rights of, 58–9, 91–2
plenishings, 62–3
simplified procedure not appropriate, 20–1
tenancy, transfer of, 66
Matrimonial property
date at which valued, 33–4
meaning, 32–3
net value of,
  division of, 35–7
  generally, 34–5
relevant date, 33–4
Medical report
evidence, as, 147
Mental capacity
party, of, 94
Mental health
curator *ad litem*, appointment of, 112–13
Minute
decree, for, 115–16
form of, 159–60
joint, 113–14
Molestation
averment, 90
order, 90
plea in law, 90

Name
defender, of, 80
pursuer, of, 80
Non-cohabitation
averment, 82
number of decrees based on, 1987 . . . 1
simplified procedure not appropriate, 17
Notice. *See* PERIOD OF NOTICE

Occupancy
matrimonial home, in, regulating rights of, 58–9
Order
access, 53–4, 88
ancillary. *See* ANCILLARY ORDER
exclusion. *See* EXCLUSION ORDER
financial provision. *See* FINANCIAL PROVISION
incidental, 29–31
interim. *See* INTERIM ORDER
made after divorce,

Order—*contd*
made after divorce,—*contd*
  capital sum, payment of, 153
  periodical allowance, payment of, 153–4
  transfer of property, 153
maintenance. *See* MAINTENANCE
Ordinary action. *See* RAISING ACTION
Overseas divorce
financial provision following, order for, 154–5

Parental rights
access. *See* ACCESS
order relating to, 49
presumptions relating to, 11–12
Parents
child, and, prior agreement on aliment, 28
splitting children between, 52
Party
conduct of, relevance of, 45–6
defended action, 136
evidence of, 141
legally-aided, style of initial writ, 73
mental capacity of, 94
one, custody to, 51–2
See also THIRD PARTY
Paternity
presumptions relating to, 7
Period of notice
extending, 102
sheriff court, 102
shortening, 102
Periodical allowance
capital assets, priority of division of, 42
disputed, 129–30
order for,
  averment, 84
  duration of, 43–4
  example, 83
  general, 42–3
  made after divorce, 153–4
  plea in law, 84
  quantum, 43–4
  recall, 45, 158
  variation, 45, 158
simplified procedure not appropriate, 19
termination, 45

Plea in law
access, 89
aliment for child, 88
assets,
  alienation, prevention of, 85–6
  recovery of, 85–6
capital sum, 84
Court of Session summons, example of, 76
delivery of child, 90
divorce, for, 83
exclusion order, relating to, 91
initial writ, example of, 79
interdict, form of application for breach of, 168–9
interim aliment for pursuer, 86
matrimonial home, rights of occupancy of, 92
molestation, 90
periodical allowance, 84
preventing removal of child, 89
resources, order to give details of, 87

Plenishings
Matrimonial Homes (Family Protection) (Scotland) Act 1981, orders under, 62–3

Polygamous marriage
presumptions relating to, 11

Presents. See GIFTS

Presumptions
aliment. See ALIMENT
gifts between spouses, 11
household goods, 7
housekeeping allowance, 7
immigrant spouse, 11
legal capacity, 8
matrimonial home, 11
obligation to adhere, 7–8
parental rights, 11–12
paternity, 7
polygamous marriage, 11
spouses,
  gifts between, 11
  immigrant, 11
succession, rights by, 10
wedding presents, 10

Process
Court of Session, transmission to, 108–9
third party entering, 130

Proof
adultery, of, 145–6

Proof—contd
allowance of, 114
bigamous marraige, of, 146
birth of child, of, 143–4
burden of, 139
defender's consent to decree, of, 147
extract conviction, of, 145
marriage, of, 143
merits of divorce, of, 114
standard of, 139
unreasonable behaviour, of, 146–7

Property
interim possession of, order for, 121
matrimonial. See MATRIMONIAL PROPERTY
transfer of,
  averment, 84–5
  disputed, 129–30
  order for, 31, 84
  order made after divorce, 153
  plea in law, 85

Pursuer
address, 80
interim aliment for,
  averment, 86
  order, 86
  plea in law, 86
name, 80

Quantum
aliment, of, 26
financial provision, of, 41–2
periodical allowance, order for, 43–4

Raising action
Administration of Justice (Scotland) Act 1972, s 1, application for order under, 98
affidavit, lodging of, 115
Court of Session,
  discretionary sist, 110
  interim order, effect of sist on, 111
  mandatory sist, 109–10
  remit from sheriff court to, 108
  remit to sheriff court from, 108
  transmission of process to, 108–9
  undefended action, 111–2
curator *ad litem*, appointment of, 112–13
expenses, 116–17
generally, 94
ground of divorce, amendment of, 115
joint minute, 113–14
Lord Advocate, involvement of, 113

Raising action—*contd*
mental capacity of parties, 94
minute,
   decree, for, 115–16
   joint, 113–14
ordinary action, commencement of,
   citation,
      Court of Session action, 99–100
      generally, 99
      induciae,
         extending, 101
         generally, 100
         shortening, 101
      sheriff court action,
         generally, 101
         period of notice, 102
   consent to decree, 106–7
   Convention countries, 103–4
   Court of Session action, 99–100, 102–3
   generally, 99
   intimation, 104, 107
   service,
      acceptance of, 99
      carrying out, 107
      documents which must accompany, 105–6
   sheriff court action, 101–3
proof,
   allowance of, 114
   merits of divorce, of, 114
sheriff court,
   remit from Court of Session to, 108
   remit to Court of Session from, 108
   transfer between, 107–8
simplified procedure,
   appeal, 97
   application after simplified divorce granted, 97
   cases to which applicable, 95
   citation, 96–7
   court fees, exemption from, 96
   extract, 97
   five year case, 95
   generally, 95
   legal aid, 96
   lodging application, 96
   recovery of documents, 98
   two year case, 95
sist,
   action, for, 109
   discretionary, 110

Raising action—*contd*
sist,—*contd*
   interim order, effect of, 111
   mandatory, 109–10
   recall of, 111
   reconciliation, for, 107
Recall
Court of Session decree, of, by sheriff court, 165–6
custody order, of, 160–1
form of minute, 159–60
orders which may be recalled, 156–8
periodical allowance, order for, 45, 158
test for, 159
Reconciliation
court's requirement to encourage, 1
defended action, 136
sist for, 107
See also CONCILIATION
Relationship
earlier, simplified procedure not appropriate in case of, 14–15
Remit
Court of Session, to, 108
sheriff court, to, 108
Removal of child. *See* CHILD
Report
access, on, 147–8
custody, on, 147–8
interim order, relating to, 125–6
medical, 147
Residence
habitual, essential basis of jurisdiction, 70
Resources
order to give details of,
   averment, 87
   example, 86
   plea in law, 87

Separation
coping with, 1–5
earlier decree of, divorce based on, 144
five years, averment for, 82–3
practical problems caused by, 2
two years, averment for, 82
Service
acceptance of, 99
carrying out, 107
defender, on, 105
documents which must accompany, 105

Separation—*contd*
interim order prior to,
  Court of Session action, 118–19
  defender, procedure in absence of, 119–20
  generally, 118
  later order, supersession of earlier order by, 120–1
  sheriff court action, 119
Setting aside
agreement between spouses, 156
financial provision, agreement as to, 28
Sheriff court
citation, 101–3
Court of Session decree, recall or variation of, 165–6
jurisdiction, 69–70
period of notice, 102
recall of orders, 162
remit from Court of Session to, 108
remit to Court of Session from, 108
total decrees granted, 1987 . . ., 1
transfer between, 107–8
variation of orders, 162
writ, obtaining interim order prior to, 119
Simplified procedure
cases where not appropriate,
  access, 18
  adultery, 16
  aliment, 19
  arrest, powers of, 21
  avoidance transactions, 21
  basis of divorce, 15
  capital assets, 19–20
  children,
    access, 18
    current marriage and, 14
    custody, 18
  custody, 18
  defender, consent of, 17
  desertion, 17
  earlier marriage/relationship, 14–15
  general, 17–18
  interdict, 21
  jurisdiction, 15
  marriage,
    brief history of, 15
    current, and children of it, 14
    earlier, 14–15

Simplified procedure—*contd*
cases where not appropriate,—*contd*
  matrimonial home, 20–1
  non-cohabitation,
    five year, 17
    two year, 17
  periodical allowance, 19
  unreasonable behaviour, 16–17
check list of questions, 14–21
court, choice of, 13–14
generally, 13
other considerations, 14
raising action. *See* RAISING ACTION
writ, 71–2
Sist
action, of, 109
discretionary, 110
interim order, effect on, 111
mandatory, 109–10
recall of, 111
reconciliation, for, 107
third party, sisting of, 132
Situation before divorce
generally, 6–7
presumptions. *See* PRESUMPTIONS
Spouses
agreement between, setting aside or variation of, 156
dependent spouse, financial support for, 39–40
gifts between, presumptions relating to, 11
immigrant, presumptions relating to, 11
See also HUSBAND AND WIFE
Succession
rights of, presumptions relating to, 10
Summons
Court of Session, example of, 73–6
Supervision order
interim, 127

Taxation
maintenance payment, of, 46–8
Tenancy
transfer of, 66
Termination
periodical allowance, order for, 45
Third party
entering process, 130
sisting of, 132

Transactions. *See* AVOIDANCE TRANSACTIONS
Two year case
raising action, 95
simplified procedure, cases where not appropriate, 17

Undefended action
affidavit, 149
Court of Session, 111–12
Undertaking
interdict, in lieu of, 65–6
Unreasonable behaviour
proof of, 146–7
simplified procedure not appropriate, 16–17

Variation
agreement between spouses, of, 156
Court of Session decree, of, by sheriff court, 165–6
custody order, of, 160–1
financial provision, agreement as to, 28
form of minute, 159–60
orders which may be varied, 156–8
periodical allowance, order for, 45, 158
test for, 159

Warrant
arrestment on dependence, for, 92–3, 128
intimation, for, 92–3
Wedding presents
presumptions relating to, 10
Welfare
child, of, evidence of, 126, 148
Whereabouts of child. *See* CHILD
Wife. *See* HUSBAND AND WIFE
Writ
address,
  defender, of, 80
  pursuer, of, 80
  unknown, 80
averment, example of, 81–3
child,
  access, 88–9
  aliment for, 87–8
  custody, 87
  delivery of, 89–90
  interdict, 90

Writ—*contd*
preventing removal of, 89
court, choice of, 68
crave/conclusion, example of, 81
defender, name and address of, 80
financial provision, order for,
  assets, alienation of, 85–6
  capital sum, 83–4
  generally, 83
  periodical allowance, 83–4
  property, transfer of, 84–5
  pursuer, interim aliment for, 86
  resources, order to give details of, 86–7
identity unknown, 80
initial, styles of,
  example, 77–80
  generally, 72–3
  legally-aided party, 73
intimation of, 107
jurisdiction,
  aliment, 70–1
  Court of Session, 69
  custody, 70–1
  domicile, 70
  generally, 68
  habitual residence, 70
  prorogation of, 71
  sheriff court, 69–70
matrimonial home, order relating to,
  dependence, warrant for arrestment on, 92–3
  exclusion order, 90–1
  expenses, 92
  intimation, warrant for arrestment on, 92–3
  occupancy, rights of, 91–2
plea in law, example of, 83
pursuer, name and address of, 80
service of, obtaining interim order prior to,
  Court of Session action, 118–19
  defender, procedure in absence of, 119–20
  generally, 118
  later order, supersession of earlier order by, 120–1
  sheriff court action, 119
simplified procedure, 71–2
Written statement
defended action, in, 149